PRAISE FOR *DON'T CALL IT A CULT*

"Berman's rigorously sourced narrative brings this über-creepy story to life, and by waiting to publish until after the conclusion of Raniere's trial, Berman has produced a more comprehensive account of the case than previous studies. This deep dive behind the headlines isn't to be missed."

—*Publishers Weekly* (Starred Review)

"Investigative journalist Berman's account is a standout. With astute research, court testimonies, and firsthand narratives from inner-circle NXIVM members, she traces the downfall of NXIVM from its roots in Raniere's first failed multi-level marketing company to the trials of each ringleader. Berman demonstrates the tactics cults use to manipulate and control without casting judgment or blame on the victims. Truly gripping, this is the definitive book on NXIVM."

— *Booklist*

"*Don't Call It A Cult* is the most detailed, well-reported, and nuanced look at NXIVM's history, its supporters, and those left destroyed in its wake. If you want to understand NXIVM—and other groups like it—reading Sarah Berman's account is essential."

—Scaachi Koul, author of
One Day We'll All Be Dead and None of This Will Matter

"Sarah Berman is absolutely fearless in *Don't Call It a Cult*. Her determination to not only tell the difficult, often disturbing story of NXIVM, but tell it right, shines through in every aspect of this gripping book. I simply could not put it down."

—Alicia Elliott, author of *A Mind Spread Out on the Ground*

"Berman has crafted a tour-de-force and powerful homage to first-person reportage. A riveting page-turner, *Don't Call It a Cult* is a must-read for anyone who is fascinated by the long term effects of cult culture, abuse, and pseudoscience."

—Lindsay Wong, author of *The Woo-Woo*

DON'T CALL IT A CULT

THE SHOCKING STORY OF KEITH RANIERE AND THE WOMEN OF NXIVM

SARAH BERMAN

STEERFORTH PRESS
LEBANON, NEW HAMPSHIRE

For information about permission to reproduce
selections from this book, write to:
Steerforth Press L. L. C., 31 Hanover Street, Suite 1
Lebanon, New Hampshire 03766

Cataloging-in-Publication Data is available from the Library of Congress

ISBN 978-1-58642-275-2

Book design by Kate Sinclair
Cover design by Kate Sinclair
Cover images: (House and street) © Erik Von Weber, (texture) © Flavio Coelho,
    both Getty Images

Printed and bound in the United States of America

1 3 5 7 9 10 8 6 4 2

*Dedicated to women who
change their minds*

Contents

PART 3: A PLACE OF SURVIVAL · 193

CAST OF CHARACTERS

Adrian* Brother of Marianna, Daniela, and Camila. All three sisters were groomed for sexual relationships with Keith Raniere at a young age.

Adriana* Mother of Marianna, Daniela, Adrian, and Camila. Moved the family from Mexico to Albany starting in 2002. Enforced Daniela's confinement in 2010.

Agnifilo, Marc Lead defense lawyer for Keith Raniere.

Ames, Anthony Actor and longtime NXIVM coach. Husband of Sarah Edmondson.

Aviv, Juval Private investigator hired by NXIVM.

Banks, Teah Girlfriend of Mark Vicente when he joined NXIVM in 2005. Pushed out by inner circle.

Bouchey, Barbara Prolific recruiter for NXIVM and Raniere girlfriend from 2000 to 2008. Bronfman sisters' financial planner. Spearheaded "NXIVM Nine" revolt in 2009. Was sued and harassed.

Bronfman, Clare Seagram heir and NXIVM bankroller since 2003, convicted of harboring a migrant for financial gain. Funded Raniere's lawsuits and failed investments.

Bronfman, Edgar Billionaire father to Clare and Sara. Outspoken critic of Raniere who became a target of NXIVM hacking and spying.

Bronfman, Sara Seagram heir who funded tens of millions in real estate and commodities trading losses under Raniere's direction. Brought the Dalai Lama to Albany in 2009 amid extreme public scrutiny.

Cafritz, Pamela Heir and long-term girlfriend who lived with
Raniere from 1989 until her death in 2016. NXIVM senior counselor. Embraced domestic servant role. Groomed young girls
for Raniere.

Camila* Youngest of three Mexican sisters who were groomed
into sexual relationships with Raniere. Was sexually exploited
by Raniere at age fifteen. Nanny to Raniere's first child with
Kristin Keeffe. Later initiated into DOS, a secret sorority that
branded women.

Chiappone, Robbie Target of Raniere's jealousy and spying.

Clyne, Nicki *Battlestar Galactica* actor from Vancouver. Early
member of DOS. Married actor Allison Mack in 2017.

Daniela* Middle sister between Camila and Marianna. Moved
to Albany in 2002. Became inner-circle girlfriend and hacker,
then victim of two-year confinement. Escaped in 2012.

Danielle* A doctor and DOS recruit who performed branding of
other "slaves."

Dones, Susan Opened NXIVM's Seattle chapter, joined Barbara
Bouchey's revolt in 2009.

Duran, Monica First-line DOS recruiter.

Edmondson, Sarah Actor and NXIVM recruiter who filled Barbara
Bouchey's shoes, opening a Vancouver center with Mark Vicente
in 2009. Secured NXIVM's young-actor following before blowing
the whistle on DOS in 2017.

Franco, Stephanie Sister to Michael Sutton. Provided NXIVM
course materials reviewed by medical experts in 2003.
Sued by NXIVM.

Garaufis, Judge Nicholas Presided over NXIVM sex-trafficking and racketeering trial beginning May 7, 2019.

Garza, Loreta First-line DOS recruiter. Oversaw Rainbow Cultural Garden, an experimental language program for children.

Hassan, Steven Cult expert who studies neuro-linguistic programming, or NLP.

Hector* Father of Marianna, Daniela, Adrian, and Camila. Enforced Daniela's confinement in 2010.

Hutchinson, Gina Fifteen-year-old alleged victim of sexual exploitation by Raniere in 1984, then early girlfriend. Believed in Raniere's spiritual teachings until she died by apparent suicide in 2002.

Hutchinson, Heidi Gina's older sister, who observed early days of NXIVM.

Jackson, Mark Middle-school classmate of Raniere.

Jeske, Barbara First-generation girlfriend of Raniere. NXIVM senior counselor until her death in 2014.

Junco, Rosa Laura First-line DOS recruiter. Wealthy heir to Mexican media empire.

Keeffe, Kristin Spy and legal liaison for NXIVM, inner circle girlfriend who lived with Raniere for more than a decade until she fled with their son in 2014.

Kreuk, Kristin *Smallville* actor, NXIVM coach, and friend of Sarah Edmondson. Cut ties with NXIVM around 2012.

Krowchuk, Chad Boyfriend of Allison Mack when she joined NXIVM in 2007.

Mack, Allison *Smallville* actor and Raniere disciple since 2007. Pleaded guilty to racketeering charges for her role recruiting women into DOS.

Marianna* Daniela and Camila's older sister and highly favored girlfriend of Raniere. Mother of Raniere's second known son.

Miljkovic, Maja Actor and writer who became a NXIVM student in 2013. Participated in a NXIVM-arranged marriage.

Myers, Ben Target of Raniere's jealousy after Daniela revealed her romantic feelings for him. Daniela's last phone call before she was confined from 2010 to 2012.

Natalie, Toni Raniere's girlfriend and multi-level marketing business partner from 1991 to 1999. Was stalked and harassed by Raniere's inner circle for decades after breakup.

Nicole* Actor recruited into DOS by Allison Mack in 2016. Became a star witness at Raniere's trial.

O'Hara, Joe Former NXIVM consultant who helped uncover NXIVM spying after he quit. Was sued and harassed by NXIVM.

Oxenberg, India DOS "slave" recruited by Allison Mack. Friend of Nicole.

Padilla, Daniella First-line DOS recruiter. Oversaw creation of BDSM dungeon.

Park, Grace *Hawaii Five-O* actor, former NXIVM coach, and friend of Sarah Edmondson. Raised in Vancouver.

Parlato, Frank NXIVM publicist turned tabloid blogger. Briefly worked on Bronfman real estate project in L.A.

Penza, Moira Kim Eastern District of New York prosecutor at Keith Raniere's 2019 trial, along with colleagues Tanya Hajjar, Mark Lesko, and others.

Piesse, Bonnie Actor and NXIVM whistleblower. Wife of Mark Vicente.

Powers, Kenny Friend of Kristin Snyder, who disappeared after a NXIVM class in 2003. Was part of an unsuccessful search-and-rescue effort.

Rambam, Steve Private investigator hired by NXIVM.

Raniere, Keith Founder of NXIVM, convicted sex trafficker. Born in 1960. Arrested in 2018.

Ross, Rick Alan Cult expert hired by wealthy New Jersey parents to rescue son in 2002. Became a target of NXIVM's civil lawsuits and spying.

Russell, Kathy Bookkeeper and long-term girlfriend of Raniere. Pleaded guilty to visa fraud.

Salinas, Emiliano Son of former Mexican president Carlos Salinas de Gortari. Top-ranking executive member of NXIVM.

Salzman, Lauren Daughter of Nancy Salzman, secret girlfriend of Raniere and persuasive NXIVM executive. Testified against Raniere and pleaded to racketeering charges for her role in secret sorority.

Salzman, Nancy Hypnotherapist who cofounded NXIVM with Keith Raniere in 1998. Convicted of racketeering.

Snyder, Kristin Disappeared after a NXIVM intensive in 2003. Friends say she suffered a psychological break. Disappearance was ruled a suicide. Target of hacking and spying.

Sutton, Michael Son of wealthy New Jersey parents. Lost $1.3 million to Keith Raniere's commodity trading bets. Subject of failed intervention by cult expert Rick Alan Ross.

Sutton, Morris and Rochelle Wealthy New Jersey couple hired Rick Alan Ross for an intervention in 2002. Son Michael was NXIVM student. Sued by NXIVM.

Unterreiner, Karen Raniere's high-achieving college classmate and long-term girlfriend. Computer programmer and founding member of both NXIVM and Raniere's first business, Consumers' Buyline.

Vicente, Mark Documentary filmmaker and Raniere's best friend from 2005 to 2017, when he discovered DOS and became a witness for the prosecution.

White, Susan Family friend of the Bronfmans who invited Clare and Sara to their first NXIVM class.

Yusko, Dennis Albany *Times Union* reporter who first wrote about NXIVM in 2003. Added to NXIVM's growing list of enemies.

*Identified by first name only in keeping with court ruling.

"The Most Ethical Man"

Keith Raniere needed sleep, that much was clear. How much sleep? Well, for decades before his arrest in March 2018, that was a point of debate. Some thought he slept only one or two hours a night. But women close to him knew he was more of a day sleeper, and that day in March, in an upstairs bedroom of a $10,000-a-week vacation rental north of Puerto Vallarta, Raniere was napping.

According to testimony at Raniere's trial, actors Nicki Clyne and Allison Mack were lounging outside on a patio overlooking an infinity pool when Mexican federal agents in bulletproof vests pulled up the cobblestone driveway. Armed with a warrant from the Eastern District of New York for sex trafficking and forced labor, the officers surrounded the property. Some of them appeared to be wearing masks and holding machine guns.

It was a big deal for Clyne and Mack—celebrities and recent subjects of relentless online gossip—to be staying so close to Raniere. Five months earlier he'd been accused in *The New York Times* of masterminding a strange blackmail scheme, and allegations that Raniere had sexually abused young girls were resurfacing online with a vengeance. The U.S. Federal Bureau of Investigation wasn't quiet about its interest in NXIVM, the secretive self-help company Raniere had founded in 1998. The feds had interviewed NXIVM associates in the United States and left business cards with allies in Mexico, asking for Raniere to get in touch. Despite all this, Clyne and Mack had come to Mexico to show their commitment to Raniere, whom they'd often called the most ethical man they'd ever met.

Raniere was technically a fugitive, but his hideout in Mexico resembled an expensive corporate retreat. A team of fixers had been buzzing around him, first in Punta Mita and now at their current location, the remote beach town of Chacala. Neighbors said they went on long walks and ordered expensive butter-infused coffees from a tourist bar; testimony later revealed they communicated through prepaid disposable phones.

Mack and Clyne had been invited to participate in a "recommitment ceremony." The plan was to show loyalty to Raniere in the most vulnerable way possible, which might have included group sex had the cops not shown up that day. Under her clothes, each actor bore a scar in the shape of Raniere's initials, burned into her skin with a cauterizing pen more than a year earlier. It symbolized her lifelong commitment to obeying Raniere's every request.

Before getting caught up in NXIVM headlines, Nicki Clyne had been best known for her role as Cally on the sci-fi drama *Battlestar Galactica*, while Allison Mack had lit up TV screens as Chloe Sullivan, best friend to Superman in the CW show *Smallville*. Those roles had become less interesting to the women as they grew more committed to changing the world with Raniere. Through thousands of hours of coursework and mentorship, Clyne and Mack had learned to break out of limiting beliefs. NXIVM students compared this process to Keanu Reeves taking the red pill in *The Matrix*; no aspect of their lives was exempt from constant study, reflection, and redefinition. Raniere taught that everything was an opportunity for personal growth—even a faceoff with federal agents.

But as police moved inside, at least one of Raniere's disciples was feeling some doubts.

For Lauren Salzman, the daughter of NXIVM's president and cofounder Nancy Salzman, Raniere's arrest punctured the bubble of secrecy and deception that had protected his reputation as someone of the highest ethical standards. Salzman was in a bedroom with Raniere when the cops came upstairs to take him into custody. As she later recalled at his trial, Raniere hid in a walk-in closet, leaving her to face the police.

"They were banging on the door," she testified. "The whole time I was thinking they could just shoot through the door."

As the door rattled in its frame, Salzman asked to see a warrant.

"Open the door and I'll show it to you," an agent replied.

Salzman didn't open the door. The cops kicked it open and pinned her to the floor. With guns pointed at her, she yelped out Raniere's name. The man known to acolytes as Vanguard, Master, and Grandmaster stepped out of the closet and was then cuffed on the floor and taken downstairs.

For Salzman, Raniere's arrest left a small but significant crack in the edifice he'd built. "I chose what I believed we had been training for this entire time, which was to choose love over everything—including the possibility of losing my life," she later testified. "There was no need to send me to shield him or negotiate with them; he could have just protected all of us and just gone."

For months Salzman felt guilty for not doing more to protect Raniere. It would take the better part of a year for her to realize that the flaw she saw in him that day went much deeper.

"It never occurred to me that I would choose Keith and Keith would choose Keith," she said.

NICKI CLYNE KEPT a cool head considering the dramatic scene unfolding in front of her outside the house. With phone in hand, she captured a short video of the police raid.

"We're going to follow them," Clyne said to Allison Mack as Raniere was installed in the back of a navy cruiser with *Policia Federal* emblazoned across its doors. Mack turned to look at Clyne with a worried crease between her brows, her green eyes obscured by shadow. Clyne told her to get out of the way.

In the following weeks, Mack would be apprehended in New York on trafficking charges and four more top NXIVM leaders would be indicted for racketeering. Their alleged crimes would amount to identity theft, forced labor, confining an undocumented migrant for twenty-three months, wire fraud, extortion, and obstruction of justice. A year later would come the charge that Raniere took sexually explicit pictures of a fifteen-year-old NXIVM student, adding possession of child porn and child exploitation to his rap sheet. These allegations laid the foundation for a massive racketeering trial beginning in May 2019.

"Let's go, you guys," Clyne called out to Mack, Salzman, and others as the cops pulled away. Raniere was on his way to becoming federal inmate #57005-177, scrutinized under the unflattering fluorescent light of the American justice system.

ON THE FIRST day of his trial, May 7, 2019, Raniere appeared diminished but not broken. He was smaller than you would expect from his photos—all head and shoulders, with a squat torso and a lower body that seemed to taper off quickly. His hair was shorter and greyer, floating in uneven waves around his temples. From a certain angle, the glare of his glasses obscured his glances across the room at a jury of his peers.

"Keith Raniere is the only defendant who will stand trial before this jury," Judge Nicholas Garaufis told the jurors settling into their places in his Brooklyn courtroom. "Please do not speculate as to why this is the case." (After many months of pretrial dealings, Judge Garaufis seemed at ease correctly pronouncing the name Ra-*neer*-ee and his organization *Neks*-ee-um.)

Raniere's codefendants had already pleaded guilty to serious crimes, ranging from extortion and forced labor to identity theft and harboring a migrant for financial gain. Three of the women—NXIVM president Nancy Salzman; her daughter, Lauren Salzman; and actor Allison Mack—had admitted that they'd participated in a racketeering conspiracy with Raniere. He was standing alone because his alleged partners in crime had agreed with the feds that Raniere was leading a dangerous mafia-like organization.

This was a big change for Raniere, who was used to the company of rich and beautiful women. Since the 1980s he'd cultivated a subculture of adoration around him in which he was compared to Buddha and Albert Einstein. The way true believers talked about him, it was as if he had magical powers, perfect recall, the keys to world peace. They commended his contributions to science, his commitment to the harnessing of human potential.

This was the myth built up over Raniere's two-decade career leading NXIVM, an international self-help movement that appealed mostly to dreamers with deep pockets. (The NXIVM name has many layered meanings, from "next millennium" to "place of learning" to the more hidden meaning that allegedly references the Roman concept of debt bondage.) Though the company began as boutique executive coaching for aspiring millionaires, over time it grew into a massive-multi-level marketing enterprise spanning the globe, with active communities in Vancouver, Los Angeles, San Francisco, Seattle, Toronto, London, New York, Miami, Monterrey, Guadalajara, and Mexico City.

Followers started daycares, yoga schools, advocacy groups, science foundations, and humanitarian funds in tribute to Raniere. They incorporated his lessons into small businesses and startups, crediting Raniere as mentor and cofounder. Federal prosecutors estimated that NXIVM had launched close to one hundred offshoot companies, many of them drawing funds up a pyramid-like hierarchy. What held them together was a feverish belief that, with the right mindset and plan, anything was possible.

Women, who outnumbered men in NXIVM's ranks, were particularly captivated by Raniere's lessons on taking responsibility for your own feelings. Students explored how they created their own suffering, and how they could use any perceived harm done to them as a teaching moment instead. People with access to vast resources appreciated Raniere's theories about value and money: as long as you were clear about your own ethical principles, each dollar spent represented an effort to change the world for good. As the "philosophical founder" of these concepts, Raniere earned immense regard and praise, and every August he was lauded at an annual retreat held on the week of his birthday.

Raniere still had access to his share of a $14 million irrevocable legal trust made available by heir Clare Bronfman in the wake of his arrest. Bronfman had been released on $100 million bail in 2018 and was one of the last defendants to plead before the 2019 trial began.

Lead defense attorney Marc Agnifilo had chatted with press gallery reporters before the jury arrived, his sky blue tie briefly escaping from his unbuttoned suit jacket. He came across as the most comfortable guy in the courtroom, exuding a kind of confidence that money can't buy.

With Raniere on his feet facing the jury, Judge Garaufis began listing off the charges, which sounded intense and technical and strangely removed from the story that all those in attendance had read in the papers. The words "branding" and "slaves" were never mentioned. Instead there was talk of an "enterprise," a "pattern," "interstate foreign commerce," and "predicate acts." There were seven charges in total, one of them a multipart racketeering charge. The United States first passed racketeering legislation in 1970 as a means of taking down mafia bosses who ordered violence but didn't physically carry out the crimes. It's since been used to prosecute bikers, bankers, cops, and politicians for coordinating complex schemes that might seem legit but obscure all kinds of illegitimate conduct, from embezzlement and bribery to murder and kidnapping.

To prove any kind of racketeering, there needs to be an "enterprise" of multiple people. Over a period of up to ten years, each member has to have agreed to commit at least two crimes in service of a common goal. Law books call this "a pattern of racketeering." The goal itself doesn't have to be criminal, as many gangs and Ponzi schemes have purely money-making ends. Raniere's goal, according to prosecutors, was allegedly to enrich and promote himself, which facilitated his access to women.

Raniere was accused of eleven racketeering acts, among them identity theft, altering court records, forced labor, sex trafficking, extortion, sexual exploitation of a child, and possession of child pornography. On top of that were separate non-racketeering counts covering similar territory: forced labor conspiracy, wire fraud conspiracy, sex trafficking conspiracy, sex trafficking, and attempted sex trafficking.

Over the coming weeks, lead prosecutor Moira Kim Penza and her colleagues would walk the jury through a gut-wrenching version of the Keith Raniere story. Raniere secretly groomed three young Mexican sisters into sexual relationships, photographing one of them naked when she was fifteen years old. He confined one of them to a bedroom for nearly two years because she dared to kiss another man. The youngest sister later became part of a secret pyramid scheme that threatened the release of life-destroying allegations and photos if women did not comply with Raniere's escalating sex games. These women, at one time numbering more than one hundred, were treated as modern-day slaves, and many of them were branded with Raniere's initials.

THE TRIAL WOULD reveal secrets that had been hidden even from Raniere's closest allies. Private messages showed how he'd threatened and manipulated women, using insults, shaming, and misinformation to break down their will to resist. Medical records and testimony would show that his many concurrent girlfriends were compelled to get abortions under the close supervision of his loyal fixers. NXIVM's inner circle arranged marriages and threesomes and secret border crossings and tax evasion, but jurors didn't learn any of this from listening to the charges. The only hint of what was to come appeared in a lengthy juror questionnaire that asked about the #MeToo movement, abortion law, tax evasion, immigration and border crossing, policing, and polyamory.

I sat in awe of the jury, who would decide what was right and wrong in a complex, potentially groundbreaking case. It had taken me more than a year to get my bearings as a reporter on the NXIVM file, and yet this newly assembled group of New Yorkers were expected to render a verdict in a matter of weeks. Though their faces would grow increasingly familiar to me as the trial progressed, they would remain anonymous by court order. How and why they reached their decision would likely remain unknowable. Whatever the verdict, it would have wide-ranging implications about power, consent, and women's agency.

In some ways Raniere was a Rorschach test for what we see wrong with the world: the right of the political spectrum sees liberalism run amok, the worst example of moral breakdown among the monied elite; the left sees textbook toxic masculinity blown up to epic criminal proportions. But like the jurors, I would try not to make up my mind until all the facts had been heard. I'd learned so much about Raniere already, yet I was prepared for the trial to turn everything upside down.

PART ONE

Theory of Everything

CHAPTER ONE

Secret Sisterhood

In late October 2017 I sat in an East Vancouver studio, writing down some of the most surreal questions I've scratched into a notebook in all my years reporting for *Vice*.

I was prepping for an on-camera interview with actor Sarah Edmondson, the first woman in Keith Raniere's inner circle to go public about NXIVM's darkest secrets. She was going to talk about being branded with his initials as part of an initiation ceremony for a "secret sorority" in which she was cast as a literal slave. It was uncomfortable imagining the words *What was it like being branded?* coming out of my mouth, but I knew I had to get there somehow.

She arrived with her own camera crew and handlers already in tow—a surprise for me and my videographer. It was the first time we'd met in person, and I immediately got the sense that she'd been preparing for the interview longer than I had.

Edmondson made direct eye contact as we shook hands. I would later learn that handshakes were practiced extensively in NXIVM workshops, broken down into subtle techniques and dissected for meaning. In retrospect I'd say that my hand as well as hers gave off signs of cautious uncertainty. She was a polished mom and green-smoothie enthusiast with a smile fit for Hallmark movies; I wrote about crime and drugs on the internet, and for a second I wasn't sure we lived in the same universe.

But I was relieved to find that Edmondson spoke my language—or at least she kept having to apologize to her handlers for cussing like a sailor. She told me that in one of the last NXIVM courses she took, on gender and identity, Raniere had taught that women, by nature, are "always looking for the back door."

"I can see all this now is just *fucking bullshit*, excuse my language," she said.

SARAH EDMONDSON FOLDED her legs and clasped her hands uneasily in front of me. Her glossy dark hair was gathered at her shoulders and she wore a key on a chain around her neck. Edmondson had spent twelve years taking almost every class designed by Keith Raniere. In all that time she couldn't recall ever speaking ill of NXIVM lessons or teachers, she said. Edmondson had thought of herself as a "good girl" archetype—eager to take on responsibility and speak "honorably" of her colleagues. She'd met her husband as well as her best friend, Lauren Salzman, through NXIVM—details she often included when retelling her own story of self-empowerment and success. NXIVM was the center of her world, and up until 2017 she'd been proud of that.

Salzman, who lived in Albany, New York, had been Edmondson's maid of honor at her wedding, and then became a godmother to her first son. As director of education, Salzman held one of the highest job titles within NXIVM. Edmondson had followed her friend's upward trajectory, advancing from an unpaid coach to opening a new self-help school in downtown Vancouver, which grew into one of the most successful satellite offices outside of NXIVM's Albany headquarters. Though they lived in different time zones, Edmondson and Salzman were in constant communication, often sharing their fears, dreams, and day-to-day plans.

Salzman was staying with Edmondson on a surprise visit to Vancouver in January 2017 when she asked Sarah to be part of something that she said had changed her life more than anything else she'd done in NXIVM.

"But before I can even tell you about it," Edmondson said, in what I now know was an uncanny Lauren Salzman impersonation, "I need to get something from you, to prove you'll never talk about it."

Salzman wanted "collateral." Maybe a family secret, or a compromising photo. She said she'd hold whatever it was for the rest of their lives—a way to make sure Edmondson would never tell anyone about this top secret life-changing opportunity.

Edmondson had good reason to be curious about Salzman's secret. Her friend was like a real-life Wonder Woman, traveling the world teaching empowerment classes, always making time for pre-dawn exercise or late-night conference calls. She thrived on next-level optimization: constantly multitasking, displaying ever more virtuous lifestyle choices while doing it, and never complaining.

Salzman had an almost wizard-like appearance, often wearing oversized tunics that engulfed her tiny frame. Like Edmondson, she was in her early forties, with dark hair and a bursting white smile. She was a walking embodiment of NXIVM's unspoken success formula, which always seemed to involve heroic acts of self-denial and sacrifice. If anyone had access to the company's most powerful secrets, it was Lauren Salzman.

Salzman said that she herself had given a nude photo as collateral, and suggested that Edmondson could do the same. Or maybe Sarah could offer a confession about something that would blow up her life if it ever got out.

Edmondson trusted Salzman more than anybody else on earth, but she was unsettled by what she was hearing—it sounded like the personal accountability techniques she'd learned and taught in NXIVM, but kicked up to a disturbing degree. Salzman sensed Edmondson's discomfort and framed it as a good thing, saying that Sarah should feel nauseated by the thought of betraying the trust between them—that it was exactly the feeling the collateral was meant to reinforce.

After a day of uneasy reflection, Edmondson wrote down a confession about her party-girl twenties. But Salzman said her indiscretions weren't damaging enough. She encouraged her to make a bigger confession—to make it up if she had to. What mattered was its weight. When Edmondson finally arrived at something consequential enough, Salzman took a photo of the handwritten confession with her phone. This was the first price of admission to the international women's group called DOS, or Dominus Obsequious Sororium—a fake Latin phrase roughly translating to "master over the slave women."

DOS, whose members were mostly drawn from the ranks of NXIVM, went by many different names. It was a vow, a sorority, a badass bitch boot camp. Some women even talked about it as if it were an elite talent agency. In Edmondson's brain it was a secret society. Salzman told her it was like the Freemasons but for women wanting to build character and change the world. The two would be making a lifelong commitment to each other, though not on the equal footing they had as best friends. Edmondson would have to take a lifelong "vow of obedience" to Salzman—to become her slave.

Obviously slavery sounded like a bad idea to Edmondson, but Salzman assured her that "master" and "slave" were just useful terms, like "guru" or "disciple." It was just another way of saying that Salzman was her coach. "She even said, 'I'm taking you under my wing. And I'm going to take good care of you.' It felt very—the way she did it—felt very loving."

It takes a certain level of privilege to overlook such historically abhorrent terminology, Edmondson admits now. She knew that Black women, Indigenous women, and other women of color came through NXIVM's entry-level courses but in many cases left quickly and quietly. The women who stayed and became lifers were mostly white or white-passing, many raised in private schools and country clubs, where subjugation was an abstraction more than a lived reality. These were glaring blind spots, no doubt, but the implicit threat of collateral blacked out Edmondson's option to walk away. She vowed to obey Salzman for as long as she lived.

SARAH EDMONDSON'S FAITH in her friend unraveled less than two months later, after a March 2017 initiation ceremony that brought together five women in the same collateral-bound situation. Edmondson and the four other women being inducted into DOS took turns holding each other down, naked, while a doctor they knew from NXIVM carved a cryptic symbol into their bikini line with a cauterizing pen. Worse, all of this was filmed.

Before the branding began, Edmondson pulled Salzman aside and said she didn't want to go through with it. She didn't know what that would mean for their friendship, her vow of secrecy, or the collateral she'd put on the line, and Salzman wasn't willing to say. Instead she turned her deep knowledge of Edmondson's fears and insecurities back on her, reminding her that she'd "always looked for a back door." This was a pattern Edmondson had identified in herself, one for which she'd learned to welcome coaching.

Edmondson had the highest rank of any of the DOS recruits that day, and Salzman said she should show it by setting a good example for the other women. Meanwhile, Edmondson told me, she was struggling to control herself—trying to justify the extreme pressure as a good thing.

"We were crying, we were shaking, we were holding each other. It was horrific. It was like a bad horror movie," she said. "We even had these surgical masks on because the smell of [burning] flesh was so strong."

Edmondson asked me to imagine someone taking a lit match to my crotch and drawing a line with it over and over again. "I really believe that the only way I did it was I disassociated," she said. "I wasn't present. I went somewhere else. I thought about giving birth to my son. I thought about how much I loved him, and I just focused on that. I just brought up a loving state."

The women had talked about a dime-sized tattoo, not the jagged two-inch scar Edmondson now had hidden under her jeans. Salzman said the composition of angled lines represented the four elements; if you unfocused your eyes, you could at least make out a mountain and a horizon.

Still in shock from the pain, Edmondson followed her master's directions, despite a rising urge to run. She was using Salzman's phone to film the fourth woman being branded when she saw a text pop up on its screen: "How are they all doing with each other?"

The message came from someone saved in Salzman's contact list as "KAR."

"I thought maybe there was another woman involved named Karen," she said. She just needed time, she told me, to "unravel the lies."

IT WOULD TAKE three more weeks to put it all together. The letters *KAR* and the symbol burned into her skin pointed back to the same person. For nearly thirty minutes of unbearable pain with no anesthetic, Keith Alan Raniere's initials had been seared onto Edmondson's body.

Was that when she realized she was part of something truly twisted? Did she think, "Maybe I'm in a cult"?

"*Cult* definitely came into my mind when [Salzman] told me that part of it was getting a tattoo," Edmondson said. Seconds later, she strongly encouraged me and my videographer to edit that part out. One of her handlers firmly agreed: the word "cult" wasn't going to work.

"Can we please? That's a legal thing for me," Edmondson said. "Be careful how you edit." Her own safety could be at risk, she added.

I was confused. We'd already talked about some textbook Cult 101 red flags: she'd told me about the sashes they wore to denote each member's rank, about secret handshakes, and about bowing to a photo of Keith Raniere, whom they called "Vanguard." In my notebook I had bullet points on calorie restriction, sleep deprivation, arranged marriage, and BDSM-style punishment. Edmondson was blowing the whistle on this group for its extreme control of women's diets and sex lives, and yet she wasn't willing to utter the word "cult" on camera?

I would later learn that Raniere was a man who knew how to double down. He'd sued many former students and adversaries just for using the "cult" label or for daring to criticize his secret self-help "technology." By the time Raniere was in prison six months later, Edmondson was more than happy to call NXIVM a cult and Raniere an abusive cult leader. But he wasn't behind bars on that Friday afternoon in October.

Over two decades Raniere had successfully ruined the lives of several people who tried to expose him, usually through lawsuits, private investigators, and criminal complaints in several states. Some of these people, usually women, were bankrupted and even jailed. One woman went into hiding with the help of a state trooper and was rumored to have fled the country.

It was reasonable for Edmondson to fear that Raniere would try to ruin her next.

A STORY THIS incendiary leaves the mind racing with questions. How is it that our brains can allow for one person to see sex trafficking and another to see self-actualization? Can concentrated social influence really change what a person thinks, feels, and experiences? Why would Edmondson, who struck me as a strong-willed, determined person, want to be part of this secret sisterhood that hurt women in disturbing ways? Why would anyone sign up for a secret group that called women "slaves"?

Edmondson was patient with my questions. On many occasions she welcomed me into her home to explain her decisions. I could sense her effort to demonstrate to me why for twelve years she loved NXIVM and its community and had seen no reason to feel any different.

I realized that most of the seventeen thousand people who took NXIVM classes thought the worst it could be accused of was *being corny.* In their minds it was like a smiley, slightly kooky summer camp for adults. There was no room in their mental portrait for sex crimes or human trafficking because everything about this group seemed as wholesome as a Thanksgiving dinner. Women didn't join because they wanted to be branded and extorted; they wanted to help people and do something important with their lives. If there was a common thread among them, it was that they dreamt bigger than their peers.

Over the years I've reviewed tens of thousands of pages of Raniere's patents, legal filings, lectures, interviews, and writings, all in search of the hook that had captivated so many women. I ultimately found that it was *other women* who allowed would-be students to talk about their secret ambitions, try on a fantasy future, and get started down a path that seemed a fast track to getting there. Former insiders who took that path say it began with a honeymoon experience, finding a sense of mission and purpose and a community that seemed to drop everything to support you. At least at first.

On a brisk forty-minute walk along Vancouver's waterfront, Edmondson explained for me how she reeled in new students. She demonstrated how her pitch would sound a lot like a gentle chat between friends, often on a walk similar to ours.

"Most of the time they'd be a friend of a friend," she said. The mutual friend would have already spoken highly of her and the work she did coaching actors and entrepreneurs. Then Edmondson would usually jump in with her own compliments—in my case, for example, telling me she's heard that I'm a great writer.

It was all in the service of fostering a meaningful, pleasant connection. NXIVM called it "building rapport"—a straightforward concept, and not particularly unique, but one that NXIVM students practiced and studied at length. I've since learned that it helps to do it while walking, since your heart rates are likely to match and you'll intuitively feel as if you're on the same journey.

"This would be five, ten, maybe even fifteen or twenty minutes of just rapport," Edmondson said. "I would do that until it feels like we're in the same world."

Next Edmondson steered our conversation toward my ambitions and dreams. She asked what I was working on, what I was excited about, and for the most part allowed me to guide the conversation. Because I had preconceived notions about how self-help works, I started listing my professional insecurities and fears around commitment, half hoping Edmondson would pounce on them. Instead she guided me back to talk of blue skies.

I got the sense that Edmondson was more focused on making me feel hope than on "finding the ruin," a technique used by Scientology recruiters to push our most emotional buttons, as documented in Lawrence Wright's book *Going Clear*. Those recruiters, having lured a subject into a private room with the promise of a free "personality test," will often cut deep with assessments of the subject's personal shortcomings.

Edmondson told me she would use her intuition and look for body-language cues to assess how to proceed. Many times she'd sense there wasn't a strong enough personal connection, and so she'd find a way to let the person gently off the hook. "I would just skip to the end and say, 'Honestly, I don't think that this is for you,' just based on energy," she said. But for an eager listener like me, she'd offer a taste of the "tech" students got to learn.

At this point Edmondson noted that she'd already been using at least one coaching technique on me, one that came from a lesson NXIVM called "Hypothesis of Language."

"I would try to mirror back the words that you used so that you felt listened to and heard. And you wouldn't even clock that, if I did it well," she said.

She would never fake it, she continued, but she'd often draw parallels to her own life to create a sense of common ground. "I would never put in things that weren't true. I would never say I was a writer also . . . I'd just bring up things I'd also gone through, so the person felt like 'Oh, there's hope for me.'"

Immediately I considered all the words Edmondson might have specifically selected for my ears. But I also got the impression that she was exceptionally perceptive in the way she noticed my verbal tics and body language. Despite my self-conscious wondering—*Is she swearing more than usual? Am I saying "like" too much?*—I did get a sense that there was hope for me, as she put it. Even though I was more than ready to get vulnerable, Edmondson didn't make me feel as though my weaknesses were being exploited. Technically, we were having a conversation about how I'd like to change my life "physically, emotionally, and spiritually," but it mostly helped me imagine an ideal future self.

"Can you imagine a world where you're more at peace with your decisions; where, if you do commit, you feel really good about that, and you're not worried about if you hadn't committed?" she asked.

I nodded and shrugged.

"So what would it be worth to you to make that go away?"

"Like, moneywise?" I asked. I hadn't expected a budgeting session, so the question threw me off balance.

"Yeah. Like, if you try to quantify it in your head, how much does that pattern cost you?"

I thought out loud about the times I'd moved across continents out of restlessness—the price of my endless need to move on to the next thing. "I don't know . . . $10,000? That's a crazy amount," I said, not for a second anticipating what was coming.

"Great! Good deal," Edmondson replied, flashing a smile. "Our program is only $3,000."

"Good sell!" I laughed, surprised by how easily I'd walked into a hard pitch. I couldn't immediately think of a way to talk myself out of this so-called deal, either.

Edmondson said that she now thinks this approach is "gross" and "manipulative." But at the time, she thought she was showing people how to invest in themselves. "When I thought it was a good end, I felt so good being able to do that for somebody," she told me. "I didn't think I was being tricky. I thought I got them a deal. I felt that way."

Edmondson admits that when she first signed up, in 2005, she too was pitched this way, and that she'd said she would have paid $100,000 to get rid of the issues she was dealing with. She knows others who claimed that their anger issues had lost them as much as $50 million in film contracts. It crossed my mind that people with more access to money and privilege would likely have felt they were being offered an even juicier "deal."

Edmondson and I weaved through a crowd of families with dogs and toddlers. A clear sky was reflecting off False Creek. I tried to imagine how I'd feel if the information she was feeding me was my only source of NXIVM info. Would it sound interesting? Sure. Would I be ready to invest *three grand* in my personal growth? Probably not.

"Let's say I was unsure," I said.

In that case, Edmondson said, she might tell me more about how the "tech" works, or move into a sales strategy that she called "specify, isolate, overcome."

If, for example, I'd said the amount of money was the only thing holding me back, she would shift the conversation into brainstorming ways to secure it. Did I know that I could get my course for free if I brought in three new students? If she were to lend me the money, would I go for it?

She was testing how ready I was to break out of my "issue." This would get me locked in while I was still excited and hadn't had time for a second thought. I knew it was coercive, but I also figured my impulsive brain might well have jumped at this kind of rare opportunity.

Edmondson said she'd been willing to go to great lengths to make that first sale. "Imagine you or someone you loved needed really expensive surgery and it's going to cost $3,000. Where are you going to find the money?" she asked.

I silently reminded myself that this was only a "fun" simulation.

"And it really should be the same emergency," she continued. "It's an emergency to resolve these things within you now, so the rest of your life is different and better. Why wait?"

Part of the brainstorming exercise included listing some ideas you wouldn't choose—like working at a strip club or sleeping with a casting director for a gig. This helped people feel as if they had more control over the situation. The exercise came from NXIVM's curriculum on self-esteem.

"We talk about how the working definition of self-esteem is your perceived options in a given area," Edmondson said. "So, for example, you may have self-esteem as a journalist. If *Vice* fired you, you could work here or there, or write your book, or do a blog, and maybe you feel good about that." But by the same token, she said, I could feel a total lack of options in another area of my life—say in my family or romantic relationships.

I wasn't quite following her unconventional definition of self-esteem, but she delivered it in a way that suggested it was a well-tested theory. "A lot of times it was actors being like, 'I don't know how to make my big break,' you know? That was common, and I would have lots of stuff to say, because as an actor, I know what you can do to take more control of your career besides waiting for your agent to call."

I WAS BEGINNING to see how Edmondson's powers of persuasion had earned her a central role in building NXIVM's Vancouver community. These pitches happened not only on long walks but also during car rides home, or in the sauna at a beachside yoga studio. Edmondson was the primary reason these classes had spread like wildfire through the local acting industry.

As we finished up our walk, she asked if I'd eaten lunch yet, and I told her I hadn't. We stopped at a high-end market around the corner from her place to pick up kefir water on the way.

Spontaneous meal-sharing also seemed to be part of the NXIVM seduction process. In a lengthy *New York Times Magazine* profile, the journalist Vanessa Grigoriadis described how Seagram heir Sara Bronfman cooked up eggs for her at Bronfman's preposterously proportioned home. We had the same thing: poached eggs, on gluten-free toast, with fermented beets, farmers' market greens, carrots, a lemon-and-ghee dressing, and the kefir water to wash it down. The greens were so fresh that Edmondson found a live bug on her plate.

"It's a worm or something," she said, "from the farmers' market. But I did wash it. . . . Oh my god, it has *legs*!"

"That is *wild*!" I said, laughing. I felt as though I'd experienced a caricature of a West Coast healthy lunch. Extra protein and all.

Edmondson followed the health and wellness trends that most give up a week after New Year's Eve. When she committed to something, she stuck with it. As she moved around her kitchen, she seemed to be living someone's ideal life, with her picture-perfect family and home. If this was a part of the seduction, I could absolutely see the appeal.

It was the kind of experience that had enticed so many young women to learn more about Keith Raniere and his so-called tech. This wasn't something you could easily say no to. It was a lifestyle, a community, and most of all a chance to think about your best self.

CHAPTER TWO

One in Ten Million

Though mentors like Sarah Edmondson did much of the work convincing new students that they could win at life, most of the credit went to NXIVM founder Keith Raniere, the purported genius who started it all.

Raniere's superintelligence was one of NXIVM's most important and persuasive myths, and one that can be traced back to a 1988 article in the *Times Union* newspaper of Albany, New York. The story was about his membership in an obscure high-IQ society, based on a self-administered intelligence test that allegedly ranked Raniere one in ten million.

Heidi Hutchinson remembers it well. At age twenty-seven, Raniere was still ten years away from launching his self-help empire, but he was already living in the Albany area and accumulating acolytes who would make that dream happen. Hutchinson's sister Gina was on the team of (mostly women) supporters who helped Raniere complete a take-home IQ test developed by Dr. Ronald K. Hoeflin. The Mega Society test was stacked with brainteasers that challenged spatial reasoning, analogical thinking, and math skills. One of the questions asked for the maximum number of individual three-dimensional shapes that could be made with three interpenetrating cubes. Hoeflin claimed the questions were so hard that even a person with the minimum IQ cutoff for Mensa would, on average, get less than half of the forty-eight questions right.

When Raniere received his results, Hutchinson recalled, he became furious that his team had gotten two of the questions wrong. According to Hutchinson, Raniere negotiated with Hoeflin to redevelop the scoring, which put Raniere at a cartoonishly high IQ score of 240.

Psychometric experts who later reviewed the Mega test found serious flaws in its scoring and weighting. For one, Hoeflin's formula relied on self-submitted IQ scores from previous tests. And unlike supervised Mensa tests, the Mega test relied on the honor system to ensure that takers worked alone and didn't use a computer to work through the massive calculations. Raniere broke at least one of those rules, if not both.

Psychologist Roger Carlson wrote in a 1991 critique that the test may have measured "resourcefulness" and "persistence" more than it measured intelligence. Any IQ score above 145, Carlson noted, is already starting to split statistically insignificant hairs. A calculation north of 170 falls more than four standard deviations away from the middle of an average IQ bell curve—theoretically possible, but not scientifically reliable.

The Mega test "violates many good psychometric principles by overinterpreting the weak data of a self-selected sample," Carlson wrote. And Hoeflin went far beyond standard "number crunching" in his calculations: "What Hoeflin has done in the norming of his test results," Carlson declared, "can be said to be nothing short of number pulverization."

IQ testing itself has since come under more scientific scrutiny, and after the proliferation of high-IQ societies in the late 1970s and 80s, new research in the 1990s moved toward theories of multiple kinds of intelligence. Intelligence testing as a whole has been criticized for its narrow, culturally exclusive definition of cognitive ability. Racists and eugenicists are obsessed with it, which is never a good sign. But in 1988, skepticism about high-end intelligence testing and Hoeflin's formula had not yet taken hold. With eye-popping results in hand, Raniere's team of supporters seemed to have no trouble finding a local Albany reporter willing to write a googly-eyed profile.

"The woman who did the write-up was completely infatuated with Keith," Hutchinson recalls of the now-infamous *Times Union* story. Raniere didn't have to brag about himself to make it happen; Hutchinson's sister Gina reached out to the paper first, talking Raniere up as a rising star in a mostly boring town. "I think the reporter was excited about it . . . being able to feature a real live true genius, right here in Albany," says Hutchinson.

Raniere told the reporter that he'd learned to spell the word "homogenized" by reading it off the side of a milk carton at age two, and that he "had an understanding of subjects such as quantum physics and computers by age four."

"By the time he was 16, the Brooklyn-born genius says he had exhausted the curriculum at his high school," read the *Times Union* story. "He dropped out of school and entered Rensselaer Polytechnic Institute where he simultaneously earned undergraduate degrees in math, physics and biology."

The piece went on to say that he played seven instruments, tied the state record for the hundred-yard dash, rode a unicycle, and juggled—"not necessarily at the same time," the writer joked. "But one gets the impression that this amazing young man, who requires only two to four hours of sleep, could do both—if he put his mind to it."

Raniere's take-home test score translated into recognition for "highest IQ" in the Australian edition of *The Guinness Book of Records* in 1989. Sandwiched between the largest-ever human chest measurements and the lowest-recorded voice, a tiny write-up mentions Raniere and two other Americans who took Hoeflin's test. Marilyn vos Savant, of Missouri, and Eric Hart, of New York, both tied Raniere's high score of forty-six. "This represents a performance at the level of one in 10,000,000," read the entry. According to the record book, Hoeflin had admitted only seventeen members to his exclusive Mega Society.

The next year, Guinness retired the "highest IQ" contest following questions about the Mega test's design and execution. In the early 1990s other high-IQ societies began rejecting the Mega test, claiming that some of its brainteasers had already been published elsewhere and that several of its problems could be solved using basic computer programming skills. Some solutions were leaked in the early days of the internet, and if you looked at M.C. Escher's lithograph *Waterfall* long enough, you could figure out Hoeflin's three-cube problem.

Despite all the inconsistency surrounding his IQ world record, Raniere committed to the one-in-ten-million super-genius narrative. Right up until his arrest in 2018, he repeated and riffed on the story of his extraordinary intelligence at an improbably young age. In one recorded interview with *Hawaii Five-O* actor Grace Park, Raniere even described having memories of infancy and early childhood. "I spoke very early," he told Park. "By the time I was, you know, a year old, I was asking questions. . . . I had some really deep, profound thoughts at an early age."

Old versions of the NXIVM website, which have since been taken down, contained more unverified claims: Raniere was an East Coast judo champion by age eleven; he learned high school math in a day at age twelve; he taught himself three years of college mathematics by age thirteen. There was the assertion that he'd been "noted as one of the top three problem-solvers in the world," another nod to his questionable Mega test score.

There are holes in Raniere's boy genius narrative. Transcripts from Rensselaer Polytechnic Institute show that he graduated with a 2.26 grade point average, the equivalent of a C+. At his trial in June 2019, Raniere's grades were projected on screens in front of a jury, showing F grades in general physiology and quantum mechanics and a D in experimental physics. The jury learned that in 1988 he was placed on academic probation and faced academic dismissal.

RANIERE WAS BORN in Brooklyn in 1960, but he was raised in the suburban sprawl of Suffern, New York, a couple of hours south of Albany.

When Mark Jackson was in school with Raniere, he didn't see anything exceptional about him. Raniere wasn't popular or extraordinarily athletic, though he clearly liked math and judo more than the average student.

Jackson and Raniere were bused together from Suffern along the New Jersey border to Green Meadow Waldorf School, an alternative school that appealed to hippie parents of the early 70s. Myths, legends, and Bible stories factored heavily into their educational diet, and the school boasted lively orchestra, choir, woodworking, and theater programs. In Raniere's telling there were gardens and crochet lessons, and none of the students were allowed to wear clothes with logos.

It would take Raniere another twenty years to fully develop his prodigy image, supposedly capable of stringing full sentences together by age one and becoming a self-taught concert-level pianist by age twelve. If Raniere really did develop above-average musical talents, Jackson didn't see it at school. "He played clarinet, but he was a bad musician," he says.

Jackson, who is a writer and actor, has the gruff outward appearance of a biker, but with kind eyes and a well-shaped graying beard. He and Raniere grew to know each other well over three years of middle school. Jackson says he sat beside Raniere on the school bus for all of fifth grade. They weren't best friends, but they spent time together outside of school at each other's houses, playing basketball, or swimming. Jackson remembers going over to Raniere's split-level house in October 1971, when they were both in sixth grade. They and three other boys went trick-or-treating together, stuffed themselves full of candy, and slept on the floor in the Raniere family's living room. Jackson says he remembers the night vividly because the light of a clock kept him up most of the night.

Raniere was an only child, but to Jackson he seemed to have a typical, healthy relationship with his parents. And even though they'd separated four years earlier, that didn't stop Raniere from boasting about his dad's skiing prowess or minding his manners when asking his mom about dinner. In interviews he has described his mother as "soulful" and said he took care of her through some serious health issues, including a heart condition. She died in 1978, when Raniere was eighteen years old.

Jackson doesn't remember ever meeting Raniere's dad in person, but he heard all about the expensive gifts he bought his son. There was a pool in the Ranieres' yard and an upscale sports car in the driveway. Raniere has said he grew up in the comfortable suburban neighborhood "surrounded by kids whose parents were all lawyers and doctors and surgeons."

Raniere didn't distinguish himself in class. "There were at least four kids who were smarter than him," Jackson says. "He was definitely smart, but not outstanding." Though math was his favorite, Raniere was beat out by higher achievers in other subjects. One of the girls in his cohort, for example, would, after being voted class valedictorian, go on to complete a PhD in biochemistry at Harvard. "There weren't exactly slouches in that class, but in terms of math and science he was bright," Jackson says.

The thing that stands out in Jackson's memory was Raniere's near-constant need for validation. He was prone to one-upping his classmates in unexpected situations, no matter how petty or point-less. In childhood photos Raniere appears to be shorter than his classmates, with ears slightly too large for his head and his chest puffed out enough to suggest a competitive streak. He would wear his judo outfit to class and practice moves on the playground, so Jackson and his friends made a point of keeping their distance when it came to schoolyard fights.

Jackson recalls one incident that became the subject of endless schoolyard gossip. One of the fifth-grade girls had apparently walked in on her older sister having sex, but being so young she had no idea what it meant. As Jackson recounts it, she was distressed and still trying to process the strange experience when Raniere apparently lunged at an opportunity to use information as a weapon.

Raniere picked on the girl for the rest of the school year, remind-ing her of the shameful secret he could expose to anyone at any time, Jackson says. Raniere threatened to tell the girl's parents and sister that he knew what she'd seen. It was only when the girl told her par-ents what had happened, and her mother intervened, that Raniere left her alone.

In middle school Raniere read the Isaac Asimov novel *Second Foundation*, which is set in a future where all human behavior is reduced to mathematical equations. Raniere later claimed he was "inspired by the concepts on optimal human communication" and as a tween began developing a "theory and practice" he later called Rational Inquiry. It was a scientific approach, he claimed, that would become the basis of his self-help methods at NXIVM. "This practice involves analyzing and optimizing how the mind handles data," he wrote in 2003. "It involves mathematical set theory applied in a computer programmatic fashion to processes such as memory and emotion."

AROUND AGE FOURTEEN, Raniere experienced "a very great perceptual shift," as he described it to actor Grace Park many decades later. He discovered that if you let go of fear and value judgments, "You can feel as much joy as you want at any time."

He'd wanted to "surrender to joy," Raniere said, but he was held back by "bungee cords" of fear. His teenage thoughts approached an epiphany: "If I were to let go of everything at this point in time—I'm a little fourteen-year-old kid, right—I may not go to school anymore, I may not have ambitions to go to college, I may just decide to try to take, you know, a pair of shorts and a T-shirt and go walking off into the sunset."

Raniere said he faced each fear in turn—fear of starving, fear of disappointing his mother—and over time the "bungee cords" holding him back started to dissolve. This was how he discovered the key to success and happiness, Raniere said. "When you remove [each fear] one by one, you know, you can feel as much joy as you want," he told Park.

Sometimes Raniere described this shift as a spiritual awakening, the moment he became "unified," or "enlightened." Decades later he would tell certain girlfriends that he recalled all of his previous lives, and that he knew he'd come into this lifetime in order to help others find enlightenment.

Barbara Bouchey, Raniere's girlfriend from 2000 to 2008, claims this transformation caused an immediate shift in the way he interacted with girls. As Bouchey first recounted on the CBC podcast *Uncover: Escaping NXIVM*, Raniere established a formula for acquiring loyalty and devotion from the opposite sex. He embraced commitment and grand romantic gestures, Bouchey learned from Raniere's father, James. And with the serial nature of his propositions concealed, Raniere benefited from always appearing ready for a lifetime together.

"Dozens of young girls were calling the house," Bouchey continued. "He was telling every single woman, every single girl the same thing: 'I love you. You're the special one.'"

More than a quarter century later, he would use a version of this formula to ensnare Bouchey herself.

Raniere transferred to Rockland Country Day School for high school, but he returned to visit Jackson and his Green Meadow friends in 1977, when they were all seniors. Jackson remembers that

Raniere's "wild, wild bragging" had gotten worse. "He was bragging mostly about girls. I think he had singled me out because I was sort of popular in class with that."

Their mutual friend Matthew, who once seemed an equal to Raniere in middle school, had somehow fallen into a "lackey" role, Jackson says. Matthew was acting the part of Raniere's hype man, teeing up Raniere's biggest brag of the afternoon. Jackson says Matthew cleared his throat and said, "Hey, Keith, what's your record like for getting a chick in the sack?"

"Twelve seconds," Raniere replied, according to Jackson.

"I was sitting there with my girlfriend at the time, and we kind of looked at each other like, 'Um, that's a little weird.'"

Raniere's habitual weirdness with women and girls was just getting started.

CHAPTER THREE

Mothership, New York

Heidi Hutchinson caught her fifteen-year-old sister Gina with a twenty-four-year-old Keith Raniere in her bedroom during the Christmas holidays.

It was 1984. Heidi and Gina lived in Clifton Park, a quiet, mostly white suburb less than a half-hour drive outside of downtown Albany, New York, where Raniere's NXIVM empire would later take root. Between the time Heidi and Gina's grandparents settled there and Gina started high school, the town's population had grown from two thousand to about twenty thousand.

Gina had met Raniere at a local theater club the year before. One of her classmates had a part in *The Barber of Seville*. Heidi was an aspiring actor herself, playing in the same club's production of *Little Murders*, by Jules Feiffer. Heidi remembers seeing her sister and her friend, also named Gina, together at rehearsals and performances, where Raniere would chat them up. The two Ginas, nearly a decade younger than Raniere, seemed to appreciate the grown-up treatment. Raniere had a way of interrogating every belief, fear, and insecurity they might have, and making it sound like the most important task in the world.

The two friends had more than a name and high school in common. In 1984 both were allegedly molested by Raniere. And when Heidi discovered the abuse that Christmas break, Raniere was already deeply entwined in Gina's life.

"I feel guilty about it to this day," Heidi says.

Gina was interested in Eastern religion, shamanism, philosophy, and martial arts, and Raniere positioned himself as a brilliant mentor in all of those fields. Heidi says she now recognizes this as a tactic predators commonly use to groom families into allowing unsupervised contact.

IN PHOTOS, GINA Hutchinson has a wide, sly smile with dark, bushy hair and blue eyes. From a certain angle she looks like a less witchy Fairuza Balk. Her journal entries have the scratchy, back-tilted print of a left-hander.

In her journal, Gina wrote about spirituality and her experience receiving energy healing from Raniere. He studied the traditions of Swami Muktananda, the founder of Siddha Yoga. (The guru, who set up an ashram in upstate New York in the late 1970s, was believed to encourage enlightenment simply by his presence.) Raniere told Gina that he recalled his past lives and had made "a commitment" to certain people to be their spiritual teacher in this life. In return, she brought him all the spiritual knowledge she could find.

Gina looked up to Raniere for his theories on Buddhism and the unexplained, but it wasn't all they talked about. At a young age Gina was excited about Jack Kerouac and E.E. Cummings, and Raniere accordingly showed off his deep knowledge of and appreciation for beat and free-form poetry. Whatever Gina thought she knew about the world, Raniere knew a thousand times better, according to Heidi.

Heidi suspects that part of what made Raniere captivating for her teenage sister was that Gina was seeking an older brother figure. Their mother had moved into their grandmother's house during a complicated marriage separation, and both of Gina's older brothers moved out soon after.

"He became what she was missing," Heidi says. "He was a friend, but then he started to position himself as a mentor, as somebody who was like our older brother, who was a genius himself." Raniere convinced Gina to drop out of high school and get a GED under his supervision. She was upgrading to a private tutor. "He went to Rensselaer, and that was a mecca of genius. It's the college on the hill, you know, a place of privilege."

Raniere took Gina and her friends on trips to Manhattan, where his dad had an apartment, or out for pizza in the suburbs. By the time Heidi realized what was happening, Gina already had her heart set on pursuing enlightenment with Raniere, in this life and the next.

When confronted, Raniere said he intended to spend his whole life with his "fiancée" Gina, and this seemed to convince the Hutchinson parents, who were somewhat preoccupied with their divorce. Heidi says she wasn't convinced; from the beginning she thought Raniere was a "megalomaniac." But Gina wouldn't hear it.

Raniere and Gina experimented with altered states of consciousness, according to Heidi, and in twilight states, Raniere guided Gina in piecing together that in another lifetime, she may have been an important Tibetan Buddhist figure. This reinforced Gina's belief that they had a strong spiritual connection, that their thoughts and actions were cosmically linked.

Heidi says she believes Gina suffered from some kind of mental health event—something close to a break—and Raniere suggested to Gina that this could be a natural result of her special spiritual sensitivity. He had a name for her experience, "disintegration," and he claimed to know how to help her become more whole again. "She needed something to cling on to, to understand what she'd been through," Heidi suggests.

Harvard researcher Susan Clancy has studied the psychological phenomena behind many fringe human experiences, from a belief in having been the subject of alien abduction to recovered childhood memories of satanic ritual abuse. The element she often sees in common in these experiences is well-meaning therapists using trance states, in some cases leading subjects toward paranormal (or repressed memory) conclusions.

Clancy's research has found that our memories are changed every time we access them, and that memories played back and recontextualized in hypnosis are at higher risk of becoming distorted, or "false." People who are higher in creativity or more prone to fantasy are more likely to have these kinds of vivid trance experiences—such as a belief that they've been probed by aliens or that they're the reincarnation of Simone de Beauvoir—committed to memory.

FOR MUCH OF the 1980s Gina didn't know that Raniere had at least one other girlfriend. He was living with a college friend named Karen Unterreiner, who would go on to play a central role in NXIVM. Though they never talked about their relationship publicly, Raniere and Unterreiner began a sexual relationship as students at Rensselaer.

Heidi long suspected that Unterreiner secretly pined for Raniere, but she hadn't imagined they'd been involved the whole time. "She was always around, and they were roommates, and they were just friends—always *just friends*," Heidi says. "She acted like his mom, actually."

Raniere and Unterreiner both worked in computer programming after finishing school. Raniere found a programming job at New York's Department of Labor and later transferred to the state's parole division.

Unterreiner and Raniere first lived in an apartment in Troy, New York, and then in 1987 moved into a townhouse together in Heidi and Gina's neighborhood of Clifton Park, a suburban town of winding streets. That second house would become a central space for Raniere's many so-called spiritual wives over the next several decades. It was the first in a cluster of NXIVM-associated properties that would later be dubbed "the mothership."

The homes of Clifton Park are strikingly uniform, and the mazelike arrangement of the streets protects them from outsider traffic. The buildings, grouped in triplets and quadruplets around small cul-de-sacs or crescents, resemble pieces of a Monopoly board game. The first NXIVM-owned townhouse is tall and boxy with pastel-colored siding and, like its many neighbors, a single-car garage. It became known to Raniere's followers by its street name, the Flintlock house.

Unterreiner was by many accounts the first long-term member of Raniere's harem, which would grow by a dozen members in just over a decade. Around 1989 she was joined by Pamela Cafritz, daughter to well-known Washington political donors Buffy and Bill Cafritz. According to Sarah Edmondson, Pam and Raniere met on a chairlift at a ski resort. When Raniere said "Follow me" at the top of a hill, Cafritz did just that.

"She was another brokenhearted stray who came into the misfits club to be healed by Keith," Heidi says. Cafritz became a starry-eyed servant for Raniere: she cooked his food, washed his clothes, and drove him to wherever he needed to be. She became known as a "defuser of bombs"—able to soften any conflict and salvage the most damaged relationships. She went on to facilitate many of Raniere's relationships with young women and girls, as Ghislaine Maxwell is alleged to have done for Jeffrey Epstein.

While Gina and Raniere liked to riff on religious and philosophical ideas, Unterreiner got an actuary certification and was seen as the business mind of the group. As long as Heidi knew them, Unterreiner and Raniere planned to launch a business around Raniere's genius.

Friends who knew Raniere at the time say he was always looking for a way to make a lot of money with minimal effort. A friend told the *Uncover* podcast host that Raniere's life goal was to set up an infinite money-generating machine, in part so he could focus on non-business interests.

Raniere studied the sales techniques of Amway and other companies that saved on overhead by turning salespeople into recruiters. He tried selling health supplements for Matol International and legal services for Pre-Paid Legal, two lesser-known players in the mostly unregulated multi-level marketing ecosystem. Raniere often said that other multi-level marketing companies were unethical and that he was working on building something better for humanity. In court filings he claimed to have invented a "new concept in marketing" that happened to resemble Amway's direct-selling structure.

On May 1, 1990, Raniere launched a new company called Consumers' Buyline, which seemed to bundle existing multi-level marketing vendors under his "open marketing" concept. Unterreiner took on the bookkeeping, and Cafritz supplied investment. Like Amway, the company sold discounted household products and services to people who paid annual membership fees.

Gina Hutchinson wasn't so interested in selling products or recruiting sellers, but she worked for an hourly wage in the company's computer programming department. Her parents allowed it because they were convinced that Raniere was preparing to marry their daughter. Meanwhile, he continued pursuing other women and girls inside and outside the growing company.

THERE ARE A couple of theories as to how so many bright, ambitious women wound up turning their lives upside down to become part of Raniere's stable of girlfriends. Cult expert Steven Hassan's theory is that Raniere used neuro-linguistic programming, or NLP, to leave suggestions in women's subconscious minds.

"I've talked to more than a few ex-members [of NXIVM] now who talked about their first meetings with Keith. They have no memory of what happened. These are two- or four-hour meetings," Hassan told me after Raniere's arrest in 2018. "As an expert who studied NLP, I think that's indicative of them being put into a hypnotic trance state, and specifically given a suggestion that they'll have no recollection of what was said or done."

Toni Natalie remembers seeing Raniere speak for the first time at a Consumers' Buyline event at a Rochester hotel in April 1991. She had decided to check out whether this up-and-coming company lived up to its marketing, which boasted about the founder's record-setting IQ. Natalie hadn't completed high school, so she was curious to learn what the smartest man in the world spent his time thinking about.

Raniere pulled Natalie aside during her tour of the Consumers' Buyline office in August 1991, and they discussed her smoking habit. "I had a small child," she said in a 2017 *Vice* interview. "I was trying to cut it out."

As she first confessed in 2006 to reporter Chet Hardin of the Albany-based *Metroland* newspaper, Natalie remembered going into a small room with Raniere, where he asked her questions about her anxieties and fears, occasionally touching her knuckles—setting an "anchor," as it's called in hypnotherapy. NLP's creators claim these anchors can be used to call up similar emotional states. "The last thing I recall was him saying, 'What relaxes you and what stresses you out?'" Natalie said. "He told me after, 'Every time you feel like you want a cigarette, press this spot on your knuckles.'" Though she remembered being in the room with Raniere for only fifteen minutes, she later learned it had been nearly three hours.

As Steven Hassan puts it, NLP is an "amoral system" that can be dangerous in the wrong hands. "If you're a psychiatrist who has sworn an oath to do no harm, and people are coming to you for help, you're being granted a license to do what's going to work and help them. But when you're talking about business and money and sex, and power differentials . . . it's so exploitative and so destructive."

Some people are more susceptible to hypnotic induction than others, and Natalie believes she was a prime candidate. "I guess something good is I never smoked again," she said.

Natalie and her husband at the time became what Consumers' Buyline called "affiliates": they sold memberships and products on commission. The couple made $10,000 in their first few months, winning a $16,000 top seller award, which in 1991 was a significant windfall on top of Natalie's regular income making gift baskets. And at night she was getting a window into the mind of the smartest man she'd ever met, chatting with Raniere for hours on the phone about philosophy and the future.

For Toni Natalie and many more women to come, the romantic advances came around the same time as a rare financial opportunity. Natalie was offered a position rolling out a new skincare line. "He told me about the job and offered me a tremendous amount of money to move me and my son and hire a nanny and do all these things," she said. Natalie tried commuting from Rochester for a few months, but eventually she went along with the relocation. She was swayed by the steady salary Raniere could offer, and was made to feel like family among his roommates and business partners. She left her marriage and moved to the Albany area to take a bigger role within the company. Like Gina, she didn't know there was already a handful of secret girlfriends in Raniere's life.

According to Natalie, the day-to-day work culture at Consumers' Buyline was charged with sexual innuendo and manic, stay-up-all-night energy. "You go in," she recalled, "and there's this flurry of young energetic people flying all over the place till two a.m. like it's noon."

The office was decked out with hulking computers and white-boards filled with equations, pulling off a proto-tech-startup vibe. Underneath it all, there was also an excitement around wanting to change the world—which is exactly what Raniere had always said he was going to do.

RANIERE'S ROMANTIC LIFE wasn't a polyamorous arrangement in the way young readers of the *Ethical Slut* might understand today. Several former girlfriends described it as more like a bait and switch: Raniere would shower each new addition with attention and praise, in many cases leading them to believe they had entered a monogamous relationship. And when Raniere's other relationships were discovered, the women worked as a team to convince the new girlfriend that her own hang-ups were getting in the way of a good thing. Natalie called this the "wolf pack" approach. "Pam would come and talk to me and say, 'He loves you. He's special. He's brilliant. He needs you to do this.'" Then the next girlfriend would make her case.

Forty-year-old Barbara Jeske and eighteen-year-old Kristin Keeffe were initiated, and went on to initiate others, this way. In some cases Raniere denied or minimized his other affairs. Unterreiner was a college friend with no interest in sex whom he promised to always take care of; Keeffe and Cafritz were just business partners living with him to save money; Jeske was actually a lesbian who was sorting out some psychosexual hang-ups. According to Heidi Hutchinson, it was Keeffe who introduced a more confrontational tactic, wherein the women already in Raniere's inner circle told new girlfriends, "You don't own Keith's penis."

Heidi overheard Keeffe confronting Gina this way on the back porch of the Flintlock house soon after Keeffe had moved in. They argued over "whether or not Gina should feel entitled to have Keith to herself." Heidi later recalled how upset her sister became as she realized that her spiritual teacher wasn't being honest about something so important. (Raniere hid inside the house as the women argued.) At the time, Heidi didn't quite grasp the private world Raniere and Gina had already built together, one in which Gina found support for her beliefs. "She accepted this whole paradigm, this worldview [with] Keith as her mentor," says Heidi. "It explained she wasn't nuts; she was gifted."

Over many years Heidi was able to observe what she calls Raniere's "ensnarement" tactics in action. Often this involved claiming unprecedented expertise in a woman or girl's area of passion, whether it was running, spirituality, lucid dreaming, or past life regression. In Toni Natalie's case, Raniere embodied the elite education she never had, while Gina was convinced she'd been a Buddhist goddess in a past life and that she and Raniere had known each other many centuries before. These were both fantasies and levers of manipulation.

As Heidi describes it, Gina became trapped in Raniere's orbit. She worked to make his business successful while he spent much of his time playing arcade games, having sex in the Consumers' Buyline warehouse, and sleeping through the day. According to an Albany *Times Union* report in 2012, one of his favorite arcade games around this time was called Vanguard, "in which destroying enemies increases the fuel in the player's tank."

HEIDI SAYS THAT Gina continued to resist the harem-style arrangement. She wanted a simple life with Raniere, to continue what she believed they'd started in a past life. She pursued a degree in Eastern religion in the second half of the 1990s, and for a time switched to another spiritual teacher, which upset Raniere. Eventually Gina returned to the community she'd helped build.

In 2002, following her mother's death, Gina's mental health started to slip. According to a police report, she had sent "personal articles and letters to family members that stated if something were to happen to her, not to worry, and that the Buddha would take care of her." The family thought she was mentally distraught and feared she might harm herself.

Police found Gina's Toyota Tercel near a Buddhist monastery in Woodstock, New York. Officers spotted a small flashlight on the ground, which led them to Gina's body at the edge of a pond. She had died of a gunshot wound. In her pockets police found a lighter, a hotel key, and a Buddhist medallion. Her death, on October 11, 2002, was ruled a suicide.

After Gina's death, Heidi learned that her sister had turned most of her modest inheritance over to the man whom she had helped turn into a self-help guru.

"I'm sure Gina died thinking Keith was a genius," she says.

CHAPTER FOUR

"Money Spilling into Your Wallet"

When Toni Natalie became a Consumers' Buyline affiliate in 1991, she believed she was joining one of America's fastest-growing companies. And from the crowds she saw at recruitment sessions, she could sense the upward momentum.

"What they presented was this amazing group of people who were running this company," Natalie says of the pitching process. Karen Unterreiner was a brilliant actuary who'd just left a big corporate firm, they told would-be members. "And you had the daughter of one of the wealthiest families in D.C., and they were financing the company," Natalie says. From one event to the next, rooms got fuller, interest keener. Long before the internet became a household necessity, Raniere encouraged attendees to look up his IQ record at the library. "It was smoke and mirrors, but it worked."

Raniere claimed that Consumers' Buyline had grown an average of 40 percent every month for two years and that by May 1992 had "gross receipts in excess of 33 million dollars of products and services." According to a biography posted on Raniere's personal website more than a decade later, he was a millionaire by age thirty, with a net worth of $50 million by age thirty-two. He attributed this success to the "human motivation and behavior model" he was developing, which allowed him to recruit and train top sellers like Natalie.

In photos from the 1990s, Raniere, then in his thirties, appears goofy and sleepy-eyed, like a sticky-fingered kid after eating too many popsicles. His hair is a mousy brown and quite a bit longer than you'd expect from a business wunderkind. He was not yet accustomed to wearing the expensive athleisure he was steered toward decades later by an "aesthetic team." Without people telling him what to wear every day, Raniere joked that he looked like "quite the creature."

People who knew Raniere say he had a "type" and that Natalie fit all the specifications. In photos she appears striking and slender, with long, dark hair draping neatly over her shoulders and back. She looks tanned and vaguely muscular next to Raniere's squishy frame. Though their relationship grew fraught, their career partnership kept it intact.

You didn't have to be smart to understand Consumers' Buyline's structure. Members paid a $39 annual fee and a monthly fee of $15, costing a grand total of $219 per year. These fees granted members access to discounts on a long list of products and services, including home appliances, electronics, furniture, health aids, vehicles, travel, financial services, real estate, groceries, and optical services. It didn't cost anything to become an "affiliate," or sales rep, for the company, though it was strongly encouraged that sellers become members so as to be familiar with the company's inventory. To buy discounted goods, members simply had to call a 1-800 number and verify their membership, and then they'd be forwarded to the appropriate vendor.

In a promotional video explaining the company's commission structure, Raniere pointed at a circle on a large sheet of chart paper. Two lines poked out from the bottom of the circle like cartoon legs, which attached to two more circles below. Raniere wore a gray suit and rounded metal-framed glasses that placed him firmly in Bill Gates's 1990s. With a marker he drew more legs coming out of each circle, fanning them out left and right. For emphasis he traced a triangle around the structure, which, it must be said, looked an awful lot like a pyramid.

Would-be affiliates sitting in a classroom-style arrangement learned that on average every person, represented by a circle, was able to recruit 2.6 new members. Years later, Raniere would tell NXIVM recruiters the same thing: on average, every student should be able to refer 2.6 people.

"So what's going to happen on the average with this structure?" he asked the room. "It's going to perpetuate, right? It's going to go and go. Because on the average this works."

Consumers' Buyline affiliates were assured that they could earn decent income with a "one-time effort." You didn't even have to be an experienced salesperson; you could get by on following a script.

"This is all found money—walkaway income—money that just keeps spilling into your wallet no matter what you're doing," reads company literature quoted in court documents. "In other words, think of it as a royalty reflecting your ongoing rights to something you've already created."

The day-to-day workings of the company often seemed impenetrable, even to members and affiliates, but in weekly meetings Raniere's team regularly rallied around wins and growth. For a select crew of Raniere's business and secret romantic partners, it seemed as if commissions were coming in like water through a fire hose. Raniere traveled from state to state, hotel conference room to hotel conference room, tapping into yet more social networks. The executive team became something of a family, with Raniere's father, James, even pitching in with advertising consulting. Complaints and troublemakers were easily explained away by jealousy. Only a few years after his IQ claim had been publicized, it seemed as though Raniere's genius was paying off.

Natalie noticed that Raniere had a special gift for finding female affiliates with vast resources and networks. All it took was reaching one wife of a well-connected Southern minister, and "her entire flock followed," Natalie wrote in her memoir *The Program*. "Keith well knew how a single convert, if sufficiently rich and prominent, could underwrite his entire business."

Arkansas was one of the first states to catch on that Raniere wasn't just running a wholesome "buyers'club." The attorney general filed a complaint in February 1992 alleging that Consumers' Buyline was an illegal pyramid scheme. By 1993, Raniere claimed to have sold $1 billion in products and recruited nearly three hundred thousand members. Raniere, Cafritz, and Unterreiner signed settlements with Arkansas and other state regulators agreeing to refund all members who asked for their money back.

By 1996, the company was facing investigations and lawsuits in twenty-three states.

CONSUMERS' BUYLINE WAS following in the footsteps of hundreds of companies with similar network-based sales structures. Though it went by many names—direct selling, multi-level marketing, chain distribution—a pyramid-like organizational chart wasn't always a red flag to regulators.

Companies like Amway first came under fire from the Federal Trade Commission (FTC) in the late 1960s and early 1970s. Any business model that relied on exponential employee recruitment was deemed inherently unsustainable and doomed to collapse. They became known derisively as pyramid schemes, and some were shut down for fraud.

The first pyramid scheme ever to be successfully prosecuted by the FTC was Holiday Magic, a soap and cosmetics company run by a flamboyant door-to-door salesman named William Penn Patrick. The government received complaints that distributors weren't actually making the money Holiday Magic recruiters promised. "More often than not, the hapless distributors ended up with basements or garages stacked to the ceiling with jars of avocado face cream," wrote journalist Steven Pressman, who charted the early days of sales-meets-self-help in his book *Outrageous Betrayal*.

Holiday Magic, investigators found, was promising that sellers could easily become millionaires as long as they signed up five new people every month. This sounded great if you didn't think about it too hard, but the math quickly became unsustainable. At that recruiting pace over the course of a year, each Holiday Magic seller would be overseeing a total of 244,140,625 new recruits, about half the population of North America. Markets across the United States quickly reached a saturation point, leaving some eighty thousand sellers on the hook for piles of products with no income. The company was found guilty of deceptive business practices and was forced to close in 1974.

Patrick's money-making empire wasn't just about pyramid selling. As reporter Dann Gallucci recounted on the investigative podcast *The Dream*, he's also credited with founding one of the first executive self-help seminars of its kind, called the Leadership Dynamics Institute, in 1967. At the height of the Summer of Love, while young people were challenging authority and leaving society, there was this other "human potential" movement bubbling to the surface, one that traded in ideas of accessing unused parts of the brain and accomplishing the previously unimaginable through psychological transformation. Tapping into the early days of this movement, Patrick claimed that his four-day Leadership Dynamics seminars would teach participants how to build the discipline and trust needed to succeed in a climate of excessive permissiveness.

"If you wanted to succeed at Holiday Magic, you had to attend the seminars," Gallucci told me. The seminars included bizarre and abusive exercises. Groups were punished for the perceived shortcomings of an individual member. Participants were beaten, mock-crucified, or put in coffins to elicit emotional responses. The company faced its own legal battles and was shuttered in 1973, though it inspired the creators of other leadership seminars, including Patrick's longtime colleague Werner Erhard, who created est, the self-help method that later became Landmark Education.

Holiday Magic's implosion did not mark the end of pyramid-shaped sales, as new companies stepped in to fill the gap. Amway changed the game by waging an expensive, politically connected legal battle against the FTC in 1975 and winning the right to continue its chain distribution sales under the banner of "multi-level marketing." The company argued it had instituted rules that distinguished its dealings from that of a fraudulent Ponzi scheme. The so-called Amway rules became an industry-led response that covered the most obviously exploitative elements of a pyramid: don't charge a huge upfront fee; don't require people to endlessly stock up; have some fine print somewhere that allows people to return product, even if restrictions apply.

While the FTC continues to prosecute smaller multi-level marketing scammers who make wildly false claims and run away with money, the industry has gained staying power, if not full-on legitimacy, through the size and influence of players like Avon and Amway.

RANIERE'S CONSUMERS' BUYLINE was part of a new wave of multi-level marketing disruptors that seemed committed to pushing the boundaries of these industry-suggested rules. Finding safety in numbers, Raniere and many others thrived in the gray area created by the government's unclear definition of a pyramid. Today multi-level marketing is a multibillion-dollar industry, even if the same unsustainable math still applies.

Internally, Raniere claimed that his company's legal troubles stemmed from either a misunderstanding or a political conspiracy to take him down. He said "Bill Clinton's people" were out to get him—a theory that would be recounted to NXIVM students decades later.

In court documents Raniere claimed that the company spent millions of dollars on legal fees, losing tens of millions of dollars in business along the way. "Throughout this process I had learned how people can cheat and win," he wrote. "In mathematical game theory cheaters, if undetected, always have the advantage because they have more options." Raniere added this finding to his "human behavior equation," later taught in NXIVM lessons.

Consumers' Buyline settled with several more states before it was forced to fold in 1996. A New York complaint argued that the emphasis of the organization "is clearly not the sale of a product, but on recruiting new organizational rows to boost memberships." Like all pyramids, read the complaint, this one was "destined to collapse."

Raniere agreed to pay $40,000 but admitted no wrongdoing. Pam Cafritz, Karen Unterreiner, and Raniere all signed a decree that they would never operate another illegal chain distribution scheme.

From that moment on, Raniere became a nonentity when it came to business records. He told his inner circle that because powerful forces were gunning for him, he needed to protect himself by not having a driver's license, not owning any property or businesses, and basically staying off the grid entirely. Instead he encouraged the women around him to put their names and bank accounts on the line.

CHAPTER FIVE

When Keith Met Nancy (and Lauren)

The beginning of NXIVM was also the beginning of the end of Keith Raniere's relationship with Toni Natalie.

In the wake of the Consumers' Buyline shutdown, Raniere and Natalie redirected their efforts to a new multi-level marketing company that sold discounted nutritional supplements. Because of Raniere's trouble with state regulators, paperwork was mostly in Natalie's name. Like Consumers' Buyline, the business relied on the constant recruitment of new sellers. And although money was coming in, Raniere wasn't living up to relationship agreements that Natalie thought had been clear. She wanted to settle down, which was why she'd bought the house that she and Raniere shared, a short walk from the Flintlock house. She wanted the workday to end at five o'clock so they could have dinner as a family. But Raniere was too absorbed in his mission to change the world, according to Natalie.

He wasn't giving up his late work nights or, she would later learn, his other girlfriends. If Natalie protested, Raniere would make it clear that the problem was her own insecurity and jealousy.

"According to Keith, the reason we had issues is because I had issues," she said. "It's never Keith's issue."

IN LATE 1997, Nancy Salzman was going through her own relationship troubles. Her second marriage had recently ended after her husband of six years came out as gay.

Salzman had worked as a nurse and a hypnotherapist trained in NLP. Another outgrowth of the human potential movement, its creators have claimed that it can be used to break addictions, resolve phobias, and even treat "psychosomatic illnesses."

Salzman studied under NLP's two founders, John Grinder and Richard Bandler, who based their techniques on the published works of psychiatrist Milton Erickson. Erickson's method was sometimes called "covert hypnosis" because it resembled talk therapy and didn't require access to deep trance states. Patients could carry on a conversation without knowing or realizing that an induction was happening.

Grinder and Bandler taught anchoring and reframing techniques in live hypnotherapy seminars. Bandler later bragged to audiences that he made up the field of NLP so that nobody could tell him he's wrong and often recounted stories of covertly manipulating and harming adversaries using hypnotic suggestion. Bandler rejected experts, and experts rejected his life's work as unscientific. But that didn't seem to slow NLP's growth in popularity throughout the 1980s and 90s.

Salzman started her own hypnotherapy practice called the International Center for Change, which she maintained until 1997. Her second husband was a doctor who had referred patients to her therapy practice. When he left, those shared clients went with him. Salzman was going through a depressive episode, according to people who knew her, and friends were eager to find her a new source of purpose and inspiration.

In a 2009 deposition, Salzman said that she and Raniere had been introduced by a woman named Sandy Padilla, who'd married

Salzman's first husband, Michael Salzman, and sold supplements for one of Raniere's companies. When Raniere put a call out to find a skilled neuro-linguistic programmer, Padilla suggested Nancy, who was already teaching communications courses based on NLP principles.

Raniere, who was still refining his "human behavior equation," began testing out various self-help methodologies on the women in his orbit, including Karen Unterreiner and Toni Natalie and then Nancy Salzman herself. "I watched him work with some individuals," Salzman recalled. "And when I asked him to mentor me, he said that if he mentored me, I would never be able to resume my career in the same way."

Raniere set up a video camera to record his early conversations with Salzman. He gave her a document that outlined the terms of his mentorship. It took her several days to make sense of the heavy-handed noncompete agreement Raniere was asking her to sign. "It just seemed like he was asking something of me that I wasn't sure . . . how to handle," she recalled. Part of the agreement stipulated that if Salzman ever left the partnership, she could never again sell self-help or counselling services. Salzman said she was convinced Raniere was onto something groundbreaking, and went on to test his theories in her consulting work in the spring and early summer of 1998.

What sales and human behavior theories was Raniere pulling from? People who knew Raniere then say he talked about Werner Erhard, the now-infamous creator of est leadership training, which later became Landmark Education. In the 1970s Erhard had carved out a path in the "human potential" movement. The likes of John Denver, Diana Ross, Buzz Aldrin, and Hollywood exec Ted Ashley had all publicly boasted about taking est's weekend leadership seminars, which promised personal transformation. The classes taught that suffering is optional, that the power of positive thinking creates reality, and that there's no such thing as a "victim."

Heidi Hutchinson recalls that in his pre-NXIVM days Raniere was also researching Scientology and neuro-linguistic programming. At one point he handed her a book on NLP, and later, when she lived in Los Angeles, he asked her to mail him all the teaching materials she could find at the Church of Scientology's renowned Celebrity Centre in Hollywood. In letters to his inner circle he used Scientology terminology and later adapted some of it into NXIVM teachings—though in court battles, he later denied being influenced by Dianetics, L. Ron Hubbard's pseudoscientific theory of mental health. Both NLP and Dianetics were marketed as "tech" that could be used to eliminate bad thoughts and behaviors and replace them with good ones.

Raniere claimed that he first became interested in establishing his own human potential school long before Consumers' Buyline or NXIVM—that back in the 1980s he'd raised almost $50,000 to fund it and had interviewed potential instructors. He abandoned the idea, though, because he couldn't find people who were ethical enough to learn and carry out his teachings. Until he found Salzman.

She was, according to his affidavit, "the ideal person to learn, duplicate and apply my model."

Salzman was already familiar with the culture of NLP-adjacent leadership training and had even led a goal-setting seminar called Advanced Neurodynamics. After months of mentorship and testing she finally agreed to launch a human potential school with Raniere. Executive Success Programs (ESP) was officially incorporated in July 1998. On January 23, 2002, it would become NXIVM, the company that connected the various parts of Raniere's self-help empire.

Nancy Salzman's coming on board was a huge win for Raniere. It wasn't just her skills; she also had a wealth of connections. Salzman would later bring in her own daughter, Lauren, as well as friend and former client Barbara Bouchey, as major advocates for NXIVM. Both would be central figures in Raniere's organization, as romantic partners and true-believer workhorses.

LAUREN SALZMAN WAS a senior at Oswego State college when she met Raniere in June 1998, a month before Executive Success Programs became official. At one point, while at home over summer break, she stopped by Toni Natalie's supplement store to meet Raniere's growing team. Nancy then hosted a dinner party to formally introduce her new business partner and friend.

Lauren knew right away that her mom admired Raniere. She learned that Nancy had been implementing some of his "innovative ideas" at one of her consulting jobs and that she was "getting good results."

Nancy made it clear that she wanted to share these good results with her daughter. "When I graduated, my mom told me they were going to teach classes that were going to be good for helping people achieve their goals," Lauren said on the witness stand at Raniere's trial. "She made a deal with me that if I came to classes for six months, then she would support me, no matter what I did after that."

Nancy and Raniere began developing therapies and coursework right away, much of it combining elements of existing psychological and self-help therapies. Raniere later claimed that traditional therapists only addressed people's reactions to the outside world, whereas his methods aimed to change the underlying meaning of the "stimulus" in people's minds. To that end, the early building blocks of the NXIVM curriculum took the form of one- or two-hour lessons, called "modules," each of which featured guided group discussion that probed and destabilized basic definitions of concepts like honesty, value, self-esteem, trust, good and bad. Raniere would file a patent application for the first twenty modules in September 2000 and develop hundreds more by 2003.

Twenty-five people, including Lauren Salzman, participated in an early trial run of classes held two times a week over six weeks at Nancy's hypnotherapy office, located in a low-slung brown brick complex that was converted into NXIVM's Albany headquarters. "At the end of the six weeks, I decided I wanted to stay," Lauren said.

NXIVM later compressed the six-week format into five- and sixteen-day "intensives" that packed five or more modules into ten-hour days, plus homework, or "outside practice." Sessions were at first facilitated by Raniere and Nancy in person, and then later taken over by coaches like Lauren, who played videos of Nancy explaining the psychological concepts.

New students were encouraged to arrive with open minds, ready to let just about anything unfold. This helped ease recruits into a set of curious rules and rituals introduced at the beginning of every class. Students were instructed to take off their shoes, put on a colored sash that signaled their rank in the organization, and bow when entering and leaving the teaching room. They learned that Keith Raniere was the leader of a philosophical movement and therefore held the title Vanguard.

When whoever was leading the session arrived, students were encouraged to stand up as if they were showing respect for a judge entering a courtroom. Everyone in the room recited a twelve-point mission statement, which began with "Success is an internal state of clear, honest knowledge of what I am, my value in the world and my responsibility for the way I react to all things. There are no ultimate victims, therefore I will not choose to be a victim." The statement ended with a hearty "Thank you, Vanguard." Then participants huddled in a circle and in unison said, "We are committed to our success!"

In the "Self-esteem" module, students wrote down areas in life where they had high and low self-esteem. Then they watched a series of videos showing that self esteem was the result of having a range of viable life choices. Between clips, coaches facilitated discussions of hard-to-answer questions like, What is reality? How do we know that it is reality? How do we know that this isn't a dream? What is honesty? What is integrity? Can you have honesty without integrity? Can you have integrity without honesty? What is a lie? These discussions often led students to find disagreement and acknowledge the limits of their own understanding of the world. At the end, coaches summed up working definitions while stressing that they weren't teaching "what to think" but rather "how to think." Honesty was the intent to "represent one's internal reality" accurately, coaches told students, while integrity was about consistency and being whole. A lie was "when one trades reality for fantasy. It is a distortion of reality that the person knows about."

When Raniere led the classes, which he often did in the early years, he would answer questions with more questions and never explicitly reveal his own position. Some lower-ranking coaches took a more prescriptive approach, following a script set out in coaching notes. By the second half of the lesson, the concept of self-esteem as a range of possibilities would start clicking into place for students: high self-esteem came from more choice, coaches said, while "people with low self-esteem feel like they have no choice and are victims." One of the last exercises in the module asked students to return to an area of life where they believed they had fewer choices and then list all the possibilities they could think of, "whether or not you would choose them." Sarah Edmondson and other NXIVM students practiced this regularly and believed it helped build confidence.

Students were assigned a coach separate from the lead trainer, someone to check in with on the commitments or goals they set during the intensive. Raniere's innermost circle, including Karen Unterreiner, Pam Cafritz, Barbara Jeske, and Nancy Salzman, fulfilled this role for many. Depending on the course, students were encouraged to call coaches twice a week, or daily. "Outside practice" often included journaling on decisions and emotions throughout the day, with the intent to explore how feelings were chosen. Students would write down every instance of pain or suffering, for example, and then ask, "How did I create this situation?"

These group exercises created powerful experiences for the people seeking help from Raniere and Salzman. They forged intense personal relationships and accountability structures that were unusual in the world of psychotherapy. Years later, NXIVM would implement a rule that no psychologists or psychiatrists were allowed to attend its courses, a rule shared with Scientology. When a former trainer asked Nancy about this, she said it was because psychologists "ruin the training for everybody else; all they want to do is argue."

Raniere's special status in NXIVM would be written right into the curriculum. Basic classes taught students to give tribute to their teachers, and that the creation of NXIVM qualified as a great human invention—a ten out of ten on a scale of human achievement, according to one exercise.

NANCY SALZMAN TOOK on the title of "Prefect" and was later honored with a gold sash and a large portrait on the wall next to Raniere's at their headquarters. Toni Natalie attended regular hypnotherapy sessions with Nancy and found that she'd become an early test subject for the one-on-one therapies Raniere and Salzman were developing. One of those therapies, later called an "exploration of meaning," led students to redefine traumatic moments in childhood by identifying flawed "attachments" and "limiting beliefs."

Natalie and Salzman weren't far apart in age, but they looked as if they were from different generations. Whereas Natalie's eyes had a bright, animated quality, Salzman's gaze was sustained and penetrating. Salzman kept her hair short, wore suit jackets, and had a disarmingly wide smile. "If a corporation were to take the form of a female human, it would look very much like Nancy Salzman," Natalie later wrote.

As Natalie and Raniere's relationship grew more strained, Natalie put more faith in Salzman's guidance. She participated in hundreds of sessions, often working through her relationship troubles with Raniere as well as her trauma from having been molested at a very young age.

Both Salzman and Raniere knew all about her deepest fears and insecurities and repeatedly used this to influence her. They offered a unifying theory of her "issues" and how to fix them. Natalie had an addiction to "taking," according to Raniere, and needed to overcome her anger, pride, defiance, and spite.

Natalie said it was an inconsequential dispute over laundry that sent their relationship into a tailspin. "I had asked him if he could throw some clothes in the dryer but not to put a particular shirt in," she recalled. Raniere put the shirt in the dryer with the rest of the laundry, and Natalie says she responded with a "Hey, I asked you not to do this." Then something snapped. "He started to scream at me: 'Don't you know who I am? I have perfect retention. You can't talk to me that way.' I remember him screaming at me and backing me into a corner."

Raniere demanded she apologize; Natalie said she refused. She left him in April 1999, but a clean break was all but impossible.

The following month Raniere sent his "sweetheart" Natalie a letter that included a tape of Beethoven's *Moonlight Sonata*. He instructed her to play it while reading. The letter, printed on marbled paper in a distracting font evoking Hallmark card calligraphy, laid out why they should get back together despite all the terrible things Natalie had done. "Although you have wronged me more than you will ever wrong anyone else, I still offer my hand to you," he wrote.

Raniere enclosed pictures of Natalie from the previous August and February, making a case that her "downward spiral" was visible in her diminishing happiness and energy. He said he'd always refused to do what was easy and had instead done what was right for Natalie's well-being and personal growth. "I gave up hope in my ability to change the situation and I surrendered 'us' to the universe to see what would happen," he wrote. "I later discovered this path leads to not very nice things for you and it appears my Sweetheart may well go to jail."

Natalie says she was immediately harassed by Raniere's inner circle. In August 1999 she reported to police that Barbara Jeske had gone through her mail. "Jeske has been harassing me for about four months, beginning after we parted company as coworkers," reads her statement in the police report. "She has written letters to customers of mine, defaming me, and has been stalking me at my residence and business." Natalie told police that she even had a video recording of Jeske's snooping.

That same month, according to Natalie, Kristin Keeffe showed up at her workplace for five hours. "She was telling people I was the chosen one, I had to come back to him," Natalie said. Another time Keeffe showed up at Natalie's house with flowers and candy. On the box was an image of a mother and child. "I had a vision that you changed your mind and you're coming back to us," Keeffe told her.

In a letter to a judge more than a decade after the breakup, Natalie accused Raniere of rape. "Prior to leaving him in 1999," she wrote, "I was raped repeatedly by Raniere, each time with him telling me it was harder on him than it was on me, that we needed to be together so that I could share his energy, and that I needed to remain silent so as to not wake up my child who was sleeping in a nearby room."

During my first phone conversation with Natalie, she surprised me by saying something that flew in the face of Raniere's genius polymath narrative.

"He's got a very small playbook; he just changes up players all the time," she said. Natalie claimed that Raniere had a pattern of constantly scouting and replacing the women in his life. He was always on the lookout for other women with better reputations, more credibility, or more money. "Once he uses them, he's done and on to the next," she said.

Toni Natalie was arguably the first person to experience every phase of the NXIVM story. She'd been captivated by a man praised as a world-changing thinker and guru. A honeymoon phase pulled her deeper into his business ventures and personal orbit. She believed the hype, participated in stoking that hype, and offered her whole self for experimentation. And then years later, to her horror, that great big money-making machine she helped build began trying to destroy her life, dragging her into courtrooms on and off for decades.

Not long after Natalie cut ties with NXIVM, Raniere and his inner circle set their sights on recruiting a new "chosen one" to be Raniere's girlfriend and business partner.

CHAPTER SIX

Albany Shrugged

Only five months after Toni Natalie walked out on Keith Raniere, Barbara Bouchey received a fateful phone call.

Pam Cafritz had picked Bouchey's asset management company out of the Yellow Pages because it listed two locations, suggesting some measure of success, according to Bouchey. It was a cold call, or so Bouchey thought, until Cafritz revealed who she was working for.

Bouchey, then a forty-year-old financial planner, learned that her old friend and former therapist Nancy Salzman was now the president of a fast-growing human potential school called Executive Success Programs, or ESP. Salzman had treated Bouchey for teeth grinding and stress management in the late 1980s, and the two had sporadically stayed in touch. Bouchey agreed to learn more about the self-help company if Salzman agreed to catch up over dinner in October 1999.

Bouchey is tall with a thick mane of blond curls and a welcoming, jolly expression. Her experience with sales calls shines through in conversation. She isn't shy about her tough upbringing, often reminding people that her mother died when she was eight years old and her father was an alcoholic. In 1999 Bouchey was still reeling from a recent divorce and mourning the death of a close friend, but she agreed to attend three weeks of seminars, starting on March 27, 2000. Salzman told Bouchey that the intensive would help with the transition and grief.

Raniere had a signature way of flirting with women like Bouchey. He handed her a copy of Ayn Rand's novel *Atlas Shrugged* and told her she was his Dagny Taggart, the heroine who wants to save unbridled capitalism. (Toni Natalie, who years earlier had also earned the "Dagny" nickname, was now being called a suppressive and a thief.)

Pam Cafritz and Kristin Keeffe both claimed they had visions that Bouchey was coming to be a leader in Raniere's project to build a new, more evolved society. "I was going to be somebody who was going to partner with Keith and be someone that he would have as a partner, companion, or somebody that would help them do this," Bouchey said in a 2009 deposition.

Near the end of the first day of Bouchey's first intensive, Raniere opened up to her about his ambition to create his own country and currency. "I know that Nancy had not ever heard that before, because she had gotten a little bit upset that night, because here I was, my first day, I didn't know Keith, and he was sharing these concepts and things with me," she said. Their Ayn Rand–inspired philosophies seemed to align, and Bouchey saw that this granted her special status with Raniere.

Unbeknownst to Bouchey, Raniere's inner circle was watching her closely, and taking notes. "They were in every breakout group, reporting everything I was thinking and feeling back to Keith," Bouchey told me. With this knowledge Raniere grew more assertive in his advances, telling Bouchey that he too believed she was destined to join him. "In the last three days of my intensive, Keith himself told me that he had dreams and visions that I actually would be in a relationship with him and have a child with him."

Bouchey says she wasn't initially all that interested in a new life partner or a career in self-help. She had a financial planning business keeping her busy and was still in the process of untangling her life from her ex-husband's. But she was drawn to the idea of becoming a central pillar of a new community, and when she returned for coach training in June 2000, she brought colleagues, former in-laws, and her own cousin.

With seven new recruits under her belt, she sailed up the ranks from coach to proctor, a paid position that oversaw coaches. Bouchey put her smooth cold-calling voice to work and helped bring in a wave of wealthy and high-profile students. She also took on the role of field trainer, teaching others new sales tactics and making a commission on new students referred by lower-ranking members. Proctors earned 10 percent on sign-ups they brought in, while field trainers earned 20 percent on every place in an intensive they sold. NXIVM's ranks would expand to include Adam Glassman, the longtime creative director at *O* magazine; Antonia Novello, New York's health commissioner and later the U.S. Surgeon General; Sheila Johnson, America's first black billionaire and cofounder of Black Entertainment Television (BET); and Stephen Cooper, the interim CEO of Enron and since 2011 the CEO of Warner Music. In a deposition, Nancy Salzman claimed to have had a one-on-one coaching relationship with all of these heavy hitters in the early 2000s.

AFTER MONTHS OF suggestion, Bouchey's role in Raniere's universe took on a romantic dimension. For the first year of their relationship, Bouchey says, she didn't know there were other girlfriends. She uprooted herself from Saratoga Springs and bought a house in Clifton Park, where Raniere slept over three or four nights a week. When friends gathered for dinner at Nancy Salzman's house, everyone seemed to know that Bouchey and Raniere were together. "People would move so I could sit next to Keith," Bouchey says.

Karen Unterreiner, Kristin Keeffe, Barbara Jeske, and Pam Cafritz knew about Bouchey and each other but were sworn to secrecy. Inside Raniere's inner circle of girlfriends, this was seen as a precaution in dealing with Bouchey's "jealousy issues." Her time spent at the Flintlock house was limited to scheduled social gatherings, like Thursday evenings spent watching *Star Trek*.

Raniere tapped into Bouchey's sense of destiny and psychological connection with him. He said he could feel her mood changes, even when they were apart. Raniere suggested this may have been because they'd both lived past lives and had been reincarnated in new roles in order to resolve what had happened in previous lifetimes. This sounded a lot like Gina Hutchinson's reincarnation beliefs, but they went to a darker place. Bouchey admits she intuitively believed Raniere when he suggested that in her previous life she had been Reinhard Heydrich, one of the architects of the Holocaust. Her name means "butcher"; Heydrich was known as the "Butcher of Prague." She accepted Raniere's suggestion that her soul might have been given a chance to repair some of the damage she'd done as a Nazi in her past life, and that she could accomplish this by joining Raniere's mission.

Bouchey wasn't alone in bearing a genocidal stain. Nancy Salzman, who is Jewish, was told she may have been Hitler reincarnated. Former associates have different ideas about how several members of Raniere's inner circle came to believe they'd been literal Nazis in past lives. Some say women were guided to these conclusions in suggestive trance states, but others say it was more about repetitive suggestion. NXIVM students were taught that resisting feedback, especially from someone with a higher rank, was a sign of "disintegration." When confronted with an uncomfortable, unprovable claim, an "integrated" person was expected to listen and consider without letting their emotions get in the way. With time and repetition these ideas seemed to grow more relevant or true to the person's experience. Most of this was useful to Raniere, who could use guilt to manipulate his true believers.

Raniere constructed a sexual component of these reincarnation ideas. More than one of his followers testified that he studied Eastern religious theories on energetic channels in the body and had mastered the path to enlightenment through sexuality. He told one of his partners that he required sex constantly, or else spiritual energy might consume him to the point of death. One way Raniere's inner circle could atone for their Nazi sins was through yogic enlightenment practices achieved through sex. "If you have sex, you can move what's called the kundalini energy," Bouchey told the CBC's *Uncover* podcast.

When I asked about the "Nazi stuff," in September 2018, Bouchey said it had been a long time ago, and that it hadn't continued past the first year of her relationship with Raniere. Today she denies that her past life theory had anything to do with hypnosis or trance.

LAUREN SALZMAN HAD her own unlikely experience with Raniere's powers of suggestion. She moved in with her mom after college, and Raniere developed a habit of checking in with her at home.

She thought he was interested in seeing her grow into a responsible, caring adult.

Raniere encouraged Nancy to start charging her daughter for rent. "That inspired me to want to move out and be more self-reliant," Lauren testified at his trial.

Lauren increasingly looked to Raniere for guidance in all areas of her life. They went on long walks together, and she told him about her goals, her family struggles, even her medical issues. He suggested she join other women in juice-fasting to lose weight. "He thought a good weight for me would be around a hundred pounds," she recalled. Raniere made the assessment simply by looking at her "body constitution," she testified. From then on, Lauren appeared increasingly waifish, made more obvious by her loose-fitting outfits and pale, makeup-free complexion.

In April 2001, Raniere initiated a secret sexual relationship with Lauren. He told her not to tell anyone, especially her mom. Lauren didn't have the same "jealousy issues" as Barbara Bouchey, and so she became enmeshed in the daily goings-on at the Flintlock house.

Having sex with Raniere meant accommodating his pubic hair preferences. "If I loved and cared for him, I would care for his preferences," Lauren testified. "His preference was that it be natural. So not groomed."

Lauren testified that she participated in threesomes with some of Raniere's inner circle, including Pam Cafritz and Barbara Jeske. "Initially I participated in them because I was curious," she said. "I had questions regarding my sexuality and I wanted to explore that." Other times, Lauren said, she went along with it because it was what Raniere wanted.

Lauren was often brought in to intervene when Raniere's other girlfriends were threatening to leave. Along with Cafritz and Keeffe, she would help Bouchey and others "work through whatever their upset was so that they would be happy with him instead." She excelled at this. Using the NXIVM curriculum, she would identify what Bouchey or another girlfriend was having an "emotional reaction" to and pitch them on an opportunity to work on that issue.

"We all believed that we are responsible for our own emotional reactions," Lauren said. "Sometimes you would talk about that, like,

'This is for your growth. This is an opportunity. How are you ever going to get through the issue if you leave?'"

RANIERE HAD MORE than a dozen other relationships over the course of nine years with Barbara Bouchey. She didn't find out about most of them until after she left NXIVM. When she suspected an affair, first with Barbara Jeske, Raniere said it was a guru–student relationship, and that they had sex only once or twice a year to exchange kundalini energy. Still, Bouchey saw herself as the one with the closest, most meaningful connection to Raniere during that time. "I was told I was the Dagny, I was the soulmate, and I was treated like his only girlfriend," she says.

Whenever Bouchey raised suspicion or protest, she says she was confronted and coached by Raniere's other girlfriends. She was getting her first taste of the "wolf pack" approach Toni Natalie described, with each inner-circle girlfriend making visits, playing good cop or bad cop.

Scientific studies of conformity have found that our minds are more prone to caving when we're outnumbered. In 1951 the social psychologist Solomon Asch set up an experiment where a single study participant believed that a group of actors were fellow test subjects. The group was asked to perform obvious "perceptual tasks," like identifying the length of a line on a flashcard. The actors were instructed to choose right answers most of the time but to uniformly get one answer wrong. Although most test subjects still chose the right answer, 38 percent of them would go along with the wrong answer.

Bouchey describes her own conformity experiment as a "mind fuck." The inner circle told her it was her own fault if she had a problem with Raniere's secretive lifestyle. They told her she was still his soulmate; she'd still been put on earth to join his mission. This was messier than Bouchey had bargained for, but she was willing to go along with it. Because when it came down to it, she was still in love with Raniere.

EVEN IF BOUCHEY had wanted to complain about the arrangement, there was no one outside the inner circle she could tell. By the mid-2000s most NXIVM students were being told that Raniere had sworn off both sex and material possessions, a claim that obscured his numerous sexual relationships from most of the community of coaches and proctors growing around Bouchey.

She began to learn more about Raniere's approach to personal and professional life—namely, that he saw absolutely no divide between them. Raniere did business almost exclusively with the people he had intimate sexual relationships with, she says. Later she would learn that this included, at different times, NXIVM cofounder Nancy Salzman and funder Clare Bronfman.

It was Raniere's way of guaranteeing forgiveness and loyalty, according to Bouchey. It gave him freedom, leverage, influence, and a window into each woman's psychology.

Each of the "spiritual wives," as they sometimes called themselves, had a different role in the company and in Raniere's domestic life. Pam Cafritz fulfilled a personal assistant role, tending to Raniere's whims with a reverence usually reserved for a religious figure. Friends described her as a soft, reassuring presence who always aimed to ease the tension in a room. Behind the scenes she spent much of her time arranging sexual conquests for Raniere and convincing his girlfriends to stay. She routinely introduced young women with big athletic dreams to her "coach," who doubled as a math and Latin tutor. When a woman told the Albany *Times Union* that Raniere had sex with her in the 1990s when she was twelve, she said Cafritz had hired her to walk her dog and suggested that Raniere tutor her in algebra.

After a stint as chief financial officer of Consumers' Buyline through most of the 1990s, Karen Unterreiner oversaw NXIVM's finances along with two other bookkeepers. Former members described her as a wallflower librarian type but with a sharp, sometimes cruel, wit. "Karen was an actual fiduciary," one long-serving senior proctor told me. "Of all the people, I think she actually has the highest IQ."

In the early 2000s, Kristin Keeffe had not yet grown into her role as "legal liaison" overseeing NXIVM's many lawsuits. According to Bouchey, Keeffe was working as a bartender and was rarely seen at NXIVM community events. She became less active as a coach and seemed to have one foot out the door. But a deluge of legal cases beginning in 2003 seemed to restore her commitment and sense of purpose, Bouchey says. As a behind-the-scenes player fighting NXIVM's perceived enemies in court, Keeffe later wound up with a victim's advocate placement in the local district attorney's office.

Bouchey was best known for enrolling hundreds of new students. She says she recruited high-profile people from all over the United States and helped build up the local community with holiday parties and music nights catering to students across a handful of Albany suburbs. Her role was expanding as both field trainer and sales closer; at one point she made $100,000 a year in commissions. She says that in the summer of 2000 she started a weekend conference that became Vanguard Week, or V-Week, an annual gathering on Raniere's birthday.

Over the years, V-Week grew into a near-mandatory engagement that spanned ten days in August. Held at a YMCA retreat center on Lake George, New York, it was an occasion for NXIVM students and coaches to test out new curriculum, participate in talent shows, run triathlons, and, most importantly, listen to Raniere speak. V-Week also became a central sign-up ground for NXIVM's new programs and fundraising efforts. Bouchey recalls raising $50,000 one year to go toward an executive library fund for Raniere. Another year she raised $350,000 to launch a new humanitarian foundation. In a show of paying "tribute," students often simply gave Raniere cash gifts.

With this crescendo of funding and activity, more people than ever were moving to Albany's suburbs to "move up the stripe path," NXIVM-speak for advancing through the ranks and earning new sashes. The so-called stripe path resembled Scientology's Bridge to Total Freedom in that it offered a graded series of rituals and teachings. All students started with a white sash, like a white belt in martial arts. If the higher-ups judged that students had advanced in their personal growth and recruitment, they earned a yellow sash, and then an orange sash, and then a green sash. Bouchey's performance had earned her a green sash, one of the highest ranks that only a few dozen people reached. The sashes represented job titles, like coach or proctor or counselor, though only the highest levels were actually paid.

NXIVM even had an affiliated real estate agent who helped facilitate more than a dozen home purchases clustered in Knox Woods,

a Clifton Park residential development. Some of these new followers had shut down their own self-help and wellness businesses and
moved across state lines to join the NXIVM mission. They populated
the organization's social gatherings, became proctors and coaches,
and often brought with them big networks of family and friends
from all over the world.

In short, the company was about to break into a whole new sphere
of money, influence, and power.

CHAPTER SEVEN

The Girls

S ara Bronfman, daughter of billionaire Edgar Bronfman, had
something that money couldn't buy for her younger sister, Clare.
Namely, people liked her.

By most accounts Sara, older by three years, was the prettier, more
popular sister. In her early twenties she developed an easy charm that
seemed singularly calibrated to quietly capture men's attention. She
had bouncy curls and smiling blue eyes that could have an immediate
impact. And if a flirty glance didn't work, Sara was perfectly comfortable walking over and getting a man's attention in a more hands-on way.

Seeing her sister work a room this way left Clare with some unre-
solved insecurities about her own popularity and self-worth, according to a family friend. She was warm around the people she trusted
but subdued and aloof in the presence of strangers. "Loyalty is one of
her strong points," the friend says.

As heirs to the Seagram liquor dynasty, the sisters had a massive
family legacy to live up to. Their grandfather Samuel Bronfman came
to Canada as a poor Jewish refugee from Russia and went on to make
a fortune distilling and distributing liquor in the Prohibition era. The
next generation of Bronfmans took the empire global, becoming one
of the wealthiest families on the planet.

By 1998, when their father published his self-congratulatory memoir *Good Spirits*, the sisters, who have five older half siblings, had barely amounted to more than a footnote in the century-long Bronfman family narrative. Their mother, born Rita Webb and nicknamed "George" by Edgar, was the Bronfman patriarch's third wife. Rita had changed her name to Georgiana and married Bronfman in the wake of his eldest son's kidnapping in 1975. The couple divorced soon after Clare was born, in 1979.

Sara and Clare's half siblings from Edgar's first marriage had a twenty-year head start establishing themselves as the high-society heirs who would take the reins of the family business in New York City. Edgar Bronfman wrote extensively in his memoir about his oldest sons, Samuel and Edgar Jr., who became leaders in the Seagram company and recurring characters in the society pages of *The New York Times*. In contrast, and not surprisingly given their young age, Sara and Clare (aged twenty-two and nineteen at the time) appear only in a brief entry about a tumultuous period in Edgar's personal life, though he calls them "wonderful" and "loving" daughters. The two shared access to extreme wealth with their half siblings, yet were separated not only by a generation but also a few unspoken social boundaries. "They really weren't always under the umbrella of the Bronfman family," a family friend told *Vanity Fair* in 2010.

The sisters were both born in New York City, but they spent much of their childhood on a farm in the English countryside with their mother. "The one rule I remember in our house was to be outside whilst the sun was up," Clare wrote in a nostalgic 2009 blog post about her mother's farm, where Webb bred horses. "I have fond memories of jumping on my pony bareback in the field, making mud pies, adventuring through the swamp and talking to the fairies in the flower garden." Between school and holidays, the girls visited their father's sprawling estates in the farmlands of Virginia, in the ski hills of Sun Valley, Idaho, and in Westchester County, New York. "We dipped, in and out of our father's world," Sara recalled in a letter describing the arrangement. "He sometimes picked us up in the corporate plane, or we were flown as unaccompanied minors or with a nanny to wherever he was so we could visit him."

Clare was passionate about animal welfare from a young age. She stopped eating meat around age nine after learning it was "dead animals," her sister wrote. By age sixteen she had sworn off all animal products, which was an uncommon choice in the mid-1990s. She put her high school education on hold and began competing in international show-jumping events the following year. According to a fellow rider Clare was always the last one to leave the barn at night, and she often referred to her horses as her "children."

Their mother moved to Kenya when Sara and Clare were still kids. On her blog, Clare described a two-week period where her mother left the sisters in the care of a remote Kenyan tribe. "I remember the children running to see us when we arrived—they were so curious; touching us and giggling," she wrote. "During those two weeks we lived very simply; in mud huts with no electricity, a hole for a toilet, and extremely simple food—however the way of life encompassed incredible richness." The memory reveals the beginning of a romanticization of poverty and struggle that would develop further in young adulthood.

"For much of my life I was ashamed of my wealth," Clare wrote to the judge that would sentence her in 2020. "I felt it made me different, when all I wanted was to be accepted." At horse shows she avoided luxury hotels and sought company with riders who came from modest backgrounds. "We joked that her horses had better accommodations than she did and laughed about her being the cheapest rich girl I'd ever met," a friend and fellow equestrian recalled.

Sara and Clare both craved a new kind of family story, ideally one that was more about helping people than getting rich. Instead of holidays in the Hamptons the sisters said they found volunteer work serving the poor. For Clare that included building huts in Nepal and spending time at a drug rehab center in Italy. In a testimonial video shown at a birthday celebration for Nancy Salzman, Sara Bronfman admitted to having felt lost in the years before she found NXIVM. By 2002, at age twenty-five, she had dropped out of university after a brief stint, grown bored of running a skydiving business in Turks and Caicos, and filed divorce paperwork soon after marrying an Irish horse jumper in Las Vegas.

Sara's friends and family knew she needed help figuring out what to do with her life. It was Susan White, a close friend of Sara's mother, who suggested she attend her first NXIVM session. White had attended an intensive in October 2002, not realizing that the company was specifically seeking out generational wealth. "I took the course purely because I wanted to see if it would be good for my kids," she says. Her stepson also signed up. "I thought it was very well put together, and I thought the kids could really benefit from it."

Barbara Bouchey says White was like a surrogate mother to Clare and Sara—someone they loved and admired. "Susan was worried about Sara's depressed state at the time and strongly encouraged her, believing it would help," Bouchey says. "Which it did."

Though White now deeply regrets signing the sisters up for something that turned out to be "predatory," she thought NXIVM's world-healing, humanitarian messaging was exactly in line with the Bronfmans' goals. On the surface, at least, she was right. Sara attended a NXIVM session in Mexico City in late 2002. "I took a training and I thought it was undoubtedly the coolest thing I'd ever done," she later recounted on Albany radio.

The following year, Clare attended her first session in Monterrey, Mexico, where coaches had a tougher time penetrating her defensive shell. "She had a defiant air about her. She was more angry than Sara—angry at the world," one source told *Vanity Fair*, adding that the heiress struggled to even look people in the eye. "My goal was to like myself—to develop a relationship with myself, and feel proud of myself," Clare wrote of the experience on her blog. The sisters became known to many in the community simply as "the girls."

SUSAN DONES, NXIVM'S Seattle center owner, first met Sara at a level two training session in 2003. "She still had a white sash on, which meant she was considered a student," Dones recalls.

Dones wasn't familiar with the Bronfman family pedigree, though she did notice that a different set of rules seemed to apply to Sara. This young woman with the bright smile was bouncing off the walls from one room to the next, and was obviously flirting with one of the high-ranking trainers, Edgar Boone.

"I was in a few groups with Edgar Boone, and she would come into the room I was in, and she would sit on Edgar's lap," Dones says, with an amused rise in her voice. "She was all over him, stroking his hair, almost like lap dancing with him . . . and I thought, 'Who is this woman?'"

Boone, who had opened the first NXIVM chapter in Mexico, was already revered by the community as a success in business and personal growth. His and Sara's flirtation developed into a relationship that fueled a brief traveling spree, where the couple tried building up new NXIVM organizations in Ireland and other regions of Mexico.

Then a few months later, "Sara dropped Edgar like a hot potato," Dones says. "I remember for Edgar it took him a long time to get over that. He didn't understand why, and I didn't understand why either. But in retrospect I think Keith didn't want them to be together; he saw Edgar as an obstacle to get to Sara's money."

In emails to Raniere, Clare asked for help in using her wealth and power to have a "positive effect on the world." "I am very un-learned in business and would love some help in that area. I feel that my family is walking into some very large business deals with their eyes closed and I do not hold sufficient credability [sic], and certainly not the knowledge to help," she wrote on May 30, 2003. "I would like you to teach and advise me in these areas. And in exchange?"

"A slave for eternity," Raniere replied.

BOTH BRONFMAN SISTERS opened up about their complicated relationship with their father, and on the advice of NXIVM coaches they persuaded him to attend a five-day VIP intensive with Nancy Salzman in Manhattan. Edgar was eager to learn more about the program that seemed to light a fire inside both of his daughters.

NXIVM later shared an unsigned testimonial letter from Edgar Bronfman that claimed Salzman to be one of the most influential people in his life. "It is my experience that when you are living life you should be learning, and when you are learning, life has much more meaning," reads the unverified April 2003 testimonial, which has circulated on news sites as recently as 2019. The letter describes Bronfman's "new way of looking at the world, not based on any hokey philosophy, but based on truth."

Barbara Bouchey claims that in 2003 Edgar Bronfman brought Nancy Salzman to his Manhattan home via private helicopter for several more private sessions. She says the arrangement was that

Salzman would provide free coaching in exchange for referrals. But Edgar didn't like the way NXIVM pressured him to pitch the courses to wealthy and powerful people in his life, and cut ties when he discovered that Clare had lent $2 million for a NXIVM-related venture. The Bronfman sisters' strained relationship with their father then became a focal point of their participation in the NXIVM curriculum.

"I am not sure where things are with my father and I," Clare wrote to Raniere in June 2003, following Edgar Bronfman's break with the group. "Yes, he walked out. I acted impulsively, and extremely mindlessly. This is where my recognition of just how mindless I can be came from."

Clare wanted badly to repair her father's impression of the company and earn Raniere's approval. "I will never know the extent of the damage I have caused, to my father, myself, you, Nancy, the organization, or the world. I would really appreciate your help in starting to try to heal the damage," she wrote.

In the same email Clare described her ideal self to Raniere: "Very clear. Very focused. A leader, but not in the public eye. Very efficient. Very strong. Very active, not hanging around."

NXIVM classes taught that the problems of the world stemmed from "parasite strategies," or individual behavior that isn't self-sustaining. The most effective way to make the world a better place was to replace parasitic strategies with "effort strategies," according to Raniere, and this included replacing all charity with investment, which he said increased value and self-esteem. With Raniere's theories on work, value, effort, and parasite strategies, Sara and Clare were able to think differently about their family's enormous wealth. Instead of being a source of guilt, each dollar they spent began to represent their effort toward building a better world. Instead of living as "parasites" off their father's fortune, they were taking responsibility for their vast resources and doing something "ethical" with them.

IN 2003, SARA Bronfman told *Forbes* magazine that the yellow sash NXIVM had awarded her "was the first thing I had earned on just my own merits." With the sash she was promoted to an unpaid coach.

A NXIVM student needed to enroll two new students to advance to a yellow sash. But if Clare and Sara wanted to advance from coach to proctor, the next step up NXIVM's "stripe path," they needed to develop six coaches each. Clare pushed through her discomfort with handling money and in the process kicked off the sisters' fifteen-year NXIVM spending spree. "What they did was they bought people's courses for them," Dones says. "So then they would get mad when someone didn't complete the course, and they would ask them to pay it back."

The sisters were expecting *Forbes* to print a glowing cover story profiling the teachers they admired, but instead, when the issue hit newsstands in October 2003, they found a critical investigation that made them look like they'd been duped. "I think it's a cult," Edgar Bronfman told the magazine.

Edgar's "cult" accusation became a massive wedge between the Bronfman sisters and their father, who instantly became an enemy of NXIVM. Raniere blamed Clare for bringing on the bad press. Clare never forgot the so-called ethical breach she'd made by telling her father about that $2 million loan, and she vowed to make it up to her mentor. "I think she felt responsible for some of the bad media surrounding our organization," Lauren Salzman testified at Raniere's trial, "and felt that part of rectifying that was to try to make that right financially, legally."

AT RANIERE'S TRIAL in 2019, prosecutors would show the jury whole file folders of financial records and dirt collected by NXIVM on Edgar Bronfman and his charities. Raniere spread the idea that Edgar was behind several supposed anti-NXIVM conspiracies. The Bronfman sisters were told that their father was funding NXIVM's enemies and even manipulating world markets to ruin Raniere's investments.

Edgar made attempts to reach his daughters on his own terms but suspected that NXIVM was mediating their every interaction. "Yesterday afternoon with the two of you was very important to me. I have a few issues with 'Albany' which we should discuss," he wrote to his daughters in June 2004, a message that was forwarded from Clare to Nancy Salzman to Raniere long before it became evidence in court in 2019.

"I have no idea how much money you've put into 'Albany' nor will I ask, but that, too, is a minor issue. Having the sessions go from 8 AM until 10 PM is extreme, and it's what cults do to gain dominance over their victims," he wrote. "I am not sure whether or not Nancy was aware of our meeting, and whether or not she's guiding you in your relationship with me."

On Raniere's recommendation in early 2004, the sisters decided to switch up their money management strategy by appointing Barbara Bouchey as their primary financial planner. Bouchey's firm recommended investments in line with the principles the Bronfmans learned in NXIVM classes.

Meanwhile, Raniere and Nancy Salzman took an interest in Clare's show-jumping career and coached her through episodes of anxiety and frustration. According to Bouchey, Raniere hoped Clare would make it all the way to the top of her field so that his coaching model would become famous.

Clare had won a prestigious Grand Prix in Rome and nearly qualified for the Olympic Games, but was not selected to compete for Team USA. In late 2005 she decided to quit her equestrian career, a choice she later described on her blog. Clare had advanced to the rank of NXIVM coach and was learning "exploration of meaning" therapy, which involved guiding a student back into their childhood memories in search of misperceptions that could be holding the adult self back. She wanted, she said, to move on to her new calling. "I felt more fulfilled than I had after the most successful victory of my riding career—I realized I had earned the privilege of connecting deeply with other humans, and was able to help change their lives profoundly," Clare wrote of the experience. "In that moment I decided it was time to join a new community."

Clare became one of Raniere's most devoted disciples, a mostly one-sided relationship, one source told *Maclean's* magazine, resembling what a "prepubescent daughter" might feel toward a father she adored. "She used to run up and kiss him and sit at his feet," the source said. "For Clare and Sara, this became their real family."

AT A V-WEEK event in 2004, Clare and Sara Bronfman presented a giant novelty check pledging $20 million toward a new "ethical" foundation. The Ethical Humanitarian Foundation was one of several similar-sounding NXIVM organizations the Bronfmans would go on to support, including the Ethical Science Foundation and the World Ethical Foundations Consortium. Bouchey, who was responsible for advising the Bronfmans on their investments, later told me that the check was just for show, and that the money wasn't set to be released for a long time.

"I had discovered that they had charitable remainder trusts, each of them did, and that they were allowed to change the beneficiary," Bouchey explained in a 2009 deposition. "I shared with them that I thought it might be a great idea that they could name the Ethical Humanitarian Foundation as the beneficiary, which would then ultimately be used to support Keith's projects or explorations or pursuits, and they liked the idea."

The giant check signaled a new era for both the Bronfmans and Raniere: the sisters had "leveled up" to a new phase of trust and cooperation, and NXIVM was no longer receiving just small-time cash contributions; it now appeared to have tens of millions of dollars at its disposal. Depending on whom you ask, the Bronfmans either added legitimacy to an otherwise kooky group or, at the very least, dumped money on the many problems Raniere was running from when he folded his other multi-level marketing ventures.

The Bronfmans made other investments that benefited NXIVM. They bought an $11 million private jet, which was used by Nancy Salzman and later for a rendezvous between Raniere and the Dalai Lama in India. Clare bought a $2.3 million horse farm outside Albany and several properties in the suburbs, which she began renting to NXIVM students. Salzman also made use of a Trump Tower condo overlooking Central Park that Sara bought in 2006 for $6.45 million. As well, the sisters started making contributions to political campaigns, both Democrat and Republican.

But all of these expenditures would pale in comparison to the legal spending and commodity trading losses they would incur in the next several years.

CHAPTER EIGHT

Us vs. Them

Keith Raniere had reason to be wary of reporters. When newspapers reached out for comment during his Consumers' Buyline days, it was usually about unflattering accusations, not the breakthroughs and achievements of his company.

Until the summer of 2003, NXIVM had successfully stayed out of the critical media spotlight. Raniere's company, still officially called Executive Success Programs, was in its fifth year of expansion without a single accusation that it was a pyramid scheme getting in the way. Barbara Bouchey was reaching new students on both coasts in record numbers, mostly through old-fashioned word of mouth, and two healthy Mexican chapters were reaching international elites. The company was in the process of rebranding as NXIVM, *Forbes* had yet to publish its skeptical cover story, and the time seemed ripe for a more public launch.

In 2003, *Times Union* journalist Dennis Yusko was a general assignment reporter covering all of Saratoga County, New York, a collection of commuter suburbs directly north of Albany. Though the state capital was a steady source of political news, its surrounding neighborhoods were sleepier and unaccustomed to grabbing front-page headlines. To fill newspaper inches, Yusko attended business association meetings and visited Saratoga's horse-racing track in search of stories.

Yusko learned that NXIVM was planning a massive 66,000-square-foot personal training center for a small Albany suburb called Halfmoon. He'd been tipped off by a planning board chairman, who simply said, "You gotta see this." What Yusko saw was an architectural rendering of clustered honeycomb-shaped structures sprawling in all directions. With what appeared to be hexagonal reflective glass sheathing tightly connected geometric domes, the property looked more like an alien village than a human potential school. And although NXIVM officials continued speaking about their plan for a futuristic new headquarters, the development was never built.

I met Yusko at a Starbucks on the outskirts of Albany in June 2019. His handshake was firm and he spared almost no time for small talk. He shifted in his seat as the gears of his memory went to work. The hand gestures he used to sculpt the greenhouse-like structures in the air reminded me of the Italians in my family.

"Halfmoon is one of the fastest growing towns in upstate," Yusko said, setting the local political scene for me. "It was kind of known for its freewheeling planning board."

NXIVM's proposal was out of character for the neighborhood, even by the Halfmoon planning board's laissez-faire standards. Yusko decided to dig up whatever he could on the proposal, completely unaware of the reporting rabbit hole he was about to venture down.

"I didn't know anything about Keith Raniere. I didn't really know anything about this group," he said, recalling the quiet before the storm. Yusko heard from neighbors that before the proposal was approved, NXIVM had hosted a ceremony on the undeveloped plot. The unofficial groundbreaking had set off alarms among some who felt the development didn't belong in the area's suburban environment.

"Halfmoon is a place where people go home and they go to sleep, and they wake up and they go to work," Yusko explained. (A resident of Knox Woods, the subdivision where NXIVM lifers had settled, told me the same thing.) "It's not where people congregate, there's no cultural places, there's no musical places. At most people will go to the local park on Saturdays, or little league games. That's why this was unusual—because these people had bought this land and talk had begun among the neighbors that they were holding these get-togethers that were unsettling to them."

"Unsettling how?" I asked, trying to imagine the scene.

"I think one neighbor had said their appearance was unusual. Again, in Halfmoon just about anything is unusual unless you're very suburban looking. So these people were wearing different kinds of clothes, and they were expressing themselves in a way that was different."

Members of NXIVM were proud of the ways they expressed themselves, and saw this suspicion as a kind of unfounded NIMBYism. A tight-knit "us" was formed, and everything outside it, Yusko included, would soon become "them."

AFTER A FEW days of research, Yusko stumbled upon the website of a cult specialist named Rick Alan Ross, who has helped hundreds of people leave fringe groups. He learned that Ross had been hired in 2002 by Morris and Rochelle Sutton, the wealthy owners of a New Jersey children's clothing company, to help extract their son from NXIVM.

Michael Sutton had quit his job with the family business to spend more time with the NXIVM community. His parents thought the classes were encouraging him to cut off communication, and they retained Ross as a consultant. They agreed to arrange an intervention at a beach resort in Florida over the December 2002 holiday.

"The point of an intervention is to stimulate critical thinking, to get an individual to reflect and think about what they're involved in," Ross said at Raniere's trial in June 2019. Ross thought Michael would be able to look at the demands the group was making on his time and bank account and think about whether it was truly worth it.

At the time, Ross put NXIVM in the same mostly benign category as Landmark Education's leadership seminars, but he was not yet familiar with the company's rules and rituals. His conversations with Michael changed that. "Michael would speak at length, and he would talk about his experience," Ross recalled of the beachside intervention, which stretched out over several days. "It was then that I learned that Keith Raniere had a special title of Vanguard. And that they celebrated his birthday during Vanguard Week."

Ross revised his assessment of NXIVM, telling Michael Sutton that he believed this was a personality-driven group "eerily reminiscent" of

Scientology and L. Ron Hubbard. Michael listened politely but wasn't swayed. "He was very courteous, very reasonable, but he kept talking on his cell phone with Nancy Salzman," Ross recalled on the witness stand. "Even in the presence of his parents and myself, he would talk to her and she would coach him. And it became obvious to me how much power and control the group had over Michael. Eventually Nancy Salzman persuaded him to discontinue the discussion."

The intervention was a failure, but the Suttons did not give up. Michael's half sister Stephanie Franco, who had attended two NXIVM intensives in the summer of 2001, agreed to turn over her class notes to the family. In January 2003, Ross recommended a forensic psychiatrist and a clinical psychologist who could assess the material critically.

Dr. John Hochman, who was teaching psychiatry at the University of California at the time, reviewed material for the sixteen-day course Stephanie had attended, identifying elements he thought were manipulative and cult-like. As points of concern, he pointed to the long hours, secrecy, inability to seek feedback from friends and family, paramilitary rituals and regalia, frequent contact with superiors, and unsubstantiated extravagant claims.

Dr. Paul Martin also audited Stephanie's class notes from a psychologist's perspective. "This appears nothing short of a religion, a system that has answers to the problems of life," he wrote in a highly critical report. Martin went on to compare the NXIVM material to Robert Jay Lifton's seminal work on what he termed "thought reform." Lifton's 1961 book, *Thought Reform and the Psychology of Totalism*, defines eight elements of ideological control, and Martin pulled out glaring examples of each from NXIVM's curriculum.

WHEN DENNIS YUSKO discovered these reports, written in February 2003 and published on Rick Ross's website in July, they solidified the journalist's suspicion that there was more to the NXIVM story than a simple building application.

Ross shared more of his critical view of NXIVM with Yusko, but when Yusko tried to get NXIVM to respond to the claims, he hit a wall of silence and misdirection. "When you're a reporter, you have instincts," he told me. "And then when you try to reach out and get the other side and it's murky and difficult, you begin to become a little suspicious, so you do more research."

Yusko knew he couldn't use the word "cult" lightly, and Ross warned him of the inevitable backlash. "He's a warrior, so he prepared me," Yusko said of Ross. "He said, 'This is going to cause a splash.' But I don't think I was fully prepared. I don't think I fully knew what I was getting into when I filed that first story."

On first glance, Yusko's initial NXIVM story wasn't the scandalous exposé you'd expect, given the years of litigation and conflict it ignited. It appeared in the *Times Union*'s Capital Region section on July 29, 2003, under the headline "'Success School' Plans Raise Concern."

"It wasn't even an A-1 story," Yusko quipped.

NXIVM reacted swiftly. "After the first time I quoted Rick Ross, days—I mean *days*—later they filed a $10 million lawsuit against him," Yusko said. "It was like a cannon shot across the bow."

NXIVM alleged that Stephanie Franco, the doctors who examined the course material, and Rick Ross had all violated trade secret laws and a nondisclosure agreement signed by all students. Yusko and the *Times Union* weren't named in the lawsuit. The suit alleged that the company was losing $10,000 per day and had suffered irreparable harm because of the breach. If Ross wasn't willing to take the offending material down, the strategy seemed to be to break the enemy financially. The case was refiled and appealed several times, even as judge after judge rejected NXIVM's requests to have the material removed. In court filings Raniere claimed that the expert analysis was riddled with "more than twenty factual falsehoods and even more logical falsehoods and errors."

"This false story with our copyrighted material released to the public through international media can never be completely reversed," Raniere wrote in August 2003. "If this is not in the least stopped it is possible it will destroy us."

Yusko immediately began preparing a story about the lawsuit, but he wasn't able to get through to anyone who would comment on behalf of NXIVM. He left voicemail messages at the company's headquarters and even dropped by the office, but for weeks he came up empty-handed. After some consideration, he decided to crash Vanguard Week, Raniere's weeklong birthday party at Lake George.

As Yusko told me this, he paused for a beat, taking a moment to look out the window overlooking the generic strip mall parking lot beside us. His expression was guarded but amused. All these years later, he still seemed excited by the idea of showing up unannounced. "I'm like, I've got to get that side of the story. At least I've got to try, got to make a stronger attempt. Phone calls and stopping by the office isn't working. So we've got to find out what this is all about, and what better place than Vanguard's birthday celebration?"

YUSKO AND A *Times Union* staff photographer headed up to V-Week, held at a YMCA conference and training center on the mouth of Silver Bay, in late August 2003. It was billed as a "celebration of the human potential to live a noble existence and to participate in a joyous interdependent civilization," whatever that means.

The V-Week visit was Yusko's first exposure to the culture of self-help, with all the power-of-positive-thinking baggage that comes with it. He didn't yet know what an extreme strain of it he was dealing with, so he fell back on comparisons to more familiar subcultures.

"Lake George reminded me of a Grateful Dead show," Yusko recalled. NXIVM followers didn't do drugs, but shared a "free spirit" type of disposition, he said. It was easy to feel lost in a sea of sports bras, sneakers, and ponytails. "People were kind of floating around, but there wasn't the love that's usually in the air. It was more confusion—just a sense of people really convinced if they take enough courses . . . they would improve themselves or their minds."

Yusko also noticed a "Latin vibe" among about a third of the crowd. High-powered families from Mexico were in attendance. "That's when I first realized that this was international."

Though many of the attendees seemed wealthy and well-mannered, Yusko saw that others were barely scraping by: "I even overheard some people talking—some guy saying he was ready to spend his last $2,400 to follow the next group of meetings. Some of them were naively following around, but the ones at the top, you know, Nancy, had their hands firmly on the steering wheel. And they were reaping the benefits."

Yusko eventually met with Nancy Salzman, first at a picnic table by the lake. Around her sat a half dozen members of Raniere's inner circle, including Pam Cafritz, Karen Unterreiner, and Kristin Keeffe.

Keeffe was younger than most of the other women Yusko met that day, but she was growing into one of Raniere's savviest fixers and would take on the role of legal liaison overseeing the Ross lawsuit. "Kristin was extremely committed at that point," he recalled. "In her eyes I saw full commitment."

"I had a complete radical shift in career capacity almost overnight," Keeffe told Yusko of the NXIVM "tech." "It improved my memory and logic dramatically." The fawning quote appeared in the *Times Union* on August 28, two days after Raniere's birthday.

Yusko hoped to interview Salzman on the record, but NXIVM's top ranks wanted to control the circumstances and context of any meeting. "They wouldn't conduct the interview unless they videotaped it," he said. "It took me like an hour to negotiate the terms of the interview."

Yusko agreed to be filmed, and the group relocated to a nearby cabin. Yusko's cameraman started snapping photos as Salzman began to speak. "One of the first things she says is, 'You never tried to call me,' and in very deliberate, slow wording. [It was] noticeably, extremely . . . What's the word . . . ?"

"Hypnotic?" I suggested.

"Yeah, that's it. That's what it was. So I'm feeling that, and then she accuses me."

Yusko was certain he'd chased Salzman and Raniere for interviews. "Trust me, I knew that I made these phone calls," he told me. Faced with a surreal situation in which what he knew to be reality was being flatly contradicted, Yusko stood up for himself. "I knew I had to establish my space, and I said, 'That's not true. You're lying.' And the only reason I remember that is because she later called my editor and complained that I said that to her. I accused her of lying."

Times Union editor Rex Smith would hear many complaints from NXIVM as their influence grew and Yusko continued reporting on the controversy that followed. And Yusko now knew from firsthand experience that Salzman was playing by different rules than the rest of the world. "The truth just didn't matter; it was all about control," he told me. "They were Trumpian before Trump."

YUSKO LEFT LAKE GEORGE with a sense that he'd witnessed injustice in some form, even if he couldn't articulate exactly what it was.

"I didn't know about the sexual abuse at that point. I thought it was more about people getting ripped off. People were getting just wrung out on a bullshit trip," he said. "I just had a real deep suspicion and sensitivity to that for some reason."

Days after Yusko's V-Week visit, he was finally offered a phone interview with Raniere. "It was awkward. He was trying to ingratiate himself," Yusko recalled. "He'd obviously done a little homework on me. I remember that."

Yusko wanted to be fair to Raniere, but he was having some trouble understanding what "Vanguard" was trying to say. "He was so esoteric with his comments," Yusko said.

Raniere talked about the noble ideals NXIVM stood for. He said he was trying to create a future society where cash registers and service workers wouldn't be necessary, because people would be so ethical that they could be trusted to leave money for the products they wanted. "He wasn't saying anything, and I clearly became impatient, and the interview kind of ended," said Yusko.

Looking back, Yusko is still unsure what Raniere expected would happen after their conversation was finished. "I felt that he thought I was a pushover . . . that a couple minutes of just talking with me and everything would be rosy again, and I would just drop off the planet and the reporting would stop. That's what it really felt like. He just needed a few minutes to convince me of his greatness and the good things they were doing. In retrospect, it was never about a better society, it was just more about him: power, control."

RANIERE DIDN'T SEEK power just from the people who came to him hoping to find new lives. His followers made connections early on with official centers of authority.

Dennis Yusko is cautious when talking about the political and social alliances that NXIVM cultivated. He reminded me that he hadn't reported on those allegations firsthand, that other reporters should be credited for digging up connections to Senate Republicans. "Their influence began to spread to official circles," Yusko told me. "They reached up to some of the top levels of government."

The community influence grew to a point where Yusko, a declared enemy of NXIVM, had a hard time planning his own wedding. "It was tough, you know. I got married in Saratoga, and we got our tuxes from this guy in Latham. Me and my father went, and little did I know that the owner of the friggin' tux place was part of NXIVM. I guess my father's number was on the tux application or the receipt, and he ended up calling my father and [making] kind of a veiled threat. And they ended up calling my wife's workplace. That rattled her."

In the coming years the Bronfman sisters would make significant campaign contributions to both the Mike Huckabee and the Hillary Clinton presidential campaigns. An Albany *Times Union* report would reveal that they contributed more than $30,000 in private jet travel to upstate Republican Joseph Bruno. "It really was difficult to report on some of these things back then, when they had so many allies," Yusko said. "And you were reporting on things that were fresh and really unbelievable for up here. . . . Who would ever think the Bronfman sisters would sink millions and millions of dollars into local coffers to, you know, keep people off [Raniere's] back? Again, a lot of it wasn't known for a long time."

Yusko was up against well-resourced dreamers who were willing to use whatever means necessary to stop his research. His friends and family started to worry that he was pouring gasoline on a blaze that was never going to end. "I lost sleep. And then, I'm not going to lie, I became mildly obsessed with the whole thing. That's just what happens when you get deep into a big story like this," he said. "There were some people who thought that maybe I had ventured too far. I was investing too much of my sanity in this.

"I consider myself lucky that, you know, I feel like I survived," Yusko added. "Some people didn't."

DENNIS YUSKO CREDITS his own survival to the reporting for a national audience by *Forbes* magazine that backed up the stories he was working on.

High-ranking members of NXIVM and their politically connected attorney were putting pressure on Yusko's editor. "I was feeling extremely vulnerable at one point, and they were coming in to talk to Rex Smith, who was the executive editor of the *Times Union*," Yusko told me. "It had been coming, I had been feeling it. They were going on the radio and saying certain things. They were trying to battle back. . . . Meanwhile they're suing Rick, and they're using all these power moves, and they come in trying this innocent routine: 'We're getting pushed around by this local reporter, you gotta get rid of this guy.'"

Nancy Salzman came into the *Times Union* newsroom with a well-connected right-wing lawyer who'd claimed that NXIVM courses had improved his law practice. Yusko knew that Smith took meetings like this in a glass-walled office in view of the city reporters. "I was sitting at my desk. I still remember to this day being really nervous, wondering if I was going to have a job after this," Yusko said.

"It was the day the *Forbes* article came out. This was ten minutes before these guys came walking in. So I read it first, and my mind was completely blown. So I printed it out and dropped it on my editor's desk and said, 'Before these guys come in, you should read this article.'"

The piece was headlined "Cult of Personality." Its author, Michael Freedman, had an impressively holistic understanding of the group's less obvious dynamics, from its preoccupation with secrecy to its theories borrowed from Werner Erhard and Ayn Rand. Freedman reported on Raniere's claims that he didn't take a salary, didn't own a driver's license, and didn't have his own bed. "I live a somewhat church-mouse-type existence," Raniere told the magazine. The article even hinted at how much money the Bronfman sisters were sinking into the group.

"I felt really vindicated," Yusko told me. "Everything and more was in this article. To the point of like, *Holy crap*, there's more stuff than we ever knew."

Rex Smith says that, inside the "glass box" where he met with Salzman and the lawyer, he listened to Salzman and the lawyer carefully but never had any doubt that he'd stand behind his reporter. "It was pretty clear to me, honestly, from meeting Nancy and then later Keith, and from reading Dennis's stories, that this was a situation that was beyond a business advisory group," he says. "It felt to me like a cult."

Whether or not his job was actually in danger, Yusko saw that meeting and the *Forbes* cover story as a turning point. "That really rescued the whole situation. That was really huge for me. And for the

paper," he said. "We were on the right trail; we weren't sensationaliz-
ing; we weren't tabloiding. This was all real. And it was in our backyard! It's here whether you want to deal with it or not."

OUT OF ALL the stories Dennis Yusko wrote about NXIVM, there's
one that still sticks out in his mind and evokes a sense of mystery
and dread.

Yusko learned that a thirty-five-year-old woman named Kristin
Marie Snyder had gone missing in the middle of a sixteen-day NXIVM
intensive in Alaska. One friend who'd interacted with Snyder before
her disappearance said that her mental health had deteriorated dramatically. Kenny Powers, who knew Snyder and her wife through the
Anchorage Nordic Ski Patrol, says that days before her February 6,
2003, disappearance, Snyder had lain down outside without a jacket
in the middle of the night but had eventually given up on an apparent
attempt to die of exposure. Powers was part of a search party sent
out to locate Snyder after she'd left a NXIVM class and didn't return
home. Following an extended search, police determined that she'd
kayaked into icy waters near Seward, Alaska. Neither her body nor the
kayak was ever recovered.

"I don't know what happened to Kristin Snyder, but the story still
haunts me to this day," Yusko told me.

Snyder's story came across his desk nearly a year after her disappearance, in winter 2004. By that time Yusko was familiar with
the psychologically exhausting techniques used to reframe NXIVM
students' worldviews. The classes went from eight a.m. to ten p.m.;
students' most private insecurities were probed and leveraged; and
none of the teachers, including Nancy Salzman, were actually licensed
to provide mental health care.

While it didn't happen in every session, some coaches were
known to introduce controversial interpretations of events that
pinned crushing responsibility on new students. Students told me
they'd heard rape victims questioned about how they may have been
responsible for their rape, or a breast cancer survivor might be asked
about how low self-esteem could have contributed to their illness.
(When questioned in 2009, Raniere said that coaches caught making
such representations would likely be subject to an ethical review.)

It wasn't unheard of for NXIVM followers to be convinced that they were partly responsible for major world events. Nancy Salzman was known to tell students that the World Trade Center attack might not have happened if she'd joined Raniere sooner. In Kristin Snyder's case, Kenny Powers had heard her talking about being responsible for the *Challenger* space shuttle explosion and suggesting that the world might be better off without her.

Forbes had already interviewed one Mexican woman who'd begun hallucinating and suffered a nervous breakdown during an intensive and was later hospitalized. An Albany-based psychiatrist also claimed to have given psychiatric treatment to two other students. Powers told me he has a medical background and had assessed Snyder's suicide risk before her disappearance. He said he'd strongly encouraged her to see a doctor but that Esther Carlson, the lead trainer for NXIVM, discouraged this. Snyder's suicide threats were described as cries for attention.

A volunteer search-and-rescue team searched through the night for Snyder on Friday, February 7, and Powers personally put in forty-eight hours straight before taking time to get some sleep. An official search, involving Alaska State Troopers, fire and emergency service workers, the U.S. Coast Guard, Seward police, and Civil Air Patrol, began the morning of Saturday, February 8.

One of the search parties found Snyder's abandoned car. In it was a chilling note in a ringed notebook. Police gave Yusko a copy of the note in 2004 when he came across the story, and the *Times Union* published a photo of it.

"I attended a course called Executive Success Programs (a.k.a. Nexivm) [*sic*] based out of Anchorage, AK, and Albany, NY," Snyder's note reads. "I was brainwashed and my emotional center of the brain was killed/turned off. I still have feeling in my external skin, but my internal organs are rotting. Please contact my parents . . . if you find me or this note. I am sorry life, I didn't know I was already dead. May we persist into the future."

A second page reads, "No need to search for my body."

Powers learned that in the months after the search, Snyder's wife, Heidi Clifford, began receiving harassing phone calls in the middle of the night. NXIVM insiders floated a theory that Snyder had simply skipped town, and later hired a private investigator to help back up the claim that she was alive and "resort hopping" in another state.

Powers tried to convince Clifford to pursue a wrongful death suit. "She decided not to do it, because she was really getting harassed," he recalls. Powers calls it "gangster intimidation-type stuff." Yusko was facing his own barrage of intimidation just for reporting on the disappearance.

ONCE THE BRONFMAN sisters' relationship with NXIVM was made public in the *Forbes* story, Sara and Clare took more active roles in managing the group's public image, which meant more meetings with the local paper, the *Times Union*. Clare Bronfman and Raniere requested a meeting with publisher George Randolph Hearst III, whose cousin Patty Hearst had been kidnapped and indoctrinated by an ideological group in the 1970s.

Rex Smith, who was included in that meeting, recalls Raniere speaking in the same mazelike aphorisms that Yusko had trouble deciphering a few months earlier. "It just reminded me of being in college," he says. "He's a few years younger than I am, but still, he reminded me of those guys who maybe smoke a little dope, would say something he thought was meaningful, and then just stare at you intently so you would absorb the importance of what they were saying."

Despite Raniere's less-than-conventional speaking style, George Hearst III took the meeting seriously and paid special attention to Clare Bronfman. "My view of George's interactions with Clare was it was as though he was almost counseling her," Smith recalls. The Hearsts and Bronfmans were of similar stature in America—morbidly wealthy, and therefore in the public eye. "I think George perceived the problem with Keith, and I think what George was doing with Clare was trying to counsel Clare to save herself from making a terrible mistake. In the way he might hope someone would counsel his own daughter," Smith says.

Dennis Yusko had no idea what words were being exchanged in the closed-door meeting, but he kept pushing to hold NXIVM to account until the story was reassigned to an investigative unit. "I was a beat reporter. I didn't have the investigative chops that other people at the paper had," Yusko says. After 2006, he returned to the daily grind of police scanner tips and city planning meetings.

It is clear from the way Yusko talks about his years reporting on NXIVM that the experience changed him. "You have to wake up every day and trust yourself and trust your instincts. You can't let them rattle your confidence. Once that happens then it begins to affect your reporting, and that's what I was just trying to tell myself."

When asked if he thought it was his job to expose NXIVM, Yusko pushes back on the phrasing. "I just thought it was a great story. I mean, here it is: it's happening in our backyard, nobody's doing anything about it, nobody's writing about it. Isn't this the purpose of our job? Isn't that what we're supposed to do?"

CHAPTER NINE

Sunk Costs

K eith Raniere had a theory for everything.

Leveraging the widely spread claim that he was a math savant, he told members of his inner circle that he was working on an algorithm that would beat the commodities market and bring in mountains of cash. This plan was in the service of his many other world-changing projects, like the one he shared with Barbara Bouchey: buy land and start a new society based on NXIVM's core values.

Raniere first started dabbling in commodities trading early in his relationship with Bouchey, though his past experiments had been decidedly unsuccessful. Between September 2000 and February 2001 he lost as much as $4.5 million on bad commodity bets, $1.6 million of it covered by Bouchey's life savings.

Bouchey didn't exactly consent to covering those losses. Raniere started off asking to open a $50,000 trading account in Bouchey's name in August 2000, offering to put in $25,000 of his own money to get it started. Bouchey thought the most she could lose was the initial seed money, but as the sole trader on the account, Raniere could dial up the risk. At first he boasted that his methodology was working, showing her charts that suggested the account had grown to $150,000. But the gains, if there were any, were soon lost to larger bets. By September the losses had ballooned to $600,000 and Bouchey became distraught.

She told Raniere to close the account, but he said that wasn't possible. Raniere, who claimed his closest followers' moods and thoughts could injure him, blamed Bouchey's "negative reaction" for tanking the markets. He said there'd been a fluke in the orange crop and that they'd have to wait until the options expired or the share prices turned around. Such losses always sounded temporary when Raniere talked about them—like a bump in the road on the way to reward and prosperity. Meanwhile, Bouchey received ongoing coaching on her "attachment" to her savings.

With help from Nancy Salzman, Raniere went on to find more wealthy followers capable of lending money to cover the losses, which continued to mount in 2001. Michael Sutton, the subject of Rick Ross's failed intervention in 2002, lent $1.3 million. Bouchey said that when she and Sutton tried to collect on their loans years later, Raniere claimed it would cripple the company. NXIVM's humanitarian mission, he said, should come before personal selfishness.

RANIERE TOOK A several-year hiatus from trading until the Bronfmans became more heavily invested in NXIVM's projects and finances. The sisters had made the switch to Bouchey as their financial planner in early 2004, and were in the middle of a spending and lending spree. Even before the $20 million novelty check incident, the Bronfmans had financed several loans—one to build the new headquarters, another to develop a winery in New Baltimore, New York.

Clare and Sara's loans weren't typical ones in that they weren't expected to be paid back. The sisters considered themselves "passive investors" who weren't focused on returns. One early loan from Clare was arranged to be repaid in coaching sessions with Nancy Salzman, which Clare valued at $2,000 per hour. Other large loans were simply labeled that way so the sisters wouldn't have to pay taxes on a gift, according to court records.

"I've always relied upon people who were advisers to me," Clare said of her financial affairs on a witness stand in 2011, during one of the company's many lawsuits. "I have never been an expert in choosing what investments, but I've always relied upon the advice of people who are experts, financial planners, financial experts, experts in different industries."

Raniere became the Bronfman sisters' most revered expert in all areas, and he had a lot of things to say about money and value. He borrowed from Ayn Rand's philosophy, focusing on creating "value" in the world and contributing to "civilization" via success in the free market. He sometimes claimed that he avoided paying taxes and getting a driver's license because he didn't buy into the social contract proposed by the U.S. government—though he seemed content living off others' wealth when his own projects were unsuccessful in the marketplace.

Amassing money and power was not unseemly in Raniere's eyes. In fact, he saw it as his ultimate ethical mission. In a 2015 recording, he talked about these aims. "If we could do one thing in this whole world, it would be educating people as to the nature of authority, power, and morality." By taking NXIVM courses, he told his listeners, a person learned how to prevent abuse of power—the root of all human suffering.

Raniere said his courses should be taught at the highest rungs of power, which in turn would inspire other, less powerful people to educate themselves in how to respect "earned authority." "You educate one common person and you have one out of seven billion educated," he said. "You educate a person of influence, who wields strong power, you have one person educated, and that inspires many others to be educated, and also the power that they wield is now used in a legitimate fashion, in an earned authority fashion."

NANCY SALZMAN APPROACHED the Bronfman sisters about paying off Raniere's trading debts with a loan. Bouchey had been through this herself, and yet she watched the Bronfmans set out on the same rocky waters—this time with a better attitude. The sisters pitched in their first $5 million in March 2004.

At his peak, Raniere was making ten to twenty-five trading calls per day, according to court records. He was spending hours on the phone with Yuri Plyam, a trading contact who would go on to become a central figure in a failed real estate scheme. Plyam's lawyers later claimed that he'd made only fifteen dollars per trade.

Raniere kept losing. "I remember myself and Sara, Clare, and Nancy all having conversations with Keith," Bouchey recalled in a deposition. "Every time we would send him money Keith would assure us: 'This is it. This is it; there won't be any more. It's going to come back. I promise you it's going to come back.'" If Raniere's trading decisions were questioned, he would brush off the concerns. "I only need five million now. I am pretty confident I will be able to give it back to the girls in thirty days," he would respond.

All the money was being transferred through a company called First Principles. Bouchey says that she advised the Bronfmans to get a loan agreement in writing, but that those requests to Raniere and Salzman were brushed aside for years. Both sisters continued to sign all the authorizations for transferred funds.

Clare later testified that she hadn't discussed Raniere's trading strategy until after tens of millions of dollars were already gone. "I did speak to him about it at one point, and he told me that his strategy was actually in some ways a hedging strategy," she said. "It's sort of like an insurance policy where if it drops below a certain amount, you have a hedged amount so you never lose that much. . . . It's a more secure way of doing things. More secure, less risk."

Around 2005, Raniere suggested that the Bronfmans would stand to learn from investing in real estate. The girls would sink another $26.43 million in a Los Angeles development before the project failed and the Bronfmans sued the developer, Yuri Plyam.

Clare testified that Salzman and Bouchey first pitched the L.A. development project to the Bronfmans and introduced them to Plyam and his wife, Natalia. The sisters met the couple in Nancy's basement and agreed to put in something like $20 to $22 million, with a promised 20 percent return on the investment. "It was to be very nice residential homes, hillside homes," Clare recalled in 2011. "Hillside, where other people weren't willing to do the building on. Very good neighborhoods. High-end houses."

"The girls knew nothing about real estate and they knew nothing about investing," Bouchey said in a deposition. "What they trusted was Keith. He had about four years of daily communications with Yuri."

Over the next two years the Bronfmans lost millions to both the commodities and real estate ventures, until they were running low on easily available cash. "There was a trust set up for them that they would not receive until their father died," Bouchey told lawyers in a sworn statement, "but they would receive a certain income per quarter. And, at one point, when the commodities losses were really great, the girls went to their father and asked if they could take $20 million out of this trust and they would pay it back."

By 2007 the Bronfmans had spent $65 million of their trust money to cover the losses.

SUSAN WHITE, THE family friend of the Bronfmans, had stopped all involvement with NXIVM but still visited during V-Week to see Sara, Clare, and White's stepson. In one of her last interactions with Sara, she asked her if Raniere had a gambling problem. "She said, 'Oh, I'll get back to you on that,'" White recalls. "I never heard from her again."

White says she was shunned by the group for questioning Raniere and was later accused of conspiring to destroy NXIVM.

When the trading scheme went down in flames and the money disappeared, Raniere once again blamed the sisters' father, Edgar, for manipulating the market to make sure they lost the money. Bouchey remembers Raniere talking about a plot that would somehow "shift the money from these accounts Keith was trading" to Edgar. "Keith felt confident that the father was involved and that was explaining the tremendous losses." According to Bouchey, the sisters believed him. Raniere has still not been made to fully account for the money.

Clare told a jury in 2011 that she didn't share major financial decisions with her father, but that she believed he knew about the commodity trading losses and the real estate scandal before it was reported in national media. "I don't tell my father about any of my finances and business ventures that I do," she testified. "I assumed at one point he would find out."

During the Bronfman sisters' lawsuit against Yuri Plyam, Clare also commented on the theory that her father was somehow behind the losses. She claimed it was Plyam's idea that Edgar interfered with the markets and was trading against Raniere. "Mr. Plyam had brought up the theory that somebody was trading against us and it was seemingly [a] very wealthy, rich, powerful individual in New York and that it could be my father," she said. "I think Mr. Raniere is more of a scientist than that. I think he believed that there could be a possibility or more likely probability, but probably a low one."

WHATEVER THE CAUSE, Raniere justified the losses as a valuable lesson in how world markets worked, according to Bouchey's deposition. "Keith was learning about moving money around. And Keith wanted to have our own country, our own currency and market, our own way of doing things," said Bouchey. "And he was learning this great body of knowledge about the world that would serve him well.

"Keith never admitted that his math formula and commodities knowledge was lousy," Bouchey added. "I never heard him say that once. It was always a plot against him and what he was doing."

The millions in losses were largely hidden from the rest of the NXIVM community. "It was set in a very tight, tight, constricted circle because what would the NXIVM community think if they found out that the leader of the mission was irresponsibly gambling millions and millions and millions of dollars and losing it?" Bouchey said. "This would shake the confidence of many people. So we all, you know, were afraid to talk to anybody about this going on because it looked crazy. And it was crazy."

Meanwhile, Bouchey was authorizing payments for the Los Angeles development scheme, often in increments of half a million dollars every couple of weeks.

WHEN FRANK PARLATO was first hired by Keith Raniere in 2007, it was to fix NXIVM's public relations troubles. The company was fighting off bad press, and Parlato was brought on to place positive stories in the media and turn the organization's reputation around.

Parlato was staying in one of the apartments owned and maintained by the Bronfmans. He became something of a fixer during his months working for Raniere, finding problems and solving them as he went.

After Parlato had spent months putting out public relations fires, Nancy Salzman asked him in December 2007 if he could help secure a $5 million construction loan for a real estate deal. The loan was to help finance Sara and Clare Bronfman's L.A. development, in which the sisters had already invested $26 million.

"I began to feel uncomfortable with the nature of the deal," Parlato told me. "It was structured entirely wrong."

The scheme aimed to buy empty lots in desirable hillside locations, build luxury mansions, and sell the developed property at a steep profit. Parlato was troubled because all the lots had already been acquired for development, but no buyers had yet been secured. Construction had started (albeit barely), and it appeared the building would be happening on spec, without input from the high-end clients who'd be buying the multimillion-dollar homes. Luxury buyers usually want a say in how their properties are constructed, especially if they're paying millions, Parlato told me.

Worse than that, Parlato began to suspect there was some embezzling going on. He claims that as much as $10 million of the Bronfmans' money was unaccounted for. Plus, the Bronfmans weren't listed on the ownership. Parlato said he wanted to investigate.

Parlato was either lent or given (this is still in dispute) a sum of $1 million to get to Los Angeles and figure out what was going on. On his way across the country he says he stopped in Las Vegas to "hire a couple actors" to pose as muscle on the trip. "These are the streets of L.A., and there are two kinds of law: legal law and street law," Parlato told me. "I wanted to be prepared to address both."

After a pause, Parlato assured me that his "muscle" routine was "pure bluff." He arrived in California in January 2008.

YURI PLYAM WAS on the scrawny side of the tough-guy spectrum, Parlato says. Plyam and his wife, Natalia, had spent the previous two years buying multimillion-dollar properties around Beverly Hills with the intention of building and reselling for a profit. The Bronfmans weren't closely supervising or holding the Plyams to a particular schedule. Yuri thought Parlato was coming over to help secure a loan.

In a deposition, the developer described Frank Parlato as a mobster-looking guy with a fedora, a long jacket, and a Sherlock Holmes pipe in his mouth, flanked by an intimidating bodyguard and lawyer. Parlato told him he'd found inconsistencies in the company's financial projection spreadsheets and that payroll records didn't match the number of workers at the sites. He'd discovered that the same workers had also been putting in time on a separate property owned by the Plyams.

One of the workers, Parlato added, admitted that he was told to rush to one of the sites and look busy ahead of an inspection.

According to Plyam, Parlato claimed to be representing Edgar Bronfman. At one point he told Plyam, "If you don't cooperate, it will be World War III."

Parlato allegedly strong-armed the developer out of the deal, making himself CEO of the $20 million–plus real estate project. In a panicked email to Raniere on February 1, 2008, Plyam claimed that Parlato had said he and his wife could go to jail if they didn't sign over the property.

Parlato admits that he intended to seem intimidating but denies he ever claimed to be working for Edgar Bronfman. He claims that Plyam made the assumption himself that Parlato had been sent by Edgar, and he didn't try to correct him. "Yuri made up a lot of fanciful things," he says. "I didn't say those words to him, but I let him believe whatever he wanted."

Parlato stands by his work for the Bronfman sisters in California. "Within a very short time I discovered a fraud and put the assets, such as they were, in the Bronfmans' name."

The Bronfmans, however, didn't see things this way. On advice from Raniere they went after both Plyam and Parlato in court. Construction on the properties was never completed.

Parlato was fired in February 2008 and was soon caught in the crosshairs of NXIVM's so-called legal department. Since that time Parlato and Raniere have been locked in an apparent battle to destroy each other. Raniere maintained a list of enemies, his trial revealed, and this latest entry would not go quietly into the night.

PART TWO

Some Very Powerful Human Beings

CHAPTER TEN

Mission in Mexico

Daniela didn't seem to be plagued with the unfortunate combination of horniness and parent loathing that usually comes with being a teenager. From a young age she'd developed a laser focus on her studies and was too shy to even think about boys.

"When I was a little younger and I used to run around with my microscope and my encyclopedia, I wanted to be a biologist," she recalled on the witness stand at Raniere's trial in 2019. "I wanted to study animals and be a marine biologist, and I wanted to join Greenpeace."

Daniela's family name is protected by court order. She comes from an unusually photogenic household, with parents Hector and Adriana, two sisters, and one brother. In beach vacation shots shown in court, they look like the surf-kissed model family displayed in a picture frame before you buy it. They lived in a small desert town with no malls or movie theaters in the geographical middle of Mexico.

Daniela was the middle sister, the "dorky, nerdy" one, as she described herself. The eldest sister, Marianna, was the popular party girl of the family, while Camila was the baby. "My family was like my center of gravity," Daniela testified. "They used to joke about our family, saying that we were like the Flanders in *The Simpsons* because we got along so well."

In 2002, when Daniela was sixteen, NXIVM was a relatively new presence in Mexico. Edgar Boone was the first NXIVM recruiter to break into the Mexican market in the early 2000s. Boone was from a prominent Mexican family and already had experience teaching meditation and studying personal growth. He and his brother Omar had an impressive degree of influence all over the country in the personal development sphere, and so they were able to bring many affluent students through the country's first NXIVM chapter in Monterrey.

Among those ultra-wealthy Mexican students was a man named Alex Betancourt, who in turn reeled in Emiliano Salinas, son of former president Carlos Salinas de Gortari. Betancourt and Salinas went on to open their own NXIVM center in Mexico City and become influential spokespeople and executive board members within the organization.

SITTING ON THE witness stand in May 2019, Daniela gave measured, understated answers to lead prosecutor Moira Kim Penza. Now in her thirties, Daniela sat tall, her posture so dignified that she seemed to levitate, occasionally leaning her angular features closer to the microphone to speak before rising up again. Her hair was long and dark, reaching for her waist, which appeared preposterously small in a fitted gray blazer.

Daniela looked relaxed and even seemed to savor memories of her childhood as she recounted her parents' preoccupation with self-help trends. They had enrolled Daniela and her siblings as kids in a couple of different personal development courses before the family got involved with NXIVM. "I had taken something called Empowerment, which was a program that connected you to your inner child, which I was a child, so it was easy to connect," Daniela joked.

Daniela scored highest in her class on a high school entrance test, which put her on course to attend a special international high school that fed students into Mexico's most competitive college programs. She attended her first year of high school in Monterrey while her parents lived in a small town a couple hours' drive away. As the weather was starting to heat up in 2002, her parents, Hector and Adriana, came into the city to attend their first NXIVM class at Edgar Boone's center. Daniela remembers that she and her sister Marianna made use of the air conditioning in their parents' hotel room while Hector and

Adriana spent long hours learning about projection and goal setting from some of NXIVM's top trainers.

Daniela testified that she'd wanted to reach even higher than Mexico's best schools and had earned a scholarship to attend an elite Swiss international school the following September for her second year of high school. She finished her first year at the top of her class once again, with new dreams of a long academic career. "I wanted to study at Harvard. That was my dream, that was my plan," she testified. "I wanted to do preventive medicine research to help people."

Hector was so moved by the NXIVM program that he bought Daniela a sixteen-day intensive as a send-off gift, to help her succeed in Switzerland. Daniela liked that the program was scientific, and apparently based on the teachings of a record holder for the world's highest IQ. This was different from the wishy-washy empowerment stuff that had come before, she thought.

Among the trainers flown in to teach Daniela was Lauren Salzman, who had risen up the NXIVM ranks to the position of senior proctor. "She was sharp. She was bubbly. She was smart and she was likable," Daniela said of her first meeting with Salzman in Monterrey. "I remember being intimidated."

In addition to learning that Raniere was the smartest person in the world, Daniela was told he was completely "unified," a word used in the same way that Scientology uses "clear," meaning that a person has resolved all psychological imbalances. "It is, in essence, like the endpoint, like the whole reason everybody is trying to go through all of these courses and removal of disintegrations, and so they can reach this nirvana, this point where there's nothing else to be fixed," Daniela testified. "And essentially, as I understood it, you no longer react to the external world. . . . You act, you think and you act."

Salzman led a NXIVM intensive module called "The Mission," which left a huge impression on Daniela's young mind. "They used a whiteboard with a marker and drew the world. Like a big circle," Daniela said. "They proceeded to, one by one, describe how every effort that humans are making to better the world is futile." She learned that it was pointless to try to save the whales or cure cancer or end world hunger, "because we're just going to keep recreating all of these problems as long as we are disintegrated."

"Disintegration" was NXIVM-speak for an emotional or psycho-logical imbalance that could be healed, or "integrated," through their therapies. Daniela recalled that an "elegant progression" of arguments led her to a conclusion that NXIVM was the only way to resolve disin-tegrations and make the world a better place. Part of the proof came from a calculation by Raniere that found if current trends continued and humanity didn't change course by spreading NXIVM's special technology, the world was going to end in the next ten to fifteen years.

Sixteen-year-old Daniela absolutely believed it. "It was a bit of a childish idea, perhaps, but I wanted to become a scientist and do all these things to help save the world," she testified. After her epiphany during "The Mission" module, trainers began paying close attention to Daniela, who was praised as a smart and speedy learner. Everyone was impressed by how quickly she was picking up the concepts, and this flattered her immensely. In a conversation near the end of the three weeks, Salzman suggested that Daniela come to Albany to join the real-life mission.

Daniela was shocked by the offer. "I was incredibly flattered but also very surprised," she said. "Like, Oh, thank you, but what do you think I can do to help? I mean, I don't know anything."

After some discussion, Daniela revealed to Salzman that she'd taught herself computer programming, and Salzman put her in touch with Karen Unterreiner, who oversaw administration and IT for NXIVM in Albany.

"I didn't jump on it right away," Daniela told the Brooklyn court-room almost two decades later. Discussion continued for weeks, until finally she resolved to take a year off school and do her part to help with the NXIVM mission.

"I decided, Okay, all right. So I'm going to take a sabbatical," she said. "A year from now, school is still going to be there."

DANIELA ARRIVED IN New York in time for V-Week in August 2002. Her parents, who were now NXIVM coaches, came along as well. Though there were plenty of summer-camp-like activities to get lost in, from painting classes to competitive sports, the main focus of everyone's week was two lectures, called Forums, given by Raniere.

Daniela's first impression of Raniere was exactly what she'd expected. He was geeky and a little weird. "He certainly wasn't normal," she said. "He was also attentive and very soft spoken, and had like a sweet presence about him."

She was surprised to find that Raniere already knew her name. "He said, 'I hear you're very smart,'" she testified. Her parents, who were by her side for that first interaction, beamed.

Raniere's words instantly became unforgettable to Daniela, who valued intelligence above everything. "I'm not one to crush on celebrities, but I mean, given my temperament and what was important to me in life, he was the smartest man in the world. So he was like a rock star. Like that moment was, like, Oh, my god."

Daniela was introduced to Unterreiner, who would become her boss. "I thought she was very sweet," Daniela recalled on the witness stand. "A little mousey, but very sweet."

After her parents went back to Mexico, Daniela moved to an apartment close to the NXIVM center that was owned by Edgar Boone, who traveled a lot between Mexico and Albany. The apartment was small and had to be shared with a constant stream of visiting students; Daniela and a NXIVM coach named Loreta Garza were the only long-term occupants.

Unterreiner showed Daniela the lay of the land. She also handed her a manual on programming languages and installed a demo application on Daniela's laptop that she could use to test out code. After a few weeks of settling in, Daniela was put to work doing data entry. For several hours every day she entered payment details and enrollment information for new students.

Daniela felt ashamed that she wasn't doing more meaningful work, or even using her programming skills. She worried that she'd let her hosts down in some way. Unterreiner never gave her lessons beyond handing over the manual and demo app.

"I started finding ways to make myself useful, you know, because there was no structure. I was used to the structure of school," she said. "I would clean refrigerators, I would clean the floors, clean the bathrooms, organize the storage room. I found ways to be useful, like a full workday."

Daniela's older sister, Marianna, had already graduated from high school but was going through a reckless, depressive phase. She was drinking and partying, and was even involved in a break-in at a supermarket owned by the parents of one of her friends. Daniela suggested that Marianna come to Albany to take ethics classes. She could also watch out for Marianna there. "I thought I could take care of her, maybe straighten her out," she said. "And she could take some classes."

Marianna and Daniela's parents paid for a Howard Johnson hotel room so the two girls could have their own space. Marianna was barely able to get out of bed in the morning, Daniela recalled. "She would get up and go to the center for the classes, but she would come right back."

On one of those trips to the NXIVM center, Marianna met Pam Cafritz. "A friendship was born. I saw it, like, overnight," Daniela said. "They became really close, really fast. At the time, it was explained to me [that] Pam was an athlete and Pam had taken an interest in Marianna as an athlete too."

Cafritz bought Marianna tennis gear and court time, and they began training regularly. "I felt happy that she was doing better, because she *was* doing better. She wasn't sleeping at the hotel all day anymore," Daniela recalled. "She had some light back in her."

DURING HER FIRST year in Albany, Daniela mostly saw Raniere from afar—either at speaking engagements at the center, where he sometimes answered students' questions, or from the bleachers at late-night volleyball games held multiple times a week at a local gym. After many months had gone by, she finally mustered the courage to approach him and express her disappointment in the work she was doing. "I was very disillusioned," she said. "I felt like there was no point to me being there and I wanted to go back to school."

Raniere asked her some "guiding" questions about her purpose and preferences, and whether she'd taken any time to write out a mission statement. Daniela recalled that he picked up on her academic interests very quickly and began testing her math skills on a whiteboard, scribbling out equations for her to identify. "The first was a quadratic equation, and there was some calculus," Daniela testified.

"I didn't take calculus in high school. I think he was gauging my level of education."

Raniere then gave Daniela a brainteaser, she said. "I don't remember what the brainteaser was, but it was simple. And I gave him the answer right away, and I thought he was very pleased." He gave her a second, much harder, problem to solve. Daniela threw her whole heart into solving it quickly.

"I wanted to impress him, I wanted to show off. I wanted him to know how smart I was," she said. "I went into one of the rooms in the back. When I want to think, I always need silence and isolation. And I thought really hard and I solved it—I think in a matter of minutes. It was fast, because I caught him before he left."

Daniela had proven herself to Raniere, who suggested she see him for more tutoring. Later, Unterreiner told Daniela that she'd been reprimanded by Raniere for not recognizing she had a genius in the admin office.

RANIERE AND DANIELA began exchanging emails regularly, with Daniela still keen to prove her problem-solving skills. "One of the problems was, How many distinct spaces can be created by three cubes that are intersected?" she said. This was one of the questions that had appeared on Raniere's record-setting IQ test decades before. Though it took longer for Daniela to reach the answer, she got it right once again.

As the end of Daniela's one-year "sabbatical" approached, Raniere encouraged her to continue with NXIVM training, suggesting she could achieve more with it than with a traditional education.

Barbara Bouchey, Raniere's girlfriend and top recruiter at the time, recalled that Daniela did odd jobs around the community and at some point also took up filming Raniere as he went about his daily activities. She continued working in the admin office with Unterreiner but was increasingly excused to work directly with Raniere.

This trend away from the admin office reached a decisive moment after Daniela admitted that she'd stolen several thousand dollars from a drawer in Unterreiner's office. Daniela felt guilty immediately about the impulsive theft and testified that she returned the cash within a day. "I felt everybody could see right through me. My heart was racing. I couldn't sleep. I felt really bad," she said. She decided to put it back and confess to Raniere. "He was a person I had started to trust. We were building a friendship."

When Daniela told Raniere about the theft, he said he already knew. "I have to say I didn't believe him," Daniela testified. "He said that, but I didn't believe that was true."

Raniere and Daniela then had a lengthy conversation about morality and ethics. "Now you know that stealing is a possibility," Raniere told Daniela. "Now you can leave it that way, or correct it."

Daniela said she left the conversation feeling she'd corrected her mistake by returning the money. And she reflected on advice from Raniere that made her feel a little better. "He said this, which I thought was interesting: 'You could actually be a better leader of people because now that you know what it's like to steal and choose not to steal . . . you can speak to it because you now know more than someone who has never done it.'"

But she soon learned that the incident wouldn't be resolved so easily. Raniere called Daniela and instructed her to speak with Nancy Salzman and Karen Unterreiner about the situation. He told her that what they had to say might be tough, but he would be there for her in the end.

What followed was a confusing several weeks of humiliation and mind games Daniela repeatedly described as "hell." Salzman grilled her on how she would "fix" the transgression but didn't accept anything she proposed—even paying back interest—as a solution. Salzman told Daniela's parents about the theft, and a number of other NXIVM members too.

"I was part of this module and breakout group that was helping me at the time," Daniela testified. "In the middle of the breakout group, I remember it was Barbara Jeske who was leading the discussion, and at some point she turns to me and said, 'So, what do you think, Daniela? How does that relate to your stealing the money?' And I was like, How does she know? Did they tell everyone? And, they did."

Daniela estimated that about a dozen people suddenly knew about the stolen money, which filled her with shame. Then, during another heated negotiation with Nancy Salzman, she heard for the first time

NXIVM's name for her actions: suppressive. "That was drilled into me," Daniela said. "I was wondering to myself maybe—maybe that's why I stole the money. Because maybe I am a suppressive."

As in Scientology, NXIVM used the word "suppressive" to describe people and forces that went against the organization's interests. In NXIVM, a suppressive person was described as someone who had their wires completely crossed, so that good things made them feel bad and bad things made them feel good.

Daniela had been fired from the admin office, and so she picked up more odd jobs to compensate for the loss. "I was running errands for people. I worked as an assistant to a real estate agent. I was dog sitting, house sitting, taking dry cleaning. I was looking to make a buck so I could, you know, continue surviving."

All the while, Daniela was confiding in Raniere, who was beginning to flirt with her in tutoring emails. He asked her if she'd ever been in love and commented on her purity when she revealed that at age seventeen she'd never been kissed. "I think he set me up," she said. "I think that he made himself the hero of the story. He created a horrible situation by which I became closer and a little more dependent on him."

Raniere first kissed Daniela during a conversation about her parents' separation. She was seeking his worldly guidance on how to navigate the split, which her father was finding extremely difficult.

"I didn't feel bad, didn't feel good, didn't feel anything, it was just like, What's going on?" she said of the kiss. They were sitting on a purple couch in Nancy Salzman's office, and the door was uncharacteristically closed behind them. But after some time passed, Daniela started to feel excited that she was special and had been chosen.

BARBARA BOUCHEY REMEMBERS the moment when she began suspecting that Raniere was grooming Daniela for a sexual relationship. She'd gone over to the Flintlock house, where he lived with his "spiritual wives" Unterreiner, Cafritz, and Keeffe. At the time, Bouchey and Raniere had a not-quite-secret romantic relationship. Bouchey was dressed for relaxing around the house, in sweatpants with no underwear. She found Daniela sitting in a chair in the living room filming Raniere while he lounged on a couch.

Daniela later testified that Raniere had a mild obsession with women's underwear, or rather, lack of it. He was a man who acted on impulse, and he apparently correctly guessed that Bouchey was going commando under her sweatpants. Bouchey recalls that, with the camera rolling, Raniere started "roughhousing" with her as if they were alone in her bedroom. It wasn't uncharacteristic of Raniere to tickle or manhandle Bouchey, but this was the first time it happened in front of a teenage girl. Bouchey was disturbed and asked Daniela to turn the camera off, but Daniela kept filming and giggled.

"It struck me as odd that he wouldn't stop," Bouchey recalled. She couldn't prove it, but Bouchey suspected he may have been exposing Daniela's two sisters, Marianna and Camila, to similar situations when they were in Albany. "I believe he had started grooming the three girls, making them more susceptible to a sexual kind of freedom or life."

Leading up to her eighteenth birthday, Daniela's conversations with Raniere turned to sex. She was too young for them to have sex yet, Raniere told her. He opened up about his own sex life, revealing that he had several long-term girlfriends. Raniere said his privacy was very important, and that he needed all of this to be kept secret.

As her birthday approached, Daniela was repeatedly asked by Raniere what she wanted, implying that she should want him. "It took a lot of him asking in a flirty way, 'What do you want for your birthday? Do you want something special?'" she testified. "I couldn't say it and I did not say it. And he noticed I was extremely shy, and he said, 'Well, if you're too shy to say it, why don't you write it on the palm of my hand?' And it was easier than to say it, so I, with my hand, spelled out *S-E-X*."

Daniela was immediately mortified when Raniere acted surprised, saying, "Ooohh, you want *sex*?" as if he hadn't considered the idea. Seeing her become so plainly self-conscious, Raniere took the opportunity to ask Daniela what body insecurities were standing in the way, suggesting she should lose weight and reassuring her that he liked natural body hair.

"I remember being really confused because I was like, How would I be insecure [about pubic hair]?" Daniela recalled. "Is the hair too curly? Is it the wrong color? And he explained, 'Some women are insecure and don't like their hair. But you know, I like natural.'"

Daniela's birthday came and went, and she didn't see Raniere. He told her he was disappointed that she hadn't reached her weight goal of 155 pounds. Raniere had shared his theory about energy exchange during sex, claiming body fat got in the way. Daniela felt rejected and disappointed that, after all this anticipation, nothing had happened.

But a few days later, Raniere followed through. He took her to an office building once used by Consumers' Buyline and led her down a second-floor hallway to a suite of offices, where he brought her into a small room.

Daniela described the room as dimly lit, with stacks of boxes everywhere. In the center of the floor, on an old, dirty carpet, was a mattress. "It had raggy, used sheets on it," she recalled. "It wasn't like—that bed wasn't made up."

Raniere asked her to undress, and she did. At first he kept his clothes on as he performed oral sex on her, and then he undressed and got on top of her. "He gave me a hug, like a long hug is what it was," she said. "And then he just kissed me, got up, helped me up and got dressed, and I drove him back to Flintlock."

Almost as soon as they'd parted, Raniere called Daniela to talk about the experience. Seemingly out of nowhere, he asked her why she hadn't asked him to use protection. "Confusion ensued because I couldn't understand why he was asking me to use protection if I didn't feel he penetrated me," Daniela testified. "He was telling me that he did penetrate me and I did lose my virginity, but I did not feel that."

Raniere later offered her theories as to why she'd "blocked out" the penetrative part of their encounter, but she was confident that she'd never felt an erection. "I feel very sure of what I felt. I was there. It's my body so it's very confusing to have contradictory information," she said. On a long walk together, when Raniere continued returning to the subject, Daniela suggested that maybe she'd blocked it out because deep down she hadn't wanted it.

"He corrected me and he gave me the right answer," she recalled. "He said, 'No, the reason why you didn't feel it was because you were too in your head. That's what you need to work on. That's why.'"

ON THE WITNESS stand at Raniere's trial, psychologist Dawn Hughes described gaslighting as "a behavior that functions to make you think you're crazy by telling you up is down and left is right." Gaslighting has become something of a buzzword in recent years, best known as the thing *Teen Vogue* accused President Donald Trump of doing to America. "It functions to make the victim not trust her own perceptions, not trust her own judgment, and not really have a sense of what really is going on, because she's continually told that she is to blame," Hughes testified.

The prosecutors would return to "up is down" moments with many of the witnesses, often spending excruciating amounts of time unpacking what the women understood as reality and what Raniere and his fixers insisted instead. This was consistent across decades, whether the witnesses were high-ranking power brokers like Lauren Salzman or the lower-ranking "slaves" who were later initiated into the secret women's group DOS with no knowledge of Raniere's role in orchestrating it. In June 2019, after watching four DOS women, including Lauren Salzman, testify, I wrote a story for *Vice* about the thread prosecutors seemed to want the jury to follow: that Raniere's slave group was in part powered by gaslighting, that he repeatedly invented new circumstances that changed and discredited women's own experiences. Raniere even told one of his partners: "Things are most maneuverable when they are most unstable."

Daniela was not part of DOS. She left Albany long before branding and blackmail became formalized rites of passage for the young women closest to Raniere. But Daniela did see her relationship with Raniere as "an ownership of sorts." And she had the most crystallized "up is down" story of all the witnesses. She didn't use the word "gaslighting," but she articulated what it felt like to have her sense of the world undermined by Raniere.

She got an uneasy feeling again when she asked him about the status of their relationship and stated her preference for monogamy. "He said we had already discussed that," she testified, adding that by Raniere's account they had agreed to a three-year relationship contract. "I felt really confused about the fact that we didn't have that conversation. . . . I thought maybe he had it with a different woman."

Though the disagreement was far from settled, their relationship moved into a new phase where Raniere initiated sexual encounters and told Daniela his beliefs about sex and monogamy. "Among the reasons presented why he could have sex with other women, but I, for example, could not have sex with other men, is because that would hurt him," Daniela said in court. "That meant we had some kind of a connection through sex; that if I had sex with someone else, he would feel it."

Raniere asked Daniela if she saw a blue light after they had sex— something that other women apparently saw. Daniela did not see any blue light and told him as much. He suggested she wasn't sensitive to the same subtle energy shifts as other women were.

Raniere also told Daniela that sex was a tool he used to fix "disintegrations" in women. He claimed to be able to see disintegrations and other weaknesses in people's bodies, and that he could heal them through sex or through NXIVM therapies.

"I found it very confusing, because the reason why I admired Keith and respected Keith was because I thought he was the smartest man in the world," Daniela said. "To me, all that mysticism, if not in contrary, at least it's not in line with what I believe science is." Daniela was bold enough to discourage Raniere from speaking publicly about his parapsychological claims, saying it went against NXIVM's mission.

In a short amount of time, Daniela was initiated into Raniere's inner circle of subjugated girlfriends. Though she didn't realize it then, she would look back at her sexual relationship with Raniere as one-sided and steeped in manipulation. "I had no other thing to compare it to," she testified. "All of the oral sex he had me give him, that was normalized. I didn't know what it was to be a woman in a relationship."

Daniela said that her concept of being a woman in a relationship was all about giving pleasure, and it didn't include receiving. "I didn't know that it was an inordinate amount of pleasure, and it was not reciprocal, and that is not normal," she said. "I mean, I'm not a sex-crazed person who wants to give oral sex all the time. That's not who I am. That's not what I wanted. All of that is a slow manipulation."

Her ensnarement would get progressively worse over the next decade. When her tourist visa was withdrawn, Daniela said, Raniere hatched a plan to sneak her back into the country using a fake ID. Whenever she would question his motives and methods, he would leverage her fear of deportation. Eventually, Daniela would be confined to a room for twenty-three months as punishment for daring to fall in love with someone who wasn't Raniere.

Daniela was, she said, "like a little deer." Raniere had set up a trap for her, "and when I fell, he's like, 'Oh, you fell in a trap.'"

CHAPTER ELEVEN

The Heist

D id Daniela really fall into a trap? If so, when was it set, and how did it work?

Though Raniere billed himself as a scientist and philosopher, his skill set was closer to that of a stage hypnotist or illusionist. Former NXIVM insiders have compared him to Derren Brown, a U.K. performer who cranks out TV specials featuring what seem like superhuman powers of persuasion.

In his 2006 special *The Heist*, Brown styled himself as a shady motivational guru and used conditioning, emotional anchoring, and other "insidious" techniques to encourage a mental state where a regular person would voluntarily participate in an armed robbery.

Brown claimed that the show's thirteen participants were drawn from the public, had steady middle-management jobs, and had no criminal record. They all met at a U.K. hotel and were subjected to a human experiment without knowing it. After dinner and several drinks, a server arrived with an unexpected food bill. "I want to see how they react: who complies, who gets angry, and who emerges as the alpha male, or female, and takes charge," Brown explained. The outcome would inform who he'd select for further conditioning and manipulation.

The next morning, Brown kicked off what the participants understood to be a five-hour seminar in "mind mastery," full of tricks taken from the neuro-linguistic programming (NLP) playbook. Among them was the scientifically unproven idea that eye movements left, right, up, or down could reveal whether a person was genuinely remembering something or fabricating it on the spot. The participants tested it out and believed they were empowered with new body-language reading skills.

NLP coaching is a growing facet of the multibillion-dollar self-help industry. It isn't taught in academic settings—more often it's experienced in hyped-up workshops like the one Brown staged for TV. Today these sessions are run by multi-level marketers, pickup artists, and business improvement YouTubers alike. They sell a chance to make more money, find more romantic partners, and unlock success in every imaginable aspect of life.

For the record, Amir Raz, a hypnosis researcher at McGill University's department of psychiatry, says the eye-movement technique, and NLP generally, is pseudoscience, talked up by the likes of self-help maven Tony Robbins and rejected by actual neuroscientists. "The whole claim on which this field is founded is completely tenuous," he said. "In many ways I find it unethical."

BROWN IS MORE transparent than you'd expect about his use of pseudoscience, misdirection, and straight-up bullshit. He admits that several techniques are effectively placebos, but claims that self-styled gurus like himself (and Raniere) are most powerful when audiences are willing to suspend disbelief and trust that something exciting and improbable is about to happen.

The Heist participants then learned to create a "motivated state" through "anchoring": "I tell them to remember when they felt highly motivated, and then to amplify that feeling," Brown said. He told them to link that go-getter feeling to the "trigger" of rubbing their leg with their hand. "They can create the motivated state on their own just by rubbing," he suggested. "And the more they do it, the stronger the association becomes." Brown later had some of them practice this while playing a Jackson 5 song, aiming to trigger their "go-time" emotional state whenever they heard it in future.

Brown's self-help seminar featured in *The Heist* was full of outlaw language. Slogans like "Steel yourself" (playing on the word "steal") and "Do it" littered his slideshow, and subjects received realistic toy guns to symbolize their new status as "thought criminals." Brown then instructed participants to steal candy from a convenience store as a fun way to harness their inner child and take an exciting risk. This amounted to simple boundary testing. Some refused, and they were eliminated from the show. But the ones who tried it and framed it as a positive experience advanced to the next phase.

After a few more experiments and conditioning exercises—including one where the participants rehearsed saying the words "Get down on the floor" in an unrelated context—Brown selected four people for the final experiment. Participants were each brought to a back alley. Unaware that they were being filmed, they had to walk alone, with a toy gun in hand, toward where an actor posing as a security guard was putting two giant cases, presumably full of cash, into the back of a security truck. The hope was that—with gun in hand, a few billboards in the vicinity that happened to display the slogan "Do it," and a passing car playing the aforementioned Jackson 5 song—one or more participants would be triggered into spontaneously robbing the security guard.

Three of the four selected participants went through with it. They pointed their guns, threatened the guard, and ran off before a crew intervened to stop them. Brown claims that each of them truly believed they were committing a robbery.

The Derren Brown special is entertainment and should be taken with enough grains of salt to garnish the rim of a margarita. Some of these participants may have caught on to the larceny theme early and knowingly played along or simply hammed it up for the camera. But Brown uses real motivation and conditioning techniques that are widely used in the field of self-help, and their employment on his show is an example of the kind of selection and manipulation "trap" ex-NXIVM members say they felt caught in.

A close read of Raniere's self-help methods shows he was guzzling from the same well of pop psychology and pseudoscience that Brown draws from. When an itemized list of books from Raniere's executive library became evidence at trial in 2019, it wasn't surprising to find

Patterns of the Hypnotic Techniques of Milton H. Erickson, which is one of Richard Bandler and John Grinder's founding texts on NLP, published in 1976; and the pop psychology juggernaut *Influence: The Psychology of Persuasion* by Robert Cialdini, first published in 1984 and updated in 2001. (Raniere also had five copies of Hermann Hesse's *Siddhartha*, Ayn Rand's *The Virtue of Selfishness*, and several For Dummies computer programming books.)

TO UNCOVER HOW these persuasion, selection, and conditioning techniques might have played out in a NXIVM curriculum setting, I took a deep dive into Raniere's patent application for Rational Inquiry, in which he sets out, for example, how lessons are conducted. Within the very first moments of a NXIVM class, ritualistic hand clapping, sash wearing, and group recitation offered an opportunity to observe students' natural tendencies toward dominance or submission to authority. Students were led through a series of handshakes, stepping into them with a different foot forward, cocking their wrist slightly downward, and "gaining control" by grasping with their middle and ring finger. They learned a special NXIVM handshake that required students of lower rank to put their left hand on top of their already shaking right hand as a sign of respect.

All of this provided helpful context for someone trained in NLP to find suggestible subjects. Just like the surprise hotel restaurant bill in Brown's made-for-TV experiment, these exercises helped proctors and coaches sort who happily accepted an unfamiliar set of rituals, who resisted, and who needed to be ejected for asking too many questions.

Raniere's neuro-linguistic programming background stands out most in lessons on one-to-one communication. Sessions focused on persuasion techniques and reading people, not unlike the eye-movement lesson in *The Heist*. "One can ascertain a tremendous amount of information about a person without them consciously transmitting it," reads one of Raniere's modules on building rapport.

Rapport is a central concept in NLP and hypnosis. Matching someone's breathing or heart rate, mirroring their movements, and watching their complexion and facial tics for signs of agreement are taught as ways to increase agreeability and trust. NXIVM students learned to "lead" a conversation by mirroring subtle movements for a while and then testing out whether the other person unconsciously mimicked them. If you took a sip of water and the person you were mirroring followed suit, you knew that person was in deep rapport.

These skills are not-so-coincidentally described in Derren Brown's memoir *Tricks of the Mind*. Brown cautions that NLP mirroring and leading doesn't work on everybody and can actually make a person uncomfortable pretty quickly, but when done with "warmth and naturalness" it can "make you oddly attractive."

Hypnosis researcher Amir Raz says these mishmashed concepts are taken from a variety of sources of varying legitimacy and give medicinal hypnosis a bad name. Even Brown, a guy who made a career for himself doing magic tricks, throws considerable skepticism at the "evangelical" tone of most NLP workshops and the over-the-top claims made by some of its practitioners.

NXIVM had its own version of the "motivated state" *The Heist* participants experienced when they rubbed their leg and got stoked. Coaches explained that enthusiasm and excitement made people better communicators. As on Brown's show, students used metaphor, memory, and role play to feel that excitement in the moment, and participated in exercises aimed at accessing those states at will. In another module called "Building Desire and Motivation," NXIVM students identified triggers that could cause a motivated state to occur. Likewise, students tried to conjure a fight-or-flight state, testing their breathing rate and posture before and after. All of this qualified as "emotional anchoring" in NLP, and would theoretically give a practitioner easy shortcuts for making a student feel scared, excited, or motivated.

Raniere's entry-level modules tackled big subjects like blame, leadership, pride, and responsibility. The group-discussion format set students up to disagree with each other on a series of hard-to-answer, sometimes contradictory, questions. Former coaches testified that these questions were designed to give students a sense that they didn't understand these concepts as deeply as they thought. After discussing in small groups, coaches would read from a script that seemed to resolve part of the contradiction. This process was repeated over and over until it stuck.

The NXIVM teachings were full of opportunities to open up about the things that scared you the most. In a module called "Honesty and Disclosure," coaches would lead students through a discussion about whether they could have honesty without disclosure, or disclosure without honesty. "It's almost impossible to be 100 percent honest," asserts part of the script coaches were instructed to read after the discussion. In Raniere's view, it was destructive to disclose "everything," and what people disclosed to others was always layered with their own "filters" and "values" anyway.

After learning how too much disclosure could create a mess for themselves and others, students were asked to reveal their deepest desires and fears, apparently in an effort to better understand their own "filters." Students were then assigned homework that essentially amounted to revealing a secret about themselves. "Find someone whom you trust and want to be close to," the assignment read. "If you've done the day's exercise properly, you already have a page full of your vulnerabilities to work from." Sharing these, Raniere said, would create "the basis for very special relationships."

Other sessions asked students to reveal the absolute worst thing ever done to them and then the worst thing they'd ever done to another person. Some students actually confessed to killing people during these sessions. "There's people who have murdered next to people who are like, 'Um, I once cheated on my taxes,'" one former student told me. "It doesn't have a hold on you," coaches were encouraged to say.

This process appears to have had a second, less obvious purpose: to dig up as much dirt as possible on all participants, young and old. High-powered CEOs and politicians spilled about their extramarital affairs, the secret child they were still paying for, their not-quite-legal deals, their growing collection of offshore tax havens—and above all their fears of being caught and held accountable. Sarah Edmondson says coaches were instructed to take notes on the worst things new students were willing to share.

Much like Scientology, the organization was collecting what Russians would call "kompromat" on students. This was used as leverage to encourage deeper participation, and in Daniela's case, her undocumented status, her use of a fake ID provided by NXIVM to cross the border in 2004, and her admitted stealing were all brought up to encourage compliance. "They had something on me," she testified. "Every time I was doing something that was not what they wanted . . . then it would be, 'Well, we brought you here.'"

If students made it to the upper levels, they were more likely to encounter Raniere's version of outlaw language. In one module called "Abuse, Rights, and Injury" participants discussed child sexual abuse. "What is abuse? What does it mean to abuse someone?" the questions begin. "If someone comes from a country where adults orally stimulate children and they find out according to American culture they have been abused, have they? Who did the abusing?" (Coach notes say the answer is yes, they have been abused, and the abuser is "our society.")

MOST CLASSES DIDN'T dig into such dark and predatory themes; students usually found the sessions practical and uplifting. I thought I understood the basic mechanics on paper, but I was missing the long days, the evangelical energy of breakout groups, the immersive experience of the intensives. These modules were designed to deliver earth-shattering personal epiphanies, and I wanted to feel one firsthand. So in July 2018, four months after Raniere was arrested and almost a year before his trial, I enlisted Sarah Edmondson and her husband, Anthony Ames, to coach me through one of her favorite modules.

As I sat down at Edmondson's kitchen table in her Vancouver condo, Ames turned to his laptop, where an exercise from Raniere's "Nature of Emotions" module was already open. This was something students initially encountered at the end of their first day, Ames said. Then he began reading to me about tracing anger to fear. "I'm going to throw a lot at you now," he warned.

"There are certain hardwired basic emotions," he read from the blurb on the screen. "People can't experience emotions without viscera, without feelings; they're hardwired into us." All emotions were "triggered," he told me, by a direct stimulus, or by a "recognition" or thought. "Like you could be driving in the car and think of something, and you react to it," he added.

Ames said emotions come from the difference between where we are and where we'd like to be. This didn't compute for me until much later, but I think he was basically saying that positive emotions come from reality exceeding expectations, and negative emotions come from reality not meeting expectations.

"Emotions are related to the fight-or-flight or satiation mechanism—satiation being *I just want to feel good*," he continued, double-checking to see whether I was following. A subtext of much of Raniere's curriculum was that this concept of constant "satiation" was a bad thing that weak people fixated on.

Even as Ames narrated the exercise description, he began shaking his head at what used to be his genuinely held understanding of human nature. "Anger is always about protecting our self-image. When we perceive our self-image is threatened, we believe we must change the world, or be shown to be less-than or not enough."

In the same breath, Ames broke out of his coaching voice and said he was no longer convinced of this. "I'm pissed my wife got branded—there's no self-image conflict going on with me there."

It was clear that Edmondson and Ames were still processing their experiences inside NXIVM, slowly calculating which parts were harmful, which parts were relatively benign, and which parts still had some value they could continue to apply in their lives. As someone who'd spent more than a decade immersed in this community, Edmondson seemed to have some difficulty rejecting the whole thing. There were essential parts of herself, her most assertive and world-savvy parts, that seemingly came to exist only because of her role in an alleged cult.

The three of us agreed that there were different reasons to be angry outside protecting a self-image, and that Edmondson's and Ames's anger over the abuses within NXIVM were justified. Still, we continued with the exercise, because it was one that had produced life-changing shifts for them. They instructed me to think of a time when I was angry, and break down what I thought I was fighting against.

As I vented to Edmondson about Twitter trolls and other journalistic irritants, I could see how the exercise was meant to chip away at my "reactionary" mind. Instead of letting anger get the best of me, I could choose to analyze the source of my discomfort and why it was manifesting in an aggressive way. This was how you became what NXIVM called an "integrated" person—to be in complete control of your emotions and not be unduly swayed by past traumas and misperceptions.

PART OF WHAT made an integration so appealing was the honest, self-assured dispositions of the people in class who said they'd had them. NXIVM's higher ranks, who often participated in these breakout sessions, never made excuses or blamed others for their problems. Ames and Edmondson did their best to recreate the atmosphere of an intensive, but without the group dynamic, I didn't, in the end, have any kind of "aha" moment.

Ames told me that some days he'd wished the program could end for students after the first week, but as coaches they were strongly encouraged to get people signed up for more classes. Coaches would often find a way to underline students' flaws, even when they weren't the issues they came in with, and upsell them on the next course. "Me saying after a five-day course, 'Your issue of wanting to be seen as a smart journalist is preventing you from being a good journalist. . . . If you want to be a really good journalist you need to finish the (sixteen-day) intensive.' That's the abuse, I think."

Many former students described this never-ending treadmill dynamic. Whatever insecurity or problem you identified in the class, the long-term solution was always more coursework. And the way to afford more coursework was to sell more classes. This is a familiar dilemma to anyone who has tried to succeed in multi-level marketing; for the vast majority of NXIVM students, the economic rewards never materialized.

AMES, AN ACTOR like his wife, has a knack for reproducing Raniere's taxing speaking style. He showed me how Raniere would stir up attention in a room with extended pauses and roving eye contact. "On my way over here I was thinking about what I would talk about," Ames, playing Raniere, said, delivering the NXIVM leader's good-natured schoolboy nods and shrugs. His pace accelerated as he suggested that his peculiar way of thinking had led him to a revelation about astronauts, the Apollo landing, and a walnut.

"You have this rocket ship, and all these great minds go into this huge rocket booster," Ames said, tracing the launchpad with his hands. "They burst off and land on the moon, just so this little man can have an experience of the moon. His experience is the size of a walnut about two inches inside his skull." At this abrupt transition, Ames pointed behind his own eye, eliciting a quiet laugh from Edmondson. "And that's consciousness," he said, leaving space again for an epiphany, "and that's what brings us here today."

Ames's performance was partly a parody, but it also illustrated a possible covert use of NLP hypnosis. NLP teaches several "confusion techniques" based on the assumption that the conscious mind can hold only about seven chunks of information at a time, give or take a couple. A simple way to leave suggestions in someone's unconscious mind is to overload them with information and hope that some of it unconsciously sticks. This got me thinking about Raniere's maze-like sermons, and his long walks spent in deep rapport with young women. (Barbara Bouchey, who studied NLP for years before she took her first NXIVM class, told me that this more insidious type of hypnosis hadn't been part of her experience.)

This overload concept seems to be supported at least in part by scientific literature. In *Thinking, Fast and Slow*, psychologist Daniel Kahneman writes about the difference between "system one," our associative brain, and "system two," our skeptical processing brain. Research tells us that the first system is quick and freely associating and linked to believing in a statement. The second system is a slower, more critical process "in charge of doubting and unbelieving."

One study by psychologist Daniel Gilbert found that participants made to hold a set of digits in their head while reading a series of nonsensical statements like "Whitefish eat candy" were more likely to think false sentences were true. "The moral is significant: when system two is otherwise engaged, we will believe almost anything," Kahneman writes. "Indeed, there is evidence that people are more likely to be influenced by empty persuasive messages, such as commercials, when they are tired and depleted."

If Daniela did fall into a trap, it was a slippery one, involving exhaustion, group conformity, conditioning, selection, leveraged secrets, and a whole lot of pseudoscience.

CHAPTER TWELVE

What the Bleep

M ark Vicente never trusted the white establishment he was born into in 1965 in his hometown of Johannesburg, South Africa. His parents supported the country's oppressive apartheid-era government, but from a young age Vicente oriented himself as an ally of revolutionary causes.

"I felt as a young child that something needed to happen," he said on the witness stand at Raniere's trial. "I had no idea what I would do."

It was the 1977 release of the movie *Star Wars* that helped Vicente's worldview snap into place. Like many kids of his generation, the twelve-year-old Vicente was smitten with the splashy sci-fi action adventure. It appealed to his budding political consciousness and inspired him to take up filmmaking as a career.

"I decided that this was the method I would try and use to express what I wanted to express, which is basically I didn't think it was necessary for people to be killing each other," he told a Brooklyn courtroom. "I hoped to make films that could affect people deeply enough that they would behave in such a way that they would make the world a better place."

Vicente is a tall man with salt-and-pepper hair and narrow rectangular glasses. He speaks from the heart, with a tendency to generalize about good and evil. He saw himself joining a rebel force for "anti-apartheid, humanitarian" good, just like in the movies. And he wanted to do it with his own camera in hand.

In 1994, then in his late twenties, this impulse carried him to the Pacific Northwest to attend a weekend retreat at a ranch in Yelm, Washington. There, at Ramtha's School of Enlightenment, a woman named J.Z. Knight taught people how to discover their own spirituality and find their purpose in life. Though Vicente would travel the world extensively over the next decade, the ranch became a place he'd return to in search of direction, purpose, and a sense of creating good in the world.

Vicente says he was never short of work, but it wasn't until much later in his career, in 2004, that he gained international recognition for his filmmaking. He'd picked up credits on commercials and feature films, but it was his indie documentary *What the Bleep Do We Know!?*—released on the heels of *Super Size Me* with the help of the same distributor—that hit a nerve with audiences.

Vicente's documentary provides a strong clue as to why the filmmaker was attracted to the intellectual atmosphere cultivated by NXIVM. "It was about pseudo quantum mechanics, neurobiology, the biology of emotions. It had to do with a certain amount of science and also we did a lot of cartoon animation about what happens in the brain and body," Vicente recalled before an unimpressed judge. The doc is heavy on jargon and janky graphics of space tunnels and neurons. Many of the scientists who appear in the film have been discredited as "quantum mystics"—theorists who became popular in the 1970s for making tenuous connections between quantum theory and parapsychological phenomena like telepathy, reincarnation, and out-of-body experiences.

The documentary featured soundbites from Judy "J.Z." Knight, a woman who claims to channel a thirty-five-thousand-year-old warrior spirit named Ramtha, and who founded Ramtha's School of Enlightenment in 1980. Students practice archery and running full speed, both while blindfolded, in the service of exploring a belief that we create the reality around us. Vicente had worked his way into Knight's inner circle and was eager to find scientific studies that supported this view of the world. The three codirectors of *What the Bleep* were all students of Ramtha's School at the time, as were some of the documentary subjects. These Ramtha connections weren't clearly disclosed in the film, despite Knight's appearing for an interview.

It isn't hard to see why NXIVM might set its sights on recruiting Vicente and bringing his mashup of science and spirituality into the self-help universe they were building. Like *What the Bleep*, Raniere traded on the urban legend that we use only 10 percent of our brains, selling students on a promise to access more of that other 90 percent.

AT THE HEIGHT of *What the Bleep*'s popularity, in October 2004, Vicente received a letter from Barbara Bouchey inviting him to a symposium involving many of the people who appeared in his documentary. Bouchey was planning a November event that aimed to bring together fifteen to twenty scientists in the fields of "science, physics and systems thinking," according to her letter, to discuss the "connection between what you think inside your mind and what's happening outside," among other topics. The invite called Vicente and his codirectors "visionaries" who would have "profound effects in the world for generations to come."

Teah Banks, Vicente's girlfriend at the time, recalls that, for much of 2004 and well into 2005, the *What the Bleep* filmmakers were flooded with similar letters and invites. Because of the film's ambitious themes tying religion and science together, many spiritual splinter groups attempted to get in touch.

When Banks had attended Ramtha's spiritual retreats with Vicente, she'd found the intense New Agey talk of "vibrations" and "frequencies" a little too off the beaten path and wanted to try something more serious. Bouchey's letter stuck out from all the hippies and kooks. She sounded professional, academic, and full of praise. Vicente testified that he replied right away.

Banks says that she and Vicente were in Los Angeles for a *What the Bleep* screening when they first exchanged phone numbers with Bouchey and Nancy Salzman, who said they were attending an event in San Francisco in the coming days. Over the phone Vicente and Banks learned that their new admirers had access to a private jet and were keen to fly down to L.A. to meet the couple for lunch the next day.

Banks and Vicente agreed, and made their way to a Beverly Hills hotel the following afternoon. As Vicente remembers it, Bouchey and Salzman complimented his film and made a case for him to come visit Albany. They told him about an "incredible mentor" named Keith Raniere—a scientist, mathematician, and all-round great person—who apparently knew how to "hack the human behavior equation." They were prepared to fly Banks and Vicente to upstate New York in the jet the following morning.

Banks says she was intrigued by the pitch but that, more importantly, she wanted to get to know Bouchey and Salzman as people. "It was strange. I don't have a lot of female role models, and I remember I just instantly wanted to be like them," she recalls of the meeting. "They just seemed so polished."

Vicente and Banks returned to their home in Ashland, Oregon, but made plans to rejoin their new friends a few weeks later. The couple agreed to travel with Sara Bronfman and Salzman to meet with the scientists who had appeared in *What the Bleep*. Vicente testified that the Bronfmans' twelve-seat jet picked them up in Oregon and flew them around the country over several days.

Banks says that most of the scientists and researchers they met on that trip weren't all that interested in NXIVM's self-help methods, but that she and Vicente grew more captivated by Salzman's talk therapy skills. Nancy Salzman was using Vicente and Banks as live guinea pigs "to demonstrate to the scientists what the methodology was," Vicente said.

When they returned to Ashland, Banks says, they went out for dinner as a group. Banks informed a server that she had a dairy allergy, which caught Salzman's attention.

"'What do you mean you're allergic to milk?'" she remembers Salzman saying.

Banks replied that she'd had the allergy since she was a little girl.

"Well, let me ask you," Salzman said. "Do you remember the first time that you were allergic to milk?"

Banks told her she did remember her first allergic reaction. "It was when I was six or seven years old, and I poured myself a glass of milk," Banks says. "And my mom came down and said, 'That's too much milk. You better drink all of it; don't waste any of that.'" The next morning, Banks woke up with a rash all over her face. "So my mom told me I was allergic to milk."

Salzman proposed a different theory. She suggested that Banks's reaction was likely a phobia caused by her mother's overbearing response. She asked about Banks's relationship with her mother and how it made her feel, which made Banks emotional. After only a few minutes of talking at the dinner table, Salzman told Banks that she believed her dairy allergy was likely now resolved.

Vicente later testified that he watched this tearful interaction with a sense of wonder and surprise. "I was mystified by the nature of her questions," he said. "I couldn't understand at the time what was happening." Salzman explained to the couple that she was using a patent-pending technique called an exploration of meaning, or EM, that helped re-examine the illogical associations our brains make in childhood. NXIVM's "technology," they learned, helped to refile everything in the brain in order to make you a more logical, ethical person.

The next day, Banks says, she tried dairy for the first time in decades, and Salzman's prediction proved true. "I was pretty impressed with that," Vicente later testified, "because, you know, a day later my girlfriend did actually try some cheese and she didn't have the reaction she had always had."

EM sessions could get to the root cause of any unhealthy behavior pattern, Banks and Vicente learned. NXIVM students often started by identifying a "stimulus" that caused trouble in their life, like a dairy allergy or fear of flying. The EM questioning process frequently led to a person's most sensitive, embarrassing, or terrifying experiences.

If an EM practitioner did it well, the student might just forget what was said. "You wouldn't even remember what your EM was about, and that was considered a good thing," one student told me. "If you're integrated, you don't need to know what your problem was—it's gone."

Scientology has a similar way of dissecting emotionally charged memories, through a process called "auditing." An auditor leads a "pre-clear" individual through a series of questions aimed to stir up emotions and insecurities. With the help of an "e-meter"—a pseudoscientific handheld device that is supposed to identify emotional spikes with a bouncing arrow—the auditor guides the person through those traumatizing places in their mind until the emotional charge is weakened or there's some kind of resolution.

THE OVERNIGHT ALLERGY cure marked the beginning of Vicente's journey into the center of an organization that would continue presenting him with modern-day miracles. It wasn't all that different from the unbelievable things he'd seen at Ramtha's School, which taught that reality was a flexible concept. Vicente decided to spend a year studying Raniere's "tech" to see whether he could harness its magic in film form.

Banks says that she and Vicente were "swept away" once they got to Albany. They'd committed to attending only a five-day seminar but ended up staying for three weeks in Salzman's house, where they talked at length with Salzman's daughter, Lauren, and other members of the inner circle.

Vicente was especially interested in meeting the Vanguard, Keith Raniere, but it wasn't until the tenth day of NXIVM classes that he was deemed ready for the experience. "I remember we spoke about dark matter, quantum mechanics," Vicente said of his first conversations with Raniere. "He was talking to me about a certain kind of mathematics. I said I had never heard about it before. He said, 'Well, actually I invented this mathematics,' and I said, 'Oh, that's amazing.' Not being a mathematician, what do I know?"

When she first met Raniere, Banks saw a gentle, humble guy who cared about plants and animals. One day during their first visit he walked into Salzman's house with a potted plant he said he'd rescued from an alley.

Another day, when Banks found out that Raniere was getting a massage from one of the community members in a bedroom in Salzman's house, she was told that Raniere didn't have a house of his own, that he'd renounced all material possessions. Salzman explained that he stayed with a rotating cast of community members, which sometimes included stays at her place. Banks was nervous about even speaking to him because of his prophet-like status among the people she'd met.

At one point, Banks says, she questioned Salzman about the way women acted around Raniere. She noticed that they'd get flustered and become fawning, sometimes competing for Raniere's attention. "I turned to Nancy and said, 'Does Keith just get to pick who he has sex with? What's going on here?'"

Salzman's swift and disapproving response took Banks by surprise. She said Raniere didn't have sex at all, that he was like a monk. Salzman added that she personally hadn't had sex in three years. Then Sara Bronfman chimed in, saying she hadn't slept with anyone in a year.

"Mark and I were weirded out by that," Banks says. But they were also sort of amazed by the apparent feats of self-restraint. Eventually this would become part of the mythology Vicente and Banks used to entice people into learning more about NXIVM. "This guy doesn't own anything, he doesn't have sex—how can you *not* be part of this group?"

Though Salzman chastened Banks for bringing up Raniere's sex life, Raniere and Salzman often talked about other people's sexual hang-ups. On one occasion, when the discussion turned to sex, Banks says that Raniere put her on the spot, asking in front of a room of people why she was getting embarrassed.

Another time, Banks says, Salzman directly questioned her about her intentions with Vicente. "She said, 'Don't you want to be more than Mark's fuck toy?'" Again, Banks was thrown off balance by the question. "We were staying at her house, and we were a new couple, so I'm sure we had sex, but we tried to be quiet. . . . I just said that's not how I view our relationship at all."

For a long time, Vicente's only access to Raniere was at late-night volleyball games. "I wanted to have a meeting with him away from the gym," Vicente recalled. "I was receiving EMs [explorations of meaning] on my overeagerness, my insistence that I should meet him." Finally, on his birthday, at seven a.m., Vicente got a call from Raniere asking if he wanted to go for a walk.

"Of course I was over the moon, because this is what I've been waiting for," he said. "It was seen as a big deal that you got to have time with him."

Despite the philosophical similarities between NXIVM and Ramtha, Raniere convinced Vicente that Ramtha's founder was a crackpot and that he should stop attending retreats in Washington. Salzman and Raniere assembled a "deprogramming team" to rid Vicente of his "mystical beliefs."

Raniere "spent an inordinate amount of time teasing me about it," Vicente testified. Pam Cafritz told Vicente that it was a big deal that Raniere had taken a liking to him. She said Raniere didn't have many male friends and suggested that Vicente could fulfill that role. Salzman echoed Cafritz. "If you're very fortunate," she told Vincente, "he may actually decide to mentor you personally, and that would be extraordinary."

"I believe I said something like 'I really would love that, that would be very important to me,'" Vicente testified.

This concentrated effort served to secure Vicente as a "true believer" in NXIVM for more than a decade to come. Banks was simultaneously pushed away.

IT WAS V-WEEK 2005 when Mark Vicente and Teah Banks finally split. Banks was out doing some errands when she had a "run-in" with Nancy Salzman that left her in tears. After Banks had left Salzman's car running with the door open for a few moments, Salzman unleashed an unsettlingly angry tirade about safety and responsibility, and then acted as if it had never happened.

When Vicente found Banks in a bedroom crying and questioning whether she even belonged at V-Week, he suggested it might be time for them to go their separate ways. "He's just like, 'Maybe it's not going to work out,'" Banks says. "Because I was kind of fed up, I was like, 'I don't know if this is the right place for me.' But he was locked in."

Couples breaking up after a short time in NXIVM became something of a running joke in the community. If couples among the new students displayed affection for each other, they were warned that they probably wouldn't be doing that for much longer. Coaches often advised that relationships were crutches and came from a place of inner deficiency—though this reasoning never seemed to apply to Raniere, who continued to accumulate partners in secret.

CHAPTER THIRTEEN

"Cracked Open"

The story of Vancouver's NXIVM chapter, which grew into one of the most active and star-studded centers of the global organization, began with a chance meeting on a cruise ship.

Thirteen years before the FBI alleged that top NXIVM members had committed sex trafficking and a variety of other crimes, Sarah Edmondson attended, in spring 2005, a floating spirituality-themed film festival with her director boyfriend Tony Dean Smith. That's where she met Mark Vicente and Teah Banks, who were both still buzzing from their first sixteen-day NXIVM intensive a few months earlier.

Edmondson had grown up in Vancouver as a theater kid with a director uncle. She got her first taste of a film shoot's craft services table when she was sixteen. Sarah's uncle Paul Shapiro, who went on to direct episodes of *Roswell* and *Smallville*, was working on a straight-to-TV movie called *Avalanche* with David Hasselhoff. "David needed a babysitter, so my uncle suggested I do it," Edmondson told entertainment blogger Ruth Hill in 2017. "I was hooked."

Edmondson caught one of her first acting breaks on the CBC teen drama *Edgemont*, appearing in ten episodes as Stevie, a laid-back, cargo-jacket-wearing girlfriend of Shannon, played by Grace Park.

When they were off set, the two women continued nurturing each other's creativity by following the advice in Julia Cameron's book *The Artist's Way*. Part spiritual practice, part how-to prompt, the text inspired regular meetups and became an anchor for a circle of Edmondson's close friends. "We worked, and had careers at a certain level, but we wanted to be more fulfilled as artists," Edmondson told me. "So we got together, supported each other."

Grace Park and costar Kristin Kreuk stayed close with Edmondson, even as they went on to bigger roles on *Battlestar Galactica* and *Smallville*, respectively. *Edgemont* was cancelled in 2005, leaving a twenty-seven-year-old Edmondson looking for her next big thing.

As she first recounted on the CBC podcast *Uncover: Escaping NXIVM*, Edmondson thought the cruise ship film festival could be an opportunity to get her life on track. At the time, she was really into "setting intentions" and was growing tired of always waiting for her agent to call.

Edmondson was trying to contain the symptoms of a nasty cold, but while she and Tony Smith were seated beside Vicente and his girl-friend at dinner, her "seal bark" coughs kept interrupting their conversation. Vicente took Sarah aside between hacking fits and asked her a bizarre question: "What would you lose if you stopped coughing?" As in, What would be the "downside" if Edmondson weren't so sick?

It was the kind of counterintuitive question NXIVM used to engineer epiphanies, and it prompted a burst of self-reflection in Edmondson. She realized that her coughs were an attempt to get her boyfriend's attention. She had subconsciously believed that sickness would earn her the care and love she craved.

"I remember thinking, 'Wow, whatever Mark from *What the Bleep* is up to, I wanna do,'" Edmondson told the CBC.

This new way of looking at health and relationships impressed her. She listened as Vicente told her about Keith Raniere, a guy with a really, really high IQ—a true polymath with concert pianist skills—bringing people together to change the world.

Vicente was still a relatively new NXIVM student, but his clear-eyed observation of subtle interpersonal dynamics gave Edmondson a feeling of hope that she could figure out her life, too. Vicente passed on Edmondson's name to Barbara Bouchey, one of the highest-ranking

NXIVM recruiters in Albany at the time. Bouchey, who oversaw enrollment, made follow-up calls to Edmondson to close the deal.

Edmondson wasn't an easy catch; she almost backed out. It was
only after Bouchey told her she needed to work on her limiting beliefs
about money in order to become "master of her own ship" and stop
helplessly relying on her agent that Edmondson made a plan to attend
her first five-day intensive in Burnaby, B.C., a few weeks later. It was
the company's first time hosting the weeklong workshop in Canada.

EDMONDSON DIDN'T THINK to Google NXIVM until after her first day
of class. After thirteen hours of hand-clapping and sashes and tears
and soul-searching, she finally looked up some of the critical media
coverage online. What she found wasn't good: the 2003 *Forbes* article suggested that she wasn't just receiving thirteen-plus hours of life
coaching, she was being initiated into a cult.

Edmondson called Vicente to ask him what the hell he'd signed
her up for. He said that anybody could write anything on the internet,
and that smear campaigns were being waged by powerful people with
a vested interest in destroying a good thing. Edmondson thought this
was a red flag, but she wasn't running away screaming. She showed
up the next day bright and early, in part just to see what would happen next.

By day three she felt "cracked open" and committed to addressing
her "self-limiting beliefs." As she began to feel the "lift" from exam-
ining her own patterns of behavior with a new set of psychological
tools, she started to imagine what her life would be like without all the
blocks she'd created for herself.

"I definitely felt like a veil of fog had been lifted: I had more clarity,
I was making better decisions, I understood people better—I thought
this was the key to success and happiness," Edmondson told me. "By
the end of the five days I thought, 'This was amazing. All my friends
need this. I want to bring this to Canada.'"

Edmondson learned that she could get the cost of her first intensive back if she brought in three new students within three months of
taking the course. She referred her boyfriend Tony, her mother, and
her actor friend Nicki Clyne, who was part of Edmondson's Artist's Way
circle and working on the set of *Battlestar Galactica* with Grace Park.

Edmondson used the money to invest in more classes, knowing that this would help her advance up the ranks and eventually make a commission. Because NXIVM didn't yet have a center in Canada, she commuted south of the border to Seattle to earn her first sashes and stripes. Edmondson and Mark Vicente couldn't help noticing how middle-aged and "schlubby" the NXIVM vibe had been when they first joined, so they set out to invite young people they'd actually want to hang out with. With sales help from Barbara Bouchey, Edmondson would take on new recruiting responsibilities, including renting hotel spaces, photocopying course materials at Staples, and burning DVDs for every workshop or retreat that happened in Vancouver.

ACTOR CHAD KROWCHUK still remembers the curious way talk of NXIVM buzzed through his social network. He first heard good reviews from Edmondson over dinner one night, and then from his acting friends Kristin Kreuk and Mark Hildreth a few weeks later. Krowchuk didn't know what to make of all his friends' hyperbolic gushing; he assumed there must be a catch. But his longtime girlfriend, *Smallville* actor Allison Mack, would eventually convince him to make the trip from Vancouver to attend a five-day intensive with her in Albany.

Krowchuk is blond, with a worried intensity about him. He's often cast as the wide-eyed dork who's underestimated by an alpha male protagonist. Mack, on the other hand, was known for swooning eagerness and golly-gee smiles. Her "sparkle," both on screen and off, put her miles out of Krowchuk's league, many thought. That he was from Alberta and she from California only added to his unspoken underdog status.

Both Krowchuk and Mack were former child actors who'd found each other in their early twenties and built a steady live-in relationship around their busy schedules. Krowchuk was working at Starbucks and bussing tables at a local restaurant in between acting gigs. He wanted to find more time to develop his career as a visual artist. Meanwhile, Mack was a household name among a certain demographic of teens, playing Superman's best friend on CW's *Smallville*, a teen superhero show watched by millions.

The couple had been living together for about three years when NXIVM "became a thing" in their group of friends, Krowchuk says, thanks in large part to Sarah Edmondson's hustle. Clyne also got to work enrolling her own network of Vancouver actors, and they made a point of regularly getting together without the usual social crutch of drugs and alcohol. "We really prided ourselves on that—how we could have fun without being under the influence of anything," Edmondson says.

Edmondson was celebrated within NXIVM for bringing coveted TV stars into the fold. "It wasn't so much a pressure to recruit celebrities; it was just kind of a whim within the company. Like, 'Oh, how great, we've got a VIP,'" she told me for a *Vice* story in 2018. "We wouldn't get bonus points per se, but it was something that was acknowledged as a good thing, because it would grow the mission and grow the company if we had whoever endorsing. . . . They were bragged about very openly."

ALLISON MACK ATTENDED a weekend retreat in late 2006. The NXIVM inner circle had come to the West Coast for the women-only event, where they rolled out the VIP treatment for her. It was like an intensive, but Raniere's new "Jness" curriculum was specifically tailored to women's experiences, and named to evoke the sound of female essence. Nancy Salzman facilitated with help from her daughter Lauren, and Sara Bronfman attended. Jness taught women to examine why they entered relationships, and suggested that dependency and inner deficiency often play a role. "By the end of the weekend, Lauren and Allison were like best friends," Susan Dones, who ran NXIVM's Seattle center, told *The Hollywood Reporter* in 2018. The next day, Mack accepted an invitation to fly in the Bronfman jet to meet Raniere and the inner circle in Albany, where she stayed for a few weeks. And in April 2007 she attended her first five-day seminar on a yacht docked in Vancouver's Coal Harbour.

Chad Krowchuk says that at first he resisted Mack's invitations to join her as a member of NXIVM, which led to a few arguments. He was surprised by how quickly she'd dropped all skepticism. "That was the part that scared me the most," he says of Mack's sudden shift in perspective. "Before, we had conversations about it, and we both thought it seemed kind of weird and creepy. I don't necessarily know if *she* thought it was creepy, but we agreed it seemed a little messed up."

Krowchuk put aside his discomfort and attended a five-day intensive in Albany. "I met some very powerful human beings," he said of his first impressions of the NXIVM community. "As in, controlling a lot of money, intellect, and influence."

Mack started a personal blog where she recorded all the new questions she was grappling with about meaning and purpose and personal connection. She was twenty-four years old, coming to terms with her own fame and attempting to foster a deeper sense of self-awareness. "I allow my insecurities to dictate the things I do in my life," she wrote in an April 2007 post. "I suppress the things within me that I think are 'bad' and then spend my time and energy punishing myself for even having these flaws in the first place. I feel like these habits are incredibly destructive and violent toward my own growth and potential."

Mack was eternally optimistic, constantly ending correspondence with multiple exclamation points. She loved Miranda July, Harry Potter, John Lennon's "Imagine," and inspirational Gandhi quotes, and she wanted to be around people who shared this romantic, starry-eyed worldview.

Both Allison Mack and Sarah Edmondson saw this kind of idealism in the NXIVM coursework—*Be your best self and help others do the same!*—but Krowchuk was on the fence about it. He thought the hand-clapping and sashes were weird, and the workshops had an intense vibe that reminded him of bad acting classes. But the people he met in Albany were impressive and kind, and they gave a name to things he didn't yet have a vocabulary for.

The courses taught that everyone was responsible for their own reactions to the outside world. That meant a NXIVM coach could turn around just about any bad situation and blame the student for their flawed interpretation. "If a course like this is in the hands of somebody who means well, it's harmless," Krowchuk says. "But I always felt like it would be really shitty if it was used in a negative way."

NXIVM SHIFTED KROWCHUK and Mack's social landscape. The classes discouraged students from revealing details of the patent-pending "technology" to anyone who hadn't paid for it. That meant not being able to share their exciting journey with the uninitiated.

Krowchuk preferred to keep a blend of industry and non-industry friends—those who knew about NXIVM and those who didn't, or didn't care for it. Others started to break away from their old lives in favor of surrounding themselves with like-minded people. Edmondson's Artist's Way group was split down the middle. Half of the women were on board, and the other half thought it was kind of culty.

Having a dinner party with NXIVM friends meant constantly dissecting your fears and insecurities. If somebody said they didn't like sharing the food on their plate, for example, other group members would chime in with probing questions in an effort to overcome the block. *What would you lose if you stopped the behavior? Is refusing to share holding you back?* Needless to say, it wasn't a welcome conversational style for everyone.

Krowchuk could see some of his friends overcoming their insecurities, like Allison's *Smallville* costar Kristin Kreuk, who battled career-stifling shyness. "I felt like I related more to Kristin than anyone there. I could see what the appeal was," says Krowchuk. But other acting friends pivoted away from the entertainment industry, like *Battlestar Galactica*'s Nicki Clyne. "Nicki—I know she was the first example of somebody who had a decent acting career, she was doing quite well, and then she took the courses and went, 'Fuck it, I want to do this thing instead,'" Krowchuk recalls. Friends saw a new self-righteous streak in Clyne, who would sometimes point out her peers' ethical shortcomings. At the time, Krowchuk thought there must have been a greater good he couldn't see, and reserved judgment.

Mack believed NXIVM was furthering her education, which had been cut short by her acting career. "I noticed recently that I have a tendency to say I am stupid," she wrote in a 2007 blog post. "I became very comfortable chalking things up to the fact that I don't have a 'proper education.'" To show her progress, Mack shared her goals with her online fans by writing about them in her blog. "I will be directing episode 20 of *Smallville* this year, and I am so intimidated!" she wrote. "Ignoring the voice inside my head that is screaming 'You have no clue how to do this!' has definitely been a challenge."

Allison was invited into NXIVM's inner circle very quickly, and in the beginning Krowchuk was able to tag along. But he knew he couldn't go much further with the coursework. "Allison paid for a lot of my courses," he says. "I would slowly pick away at paying her back, but I couldn't afford to do it. Most normal people couldn't afford to do this."

All told, Krowchuk says he probably spent between $20,000 and $30,000 on NXIVM courses, and by then, he and Allison were already on the verge of breaking up. Their friends could see it coming; one heard Mack speculate that she might be asexual. Mack and Krowchuk had different ideas about where their lives were headed, and around 2009 they ended things for good.

Sarah Edmondson was nearing a similar crossroads in her relationship and career. She was pushing harder than ever to advance in the company, and in July 2009 she was finally rewarded with a license to open a permanent space in Vancouver with Mark Vicente. Under the guidance of her NXIVM coach, Edmondson split from her boyfriend and fully immersed herself in work. This was a common story among women in NXIVM's upper ranks, as boyfriends and husbands were often interpreted to be standing in the way of success. Like Mack, Edmondson was feeling the gravitational pull of Albany and began making trips there several times a year. Clyne and Mack went on to live in Albany full time, but continued inviting their Vancouver networks into the fold.

That meant the stage was set for Vancouver to outpace all the American centers—even Albany—in attracting younger creative types to NXIVM.

CHAPTER FOURTEEN

An Ethical Breach

In many ways, Daniela was the perfect candidate to act as accomplice in Keith Raniere's secret mission. She was a fast learner and a capable computer programmer. But more importantly, she didn't "cause problems."

Initially she seemed at ease with the one-sided sexual arrangement Raniere had introduced during the week of her eighteenth birthday. Whereas the other women in his life would "go off" (Raniere's words) on emotional tirades supposedly propelled by their issues of jealousy and pride, Daniela obliged him with sexual favors and seemed content to watch other women constantly seek his attention and approval.

"I felt I was Keith's friend," she said on the witness stand at Raniere's trial in 2019. "I felt like he could be with women in front of me; I wasn't jealous. I really wasn't." When asked to name the women who were regularly part of Raniere's sex life, Daniela testified that she knew of at least eleven, including her own sister Marianna.

Daniela had accepted that some kind of inverse relationship existed between intelligence and adherence to social norms. What Raniere lacked in social skills or conventional attractiveness he made up for in brain power. Daniela herself didn't seem to fit into her own theory: she had nerd credentials and was also a striking young woman with a collection of miniskirts. But the momentum of her own ambition and idealism pulled her away from a typical young person's social life and thrust her deeper into Raniere's.

This combination of forces made Daniela a regular fixture at the Flintlock house in 2005. "I was spending almost every waking moment I had there," she said.

Marianna was also a regular presence, making a home at the Flintlock house in Pamela Cafritz's room. The rest of their family's living situation was more complicated. The youngest siblings, Camila and Adrian, had come to Albany for the 2003–2004 school year but lived separately in shared NXIVM homestays. Camila was placed with Monica Duran, another transplant from Mexico, and her roommates, while Adrian lived with Mark Vicente and other men. Eventually their parents bought a family home in Clifton Park—but not before most of the kids ran into visa troubles. NXIVM had always offered help with visas and advised against leaving the United States even to renew their tourist status, but the help never seemed to materialize.

The Flintlock house in its natural state was a "pigsty," Daniela testified. When Cafritz hired a cleaning service, workers left a note saying they refused to deal with the mess that had greeted them. Daniela took it upon herself to make the space more livable. In the process she became a fly on the wall for more of Raniere's high-stakes conversations, whether it was about his commodities trading, the legal cases NXIVM was initiating, or illicit spying activities.

Daniela testified about the inner circle's many attempts to hack into enemies' email and bank accounts. On a typical morning, Kristin Keeffe would come downstairs in her bathrobe to make coffee and start the day, knowing that Raniere would be waiting for her to report on various information-gathering missions. In the beginning these kitchen strategy sessions would mostly focus on cult educator Rick Alan Ross or Raniere's ex Toni Natalie, but they expanded to include others over the years. According to Daniela, Keeffe would propose some next steps and Raniere would choose among the options.

"He would ask, 'How much is this, how much is that?'" Daniela recalled on the witness stand. By the mid-2000s, Raniere's attention had turned to the Kristin Snyder incident. He was interested in accessing Snyder's email account, years after the NXIVM student had gone missing in February 2003. Daniela recalled that Raniere had a theory about her disappearance he wanted to test by reading her inbox. He believed the disappearance had been a plot to create negative publicity for the company, and that Snyder was alive and in hiding.

On the stand, Daniela explained that Keeffe was Raniere's legal liaison, and that part of her role entailed digging up dirt on enemies NXIVM could potentially face in court. It was a proactive job, which meant that Keeffe sought the services of private investigators who might be willing to go around U.S. privacy laws to get passwords for email accounts. With access to Snyder's email, Raniere wanted to prove that she hadn't committed suicide.

From what she'd already seen at NXIVM, Daniela was familiar with this kind of plotting bordering on criminal conspiracy. What stood out most for her wasn't the hacking plot but the price tag Keeffe attached to it: a steep $24,000 for access to one email account. "I remember it was a very large amount of money they were willing to pay for a password," she said. "That was the shocking part for me." And no wonder: in all the odd jobs Daniela had performed around the NXIVM community since she was sixteen—cleaning, cooking, and babysitting for handfuls of cash—the most she'd ever earned was $3,000, also paid in cash, for building a website for Pam Cafritz.

Daniela was soon enlisted to find a new, less costly source of assistance for NXIVM's investigative needs. In her search to save Raniere money on hacking, she first reached out to friends who had computer programming skills. One friend passed her on to a software wizard who called himself the Dark Lord. "I sent one of the addresses to the Dark Lord and he wrote back and asked me if the email address belonged to me," Daniela recalled. "I told him very honestly: I said no. And he said, 'Then I can't help you.'"

Hacking would soon become a major theme in Daniela's conversations with Raniere. She began reading forums on the subject and downloading software from the internet. "I played with them and I started testing, and pretty quickly I zoned in on a strategy that I thought would be successful," she said. "I thought I could, in all likelihood, get a password—hack a computer and get a password."

At first Daniela saw hacking as being at odds with NXIVM's stated mission of raising the ethics of the world, and she said as much to Raniere. "How do we get to do this?" she asked him. "Why are we breaking the rules? I didn't understand."

Raniere addressed her concerns with a thought experiment—something he said was derived from game theory. As "good guys" with world-changing ideals, NXIVM would be limited by their own ethics. "We're going to be good people, and there are certain things that we're not willing to do because they're wrong and they're unethical," Raniere said. "So we have a certain number of options of choices we can take. And then you have these bad people, the suppressives, the people who are out to get us and destroy the good things in this world," he continued. "These people are going to do everything we're going to do and then more. They're going to break the rules and do illegal things and destroy. These bad people have all the options in the world and we have only these options."

Daniela was intrigued, even excited by this response. The math made sense in her head—sticking to the rules only limited the total number of options available in a given situation. That meant bad people were always going to win.

"Ultimately this is to do good," Raniere told Daniela. "So we're going to have to break some rules in order to make that happen."

She would be applying her coding skills to further the NXIVM mission, even if it wasn't anything like what she expected when she'd first taken a course at age sixteen. She was nearing her twentieth birthday now, and her days mostly consisted of listening to war room debates, overhearing heated commodities trading calls, and giving Raniere blow jobs anytime he thought to drop his pants. Manipulating software to achieve a special secret mission felt like a level up in her life.

Daniela took extra care to ensure her hacking efforts wouldn't be detected. Cafritz gave her $500 to buy a new refurbished computer that wouldn't be linked to her name in any way. She would use public wifi and a set of brand-new anonymous Gmail accounts to send test emails with spyware embedded in attachments. If the targeted person clicked on the attachment Daniela had sent, the code she'd created would log every keystroke they made and upload those records to a server.

Daniela hid the spyware in Excel spreadsheets and image files. To bypass spam filters, she learned to mask her email address with a less conspicuous one. Her first attempts weren't successful, but she refined her process over time. "I would code it in a way that it would self-destroy if it wasn't opened in a certain amount of time, so that there would be no evidence sitting there in someone's inbox," she said.

BY 2005, RANIERE and Clare Bronfman had a new enemy they wanted Daniela to target: Clare's father. Daniela knew that Edgar Bronfman was a powerful man and that she'd need to be extra careful to avoid getting caught. So instead of sending an infected email from one of her anonymous Gmail accounts, she worked directly with Clare to attach the code to a message from his daughter—an email he'd be more likely to open.

"Clare hacked her father's email account," Kristin Keeffe said in a 2015 phone call that would later become evidence in court. Together, Clare and Daniela sent Edgar an email with a photo attachment that contained a key-logging virus. She chose a photo of a bear, playing to her father's pet name for her: Clare Bear.

"Clare went so far as to send the email to her father—'Oh, look at this thing' . . . but he never opened the picture," Keeffe alleged. "So she went down to his office and met with him, and specifically said, 'I want to show you this picture.'" She then "went on his email with him and downloaded the virus onto his computer herself."

After Clare had opened the infected file, Daniela started receiving all the keystrokes Edgar Bronfman was making. "Very rapidly, as I remember, I get the username and password that I'm looking for, which was, as I remember, his AOL account," Daniela testified. "And, I mean, this was a high-profile person as I understood, so immediately after I had that access I killed the back door. . . . I didn't need any more key logs being uploaded." She recalled that Bronfman's password was "miles75"—his middle name and the year he married Clare's mother (also, more darkly, the year his eldest son, Samuel, was kidnapped and held for ransom).

Daniela testified that she logged on to his AOL account and read his emails. From then on, anytime Raniere requested an update on the Bronfman email account, Daniela would log on late at night, copy and paste a selection from his inbox and his "sent" folder into a document, and pass it on to Raniere.

"There were communications between him and his family, there were a lot of emails about scheduling—whether he was going to travel to this place or that place. There was a great deal of, like, political emails. I noticed he was a man with very good manners. It seemed he always sent thank-you emails after meeting someone, or having an event and running into someone," Daniela recalled. "He followed up on things like that at a very personal level. I remember that."

AS PART OF Daniela's work for Raniere, she had access to his executive library and his hard drives. At trial, prosecutors showed video clips of Raniere in his library, which was really a dimly lit condo that housed his Steinway piano, his books and whiteboard, a sauna, a hot tub, and a loft space containing a bed with a TV mounted on the ceiling. Raniere frequently ordered books on Amazon, and when they arrived it was Daniela's job to catalog them. She would also digitize music files or back up computer folders at Raniere's request.

Daniela testified that it was during one of these digitizing assignments that she came across a folder of naked photos. It wasn't hard to figure out they were Raniere's, as she recognized some of the women. "There was one that I distinctly remember because I didn't know Keith was having sex with her," Daniela said. It was her younger sister's first roommate, Monica Duran.

Seeing the photos triggered a not-too-distant memory for Daniela. She'd been sitting on the Flintlock couch when Raniere had insisted she pull her pants down and let him take a close-up picture with his new camera. "I knew he had taken pictures of me, so I asked him to delete my pictures. I didn't click through [the folder], so I don't remember having seen myself."

That backup folder, or some later version of it, is likely what became key evidence in the sex trafficking and racketeering trial against Raniere, containing graphic photos of Daniela's sister Camila, taken when she was fifteen. Daniela said she didn't see her sister's pictures, but she told Raniere to delete the folder. "I remember my approach when I went to him was like in a 'I'm looking out for you' kind of way, like, You really shouldn't have that there. You really should be more careful. I found it. Anybody else could find it," she said.

Though she didn't see Camila's photos, Daniela soon learned that Raniere was having sex with her younger sister. Daniela had noticed that Camila was looking unwell and was leaving small self-inflicted cuts visible on her skin. On top of the cutting, she was wearing ragged clothes and writing dark poetry. "She didn't look good," Daniela testified. "It was very concerning to me, so I went through her stuff."

Daniela read Camila's private writing, including a letter that revealed her sexual relationship with Raniere. "It said things like she was sexually unsatisfied. It said things like she really wanted to have a baby," Daniela said. Camila was sixteen years old.

Daniela confronted Raniere, but she didn't put a stop to the relationship. Exposing it would have meant exposing her own secret. She testified that Raniere convinced her to put the letter back and let him handle it. "I deeply regret that I didn't at that moment get my sister out of there," she said. "But that's how it happened."

IN 2006 DANIELA realized she was pregnant, which became another secret that ate her up inside. She testified that Raniere had joked about one day having really smart kids with really big heads, but she never wanted that for herself.

"I thought he was a great man, but he was with a lot of other women and he was with my sisters and that was not something that I wanted the world to know," Daniela said. "That was something that caused me a lot of shame."

Daniela needed time to process the news, though her instincts leaned toward choosing an abortion. When she told Raniere about the pregnancy, she learned the decision had already been made for her. "He very matter-of-factly stated that we already talked about that if I got pregnant, I would have an abortion," she recalled. "We had never talked about that before. Never. I would have known.

"That interaction was very shocking to me, and I was very emotional and I was very scared, but it was also what I wanted," Daniela said. "I could not imagine having a baby. So I didn't push back. Even though I knew we did not have that conversation."

Daniela said she went through with the abortion, and that Pam Cafritz coached her on what to say to the staff at the clinic. Because she couldn't talk about it with anyone except Pam and Raniere, she was alone for the two days the doctor told her she would bleed and feel intense pain. She would later learn that both of her sisters also had abortions, and that all three of them were coached through the process by Cafritz.

Within days, Raniere was looking for an upside to Daniela's abortion. "I remember just a few days after, we were on a walk and he told me this was a great opportunity for me to lose weight and get fit."

"What do you mean?" Daniela replied.

"There are Olympic athletes that get pregnant on purpose just to have abortions as part of their training," Raniere said, according to Daniela.

IT'S NOT CLEAR whether Raniere's response to Daniela's abortion was the catalyst, but after that exchange Daniela said her heart wasn't in the relationship. That fall she started to develop feelings for someone else. Ben Myers, a fellow NXIVM student and employee who attended all the same volleyball games and social gatherings, became the focus of her romantic attention. Myers was a few years older than Daniela, with an awkward computer geek disposition. He worked in the IT department and attended weekly *Star Trek* screenings at the Flintlock house.

"It happened one night at *Star Trek*," Daniela testified. "I had never felt attracted to him before. It was really just like a friendly relationship." She recalled that over the course of the episode they were watching, they had naturally inched closer to each other, and after everyone else left, they almost kissed.

"I felt something for him, and I think he felt something for me, and there was this brand-new feeling for me of attraction. Which was new. And it was an intense moment," Daniela said. "We didn't even kiss, but it was really close. So there was this tension that built up."

Daniela tried to articulate how she felt about Ben Myers to Raniere. Raniere was her best friend, her closest confidant, she testified. "I had nobody else to tell. It never crossed my mind to hide it."

But Raniere was not the supportive friend she thought he would be. He told her she was wrong about her own feelings. "His direction was, 'No, no, no, no, no, that's not what it is. You are making it up. You cause every single feeling you have and you should have that for me, not for him.'"

Not only did this reaction not make sense to Daniela, it also didn't work. She went to *Star Trek* night the next week full of anticipation and curiosity. Would she and Ben finally kiss? Did he feel the same way as she did? She distinctly remembered what clothes she put on for the occasion: a white crew-neck top and a long Ralph Lauren skirt with two buttons on the side.

Daniela and Ben stayed on the couch together after the screening. They talked and moved toward each other, and then finally it happened. They kissed, or more accurately, they made out. "I liked the way I felt with him and I liked what happened," she said.

Daniela didn't want to hide this blossoming crush from Raniere. Her sense of justice led her to think he'd come around to seeing her perspective. How could he stand in the way of something so innocent and lovely? With the right negotiation strategy, she thought she could persuade him that he didn't need her as a romantic partner, that he had plenty of women in his life already.

"The way I saw it, Keith didn't really love me. Keith loved my sister Marianna. Keith loved Pam. He spent a lot of time with them," Daniela said. "He spent time with me but it wasn't romantic, it wasn't sexual. I mean, he had me give him oral sex but that was very robotic and mechanical."

Daniela thought Raniere would be willing to compromise, to trade in their life commitment for a lifelong friendship. But it didn't go that way. "He was angry. I had never seen him angry," she said. "It was dramatic. It was irrational. It was illogical. I remember that night, and I remember there was no reasoning with him."

Raniere told Daniela that she was no longer pure. She had broken her word and in the process had destroyed so many things that she didn't even realize it. To understand what Raniere was accusing Daniela of destroying, another lesson in NXIVM jargon is necessary. NXIVM taught that reality is separate from our perceptions, and that our perceptions can influence others. NXIVM students called the mental image of a person a "thought object." Daniela had learned it was important to speak honorably of others; otherwise, you could harm the "thought object" of a person in other people's heads.

"I had destroyed the thought object of him," Daniela explained at Raniere's trial. "He is telling me that the way I think of him, I've changed forever and I've destroyed it, and that is my fault and that is an ethical breach for me."

Daniela did not accept this ruling without putting up a fight.

"Why can't we just be friends? You can still teach me. We can still do science together. We can still do great things together," she pleaded. "There was just no reasoning with him. He would not let it go. It was, 'No, you can't, you're destroying me. I've done everything for you and you are now damaging me. You're hurting my heart.'"

"You are going to *kill me*," Raniere said.

UNLIKE MANY IN Raniere's harem, Daniela didn't give much weight to the metaphysical link he claimed to have with women in his inner circle. He said their actions could give him chills, sap his energy, cause him physical pain, and make him feel sick. Daniela had seen and heard him manipulate others this way. Now he was turning his arsenal of manipulation and discipline tactics on her.

"I remember standing there telling him, 'Hey, don't use that on me. I'm your friend. I've seen you use this with everybody else,'" Daniela said.

Raniere told her she was choosing pride over her life commitment. He called her destructive. He told her she was wrong about her own feelings. "You say that about Ben but you're wrong. You don't even know what you feel. You're not honest with yourself," she said he told her.

Daniela resisted Raniere's attempts to confuse her. She went with him when he tried to storm off. She followed him to the executive library, and then back to the Flintlock house, where Karen Unterreiner and Pam Cafritz heard them. "Honestly, maybe I was stubborn but I couldn't let it go. I was very clear what I felt and what I thought about it," Daniela recalled.

Raniere suddenly lunged for the bathroom and locked himself inside. Unterreiner asked Daniela to leave, but she refused. "I was like, 'No, I want to figure this out.'"

Eventually Raniere opened the bathroom door and ran up the stairs. Daniela ran up after him. He ducked into Pam's room with Daniela close behind him. Daniela recalled Raniere grabbing her by the arm as she approached and pushing her to the floor, where she fell on a mattress.

Raniere ran out of the room and Daniela stayed on the floor. The confrontation was over. After that night, in November 2006, Daniela would never have another face-to-face conversation with Raniere, but she would stay involuntarily fixated on the exchange for many years to come. Nobody knew what her "ethical breach" had been, but the breach became the justification for escalating intervention and discipline at the hands of her family and community.

The argument also marked a turning point in Daniela's thinking about Raniere. Just as Lauren Salzman would realize during Raniere's arrest a decade later, Daniela saw that Raniere did not live up to his own ethical principles. "I can say this now but I didn't grasp it fully then . . . that Keith was a regular man, a fallible human, and all of those characteristics that I attributed to him, a better being in a way, wasn't true."

Though the doubts were beginning to set in by 2006, another six years would pass before Daniela escaped Albany for good.

CHAPTER FIFTEEN

Golden Boy

D aniela didn't want to have Keith Raniere's baby, but there were many women in the NXIVM community who did.

Publicly, Raniere maintained that he'd renounced all physical pleasure and material things. His fixers called him a "renunciate," but at the same time he was sleeping with a dozen or more women, secretly promising many of them that he'd one day give them his first-born child.

One of those women was Nancy Salzman's daughter, Lauren. Since her late twenties, Lauren Salzman had been dedicated to proving herself a worthy mother to Raniere's children. The two began a secret relationship in 2001, when Lauren was fresh out of college. By 2006 Raniere was showing less interest in her—and by 2009 they'd stopped sleeping together entirely—but her loyalty and wish for a family only grew stronger.

"When I started getting closer to thirty, I started pushing that I thought I wanted to do it sooner," she testified. Raniere often told would-be mothers like Lauren that they just weren't ready. They needed to work on their issues first.

Privately, Raniere often said he took on new sexual relationships for the benefit of his partners. He told Salzman it was sometimes difficult to take on new women, but that it was best for their growth. Salzman too thought she was overcoming her attachments and hang-ups through their complicated, mostly one-way relationship, but becoming a mother was not an attachment she was prepared to give up.

At times she even suggested that Raniere allow her to break off their lifetime commitment so that she could fulfill her dream of being a mother with somebody else. She testified that he strung her along with a pledge to "reinvest" in their relationship but later found new reasons not to pursue having a child. "It was just this never-ending thing that got put off and put off and put off," she said.

Salzman testified that the conditioning instilled by NXIVM's women-only "Jness" curriculum planted suggestions that women should want to have kids with Raniere. Talking points at some meetings raised eugenicist ideas about prioritizing the genetically fittest mate—Raniere naturally being the smartest, most evolved example on everyone's mind. This kind of conditioning was part of the reason why Salzman and many other women in NXIVM's inner circle held on to the hope that they would one day have Raniere's child.

IT'S UNCLEAR WHETHER Kristin Keeffe was ever promised, as Salzman was, that she could bear Raniere's first-born child, but she was definitely not supposed to be pregnant. Daniela was one of the few people to notice, in 2006. It was a short time before her blowout argument with Raniere. "I was spending a lot of time in Flintlock," she testified. "At one time, I noticed her belly was very swollen—like, very, very, swollen—and I thought it was strange."

When Daniela noticed Keeffe's belly a second time, she decided to mention it to Raniere. "I asked him if Kristin was pregnant and he said no, he had talked about that with her, but no."

Keeffe had good reasons to hide a pregnancy if she intended to keep it. During the jury selection process preceding Raniere's trial, defense attorney Marc Agnifilo conceded that his client used abortion "cavalierly." According to testimony in the trial, these abortions were sometimes carried out despite the wishes of the woman whose pregnancy was terminated.

"There are a lot of abortions in this case," Agnifilo remarked, out of earshot of a potential juror who'd said he was against abortion. Raniere had compelled "dozens" of abortions, Agnifilo revealed. The would-be juror was later dismissed.

Why so many abortions? As Daniela learned firsthand, Raniere advised against hormonal birth control because weight gain was a common side effect. Abortion became a de facto birth control for Daniela and her sisters, and Cafritz, herself promised a child, was enlisted to ensure the procedures were carried out.

Each time, Cafritz coached the sisters on what to say to doctors at the women's clinic. They were instructed not to mention Raniere's name or their undocumented status. On medical records presented at Raniere's trial, Cafritz was listed as Camila's only emergency contact when she was seeking a pregnancy termination in 2008.

When clinic staff noted that the three sisters had all been accompanied by Cafritz and asked a few standard domestic abuse questions, Cafritz complained that the clinic was violating its patients' privacy, which seemed to take care of the issue. By the time Marianna had her second pregnancy terminated, Cafritz and Raniere were well-practiced in making a pregnancy problem go away.

So if Keeffe had told Raniere about her pregnancy, this apparently well-oiled abortion machine would likely have whirred into action. Instead, Daniela testified, the pregnancy announced itself with a pool of blood. "Kristin was upstairs in her room, and she hadn't come out of her room," she recalled. "I think Keith found her."

Keeffe was immediately taken to the hospital, likely by Cafritz. "It was a very serious situation," Daniela said. "And Keith hadn't gone. Keith had stayed back."

Daniela told the jury that Raniere received a phone call from the hospital that confirmed not just a pregnancy but a newborn baby boy. "I think Keith was talking to Kristin, but I remember the conversation being, like, 'Well, how pregnant?' Like, 'How late in the term, how many months pregnant?'"

GAELYN WAS BORN several weeks premature in October 2006. As if that weren't enough shocking news for one day, Keeffe also learned that she had cancer, according to testimony.

Daniela and her younger sister, Camila, spent time with Keeffe in the intensive care unit, and assisted with childcare while Keeffe was undergoing cancer treatment.

Camila grew especially close with the tiny, bright-eyed infant. "I even came to see her as Gaelyn's second mother," Daniela said of her sister. "She really was the one who took care of him since he was very, very little. She would go to the NICU, too, and she was doing a lot more of the babysitting."

When Gaelyn could finally come home, Raniere didn't want the community to know the baby was his. And so, before Keeffe returned from the hospital, the inner circle hatched a plan to protect his reputation.

"To the community, Keith was celibate," Daniela noted. "Keith's relationships with everyone were secret. Nobody knew. This was part of Keith's image in the NXIVM community, so it would completely counter all they knew about him. If he had a baby, it means he had a relationship, and all of that would have to be explained.

"It was plotted and planned that this baby was going to be in Barbara Jeske's home," Daniela continued. "That was a cover story, that she had adopted him, and that Kristin would be living there."

"I was there when it was told to the community," the Seattle center's Susan Dones recalled of the strange baby announcement. "It was during a training, and Nancy tells this story from the front of the room about this child. She said a friend of Barbara Jeske's had a daughter who had been killed, she had a baby, and the parents couldn't take care of the grandchild."

The NXIVM community apparently welcomed the child with open arms, many of them wholeheartedly believing the baby was being fostered. By the time Keeffe was out of the hospital, the story had already circulated widely. Keeffe said she accepted the cover story because she was convinced Raniere's enemies would harm the baby if they knew he was the father.

Jeske was declared the adoptive mother. Some questioned why a child was being handed over in this way—Dones worried Barbara Jeske could barely take care of her own dog—but most embraced the lie as a heartening rescue story following a terrible tragedy. Later, Keeffe quietly moved to her own townhouse next door with the baby.

WHEN NXIVM CRITIC Joe O'Hara heard about the mysterious adoption, he immediately knew something was amiss. O'Hara was a

Washington lawyer who'd learned about Raniere's unconventional business practices while working for him as a consultant.

O'Hara had worked in child welfare and suspected the adoption was illegal. "You can't trade kids like playing cards, there's a process you have to go through," he told me. O'Hara reached out to the Saratoga County Department of Social Services and the New York State Office of Children and Family Services.

"I got zero response, and I mean zero, nothing, *nada*," he said. Undeterred, he wrote a letter to the New York attorney general, Andrew Cuomo. "I probably wrote three letters, which got increasingly aggressive and increasingly detailed." Finally, the government got sick of hearing from him and called state police to have a look.

State trooper Rodger Kirsopp was brought in to investigate what he called the "golden child." O'Hara gave Kirsopp all the information he had about NXIVM and the adoption story that Nancy Salzman and Barbara Jeske were spreading. After more than six months of investigation, Kirsopp finally confirmed that Kristin Keeffe and Keith Raniere were the parents.

"Whatever story had been put out there by NXIVM was a fallacy," Kirsopp said in a *Vice* interview in 2017.

GAELYN BECAME THE center of a new language program Raniere developed called "Rainbow Cultural Garden." This "system of education" proposed to hire half a dozen nannies to speak different languages to a child at the early stages of development.

"Even before Rainbow, we had heard that Gaelyn was being experimented on," Joe O'Hara says about the language program Raniere was testing on his son. NXIVM critics heard that Gaelyn was on a bizarre diet and was limited in his interactions with other children.

The Rainbow program was offered to other pre-kindergarten kids in the NXIVM community at a steep price. It was marketed to wealthy families who believed that kids with language skills would probably have more empathy and would maybe score higher on intelligence tests. No research was produced to support these claims.

"My sister Cami was the first teacher in the program," Daniela testified at Raniere's trial in 2019. Nannies like Camila were called "multicultural development specialists," and the program cost parents upward of $120,000 per year.

Loreta Garza oversaw the hiring of several nannies with various cultural and linguistic backgrounds. Other "specialists" spoke German, Hindi, Mandarin, and Arabic. The "full rainbow" included a different language every day of the week, and parents who paid for this service were sometimes asked not to interfere with the nannies during full-day teaching sessions.

NXIVM's critics were disturbed by the development. Again, O'Hara's experience with child protection suggested that there were urgent reasons to investigate. The program would have to be registered, either as a school or a daycare, and O'Hara couldn't find any evidence that NXIVM had taken these basic steps. He contacted the appropriate offices to complain, but it went nowhere. O'Hara began to suspect NXIVM had government backing.

"I knew at some level they had some protection," O'Hara told me. "Child welfare workers are among the most aggressive in government. People in that business really do care about kids. They put their own lives at risk going into abuse and neglect situations." O'Hara thought the only way to explain the government's failure to shut Rainbow down was that someone with insider influence had put a stop to any investigation. "Somewhere in the hierarchy the dogs weren't being let loose," he said.

FOR MORE THAN a decade, Rainbow continued to expand. Daycares opened in Monterrey, Miami, London, and Guatemala City. Sara Bronfman headed up Rainbow's U.K. operations, and in 2017 she gave a rare interview to a British education consulting group called Quintessentially Education. Bronfman claimed that Rainbow's "bespoke, in-home service" allowed children to speak four to seven languages fluently.

"This service replaces a nanny or other childcare options from as early as three months to school age and beyond," Bronfman explained. "As an example, a child might have a Spanish development specialist from eight to eleven a.m., Chinese Mandarin from eleven to two p.m., and Russian from two to five p.m. each day of the week, to introduce age-appropriate exercises in each language."

For many NXIVM followers, Rainbow was the calling card for the company's world-changing credentials. Here was proof that they were literally breeding a new, more evolved generation that would speak more languages, live according to higher principles, and score higher on intelligence tests. Gaelyn was the "epitome of a Rainbow child," former students told me. People told fantastical stories about him reading books as a toddler and speaking a dozen languages fluently. At V-Week and other community events he was held up as a prodigy— until he and his mother fled the community in 2014.

"Keith was experimenting on him. I had to get Gaelyn away," Keeffe wrote in a panicked April 2014 email to a lawyer she trusted. "The state police arranged a series of safe houses for me to stay in with Gaelyn and they moved us out of the Northeast."

Keeffe went into hiding, and Rodger Kirsopp, the state trooper who'd first investigated Gaelyn's birth, helped her exit quietly. "We did help Kristin Keeffe," he confirmed. "She came to us and asked us to help her get out of the situation that she was in. She was placed in a shelter."

When Keeffe left NXIVM, she took Rainbow's shining case study with her. The wider community was told that Keeffe had taken over as Gaelyn's foster parent but had "gone crazy" and kidnapped him. The company never completed a documentary that was supposed to showcase Gaelyn's genius and the Rainbow program's effectiveness.

It wasn't until after Raniere was arrested on sex trafficking charges in 2018 that some Rainbow schools finally began to close. The state of Florida's Department of Children and Families issued a statement saying that the agency "has no tolerance for any activities that put children at risk, including operating an unlicensed child-care facility." A spokesperson for the department told the *Miami New Times* that operations at a midtown Miami Rainbow school had been halted until a thorough investigation could be completed.

Yet even at the time of Raniere's trial in 2019, sources familiar with NXIVM's operations in Mexico said that Rainbow schools were still alive and well. When she testified in May 2019, Daniela said she thought her sister Camila might still be working as a "multicultural development specialist" in Mexico while her first student remained in hiding with his mother.

CHAPTER SIXTEEN

His Holiness

By 2006, Daniela wasn't the only girlfriend of Raniere's who was asking questions and "creating problems." Barbara Bouchey, one of NXIVM's most prolific enrollers and sales trainers, had some growing doubts about the company's leadership.

For three years before she left NXIVM for good, Bouchey was in survival mode. Even from a distance she looked like she was suffering. The wit and energy she'd radiated at early V-Weeks had faded. "Something had happened, and her demeanor had deteriorated," former member Susan White told me. Behind the scenes, Bouchey suspected the inner circle was plotting to shun her.

Specifically, Bouchey guessed that Raniere wanted to turn key people against her because of her tendency to speak up when she didn't like what she saw. As the Bronfmans' financial planner, she'd witnessed millions of dollars pulled out of the sisters' trust funds for failed commodities trades and real estate deals. That was after she'd lost $1.6 million of her own life savings to an earlier bogus trading scheme put in her name. She maintained that all this money had been lent, and that the company should make efforts to repay it.

Former members say that NXIVM's financial records were closely guarded by bookkeepers Karen Unterreiner and Kathy Russell.

Daniela testified that, during her early days working for Unterreiner, in 2002 and 2003, she was instructed to record cash payments separately from the others. Cash went directly into the top right drawer of Unterreiner's desk and was logged as "scholarship admin." "The point was to not pay taxes on the cash," Daniela said matter-of-factly. "So the cash would not be on the books."

For anyone who'd watched Raniere lecture about unjust taxes, this may not have come as a surprise. Consultants were brought in to help NXIVM achieve its goal of paying as little tax as possible. But Bouchey says she never actually saw evidence of illicit tax evasion. "I was never allowed in their financial office," she told me. Bouchey claims she would have left the company if she knew the extent of NXIVM's evasion, and that Raniere knew this and deliberately kept her in the dark.

NXIVM enrollment was nonetheless a steady stream of income for Bouchey, on top of her financial planning income. She was a field trainer earning tens of thousands every month on top of asset management income that at times exceeded $1 million a year. For a long time she was willing to accept that NXIVM's books were a black hole for reasons she didn't need to know. Until, one day, she couldn't do it anymore.

IN JANUARY 2008 Bouchey decided to step down from NXIVM's executive board. One of her top concerns was that the business model wasn't working: enrollment was sagging and people weren't properly advancing through the "stripe path."

NXIVM coaches worked for no pay until they advanced far enough to become proctors. Coaches would arrange for participants' food, facilitate the training exercises, and pay for their own travel, essentially just to maintain their standing within the company. It was only by hitting an exceedingly tough recruitment goal—developing six new coaches with at least two students under each—that NXIVM lifers could actually start making an income.

"Nobody got to the proctor level," Bouchey says. "Over nine years, only twenty or so people made it to proctor, and what that meant was we had a couple hundred people at the coach level who weren't making any money. In my opinion, that was a fatal flaw in the business model."

There was more going on that Bouchey didn't like. She thought Nancy Salzman was abusing her power at times, and that there was too much pressure for members to work on the "inner deficiencies" they identified in coaching sessions. For Lauren Salzman, her issue was that she indulged in sadness too often, earning the nickname "Forlorn." For Nicki Clyne, it was always needing to be right. "I never saw a group of people work harder on their issues—to root out any issues of anger and fear and lack of forgiveness," Bouchey says. "These people were amazing at this."

But Bouchey's biggest concern was that Raniere seemed to be abusing his position as leader in order to sexually manipulate women in the company. At the time, Bouchey, Loreta Garza, Lauren Salzman, and Karen Unterreiner were all on the executive board and secretly maintaining sexual relationships with Raniere. Edgar Boone was the only board member who wasn't also a sex partner. Bouchey thought Raniere was leveraging these relationships, and that it was affecting day-to-day decision-making.

Bouchey stopped enrolling new students, hoping the financial pressure might encourage Raniere and Nancy Salzman to address what she called the "elephants in the room." But her plan backfired. She noticed her ideas were being shot down in every facet of NXIVM activity. When she criticized how Raniere ran the business, others in his inner circle would jump to his defense, telling Bouchey, "How dare you speak to him that way."

For the next two years, Bouchey claims, Raniere's most loyal followers, including filmmaker and Vancouver center cofounder Mark Vicente, waged a smear campaign against her. People whispered horrible things about her—that she was a troublemaker and blamer and might have an undiagnosed mental deficiency. NXIVM taught that it was an honorable thing to keep a secret, so the damaging rumors were spread quietly. Bouchey had no idea what was coming her way.

"What Keith Raniere is masterful at is using secrets and lack of transparency to not allow people to know the whole story, or to discredit someone who might," Bouchey says. "NXIVM was all about teaching people how to be more honest, honorable, forthcoming, and genuine. So nobody ever expected that the leadership were all liars."

In NXIVM-speak, Bouchey had become "suppressive" and was in danger of taking a fall, like the angel Lucifer in Milton's *Paradise Lost*. Raniere had created an entire module about what happens when brain wires cross to create a suppressive. Bouchey was also a danger to NXIVM's bottom line, which meant she was probably evil, the kind of sociopath who thought good things were bad and bad things were good.

AROUND 2008, SUSAN Dones noticed the way Barbara Bouchey was becoming an outcast in the company. She heard that Raniere wasn't speaking to Bouchey and wondered why. "People were going around and saying, 'What do you think Barbara did that was so bad that even Keith won't talk to her?'" Dones recalled in a 2010 deposition. "I didn't know. And so finally I went to Barbara, and she said, 'All I can tell you is I'm renegotiating my contract with him.'"

This was an interesting choice of words on Bouchey's part, given that her renegotiation wasn't just about the business; she'd also taken her sexual relationship with Raniere off the table. Like Daniela, Bouchey was snubbed and silenced for breaking up with Raniere, and she began to be more openly accused of trying to destroy him and the company.

Bouchey's criticisms about the executive board were partly answered in 2009 when new members were appointed, including Mark Vicente, Clare Bronfman, and Mexico City center owners Emiliano Salinas and Alex Betancourt. Though Lauren Salzman had been removed from the board following Bouchey's claims of inappropriate relationships, she was allowed to return a few weeks after the shakeup.

Bouchey wasn't the only troublemaker on NXIVM's watch list. In April 2009 Nancy Salzman and Karen Unterreiner paid a visit to the West Coast, where Dones and her wife, Kim Woolhouse, operated the Tacoma and Seattle chapters of the company. "Nancy came out to the Pacific Northwest and met with all the proctors," Dones told me. "What she wanted to do was take the center away from me and give it to the proctors in the Pacific Northwest."

Dones thought the proposed deal went against everything NXIVM taught about business. Not only would it take income away from her and her partner, but it would turn several proctor colleagues into what NXIVM termed "parasites." They hadn't earned their position, the teaching went, and knowing this would damage their self-esteem.

Dones looked to Bouchey as an ally within the company, and after some protest Bouchey was allowed to be her coach. Dones told Bouchey about Nancy Salzman's plan to push her out and promote her proctor colleagues. Dones decided that if Salzman went ahead with it, she would leave the company and take her recruiting contacts with her. "Nancy knew the proctors aren't enrollers," Dones says. "I just called her bluff."

Salzman did not take this news well. "She said, 'You've ruined everything,'" Dones told me. "I said, 'I haven't ruined everything. I've made a decision about how I want to participate, or not participate, if you do what you said you're going to do.'" Salzman relented and allowed Dones to keep ownership of the center.

Dones called Bouchey after the exchange and told her coach that, even though Salzman had given up on her West Coast coup d'état, she wanted to quit anyway. Salzman had let it slip that untaxed cash was coming across the border from Mexico. "I told her what had happened. I said, 'There's a lot of weird shit going on, I think illegal shit, and I can no longer be a part of this organization.'"

Bouchey and Dones would take unprecedented action together within a matter of days. In court filings, NXIVM would later allege that Dones took 120 clients and coaches with her, leaving only eight members in the Seattle area.

THOUGH THE COMPANY'S foundations were shaking in that early spring of 2009, NXIVM was in the international spotlight more than ever before—for better and for worse. Clare and Sara Bronfman had spent over a year planning the details of the Dalai Lama's first-ever visit to Albany at the invitation of the World Ethical Foundations Consortium, the organization financially supported by the Bronfmans and whose "conceptual founder" was Raniere.

In an interview with local Albany radio personality Paul Vandenburgh in 2009, Sara Bronfman said she'd always wanted to meet the spiritual leader. "I was literally in my bedroom one day listening to his tapes and thought to myself, 'Wow, this guy is amazing!'" she gushed. "I always had this calling, or this vision, to find people who were humanitarian."

In interviews, Sara said she'd seen parallels between the teachings of the Dalai Lama and of Keith Raniere, and so had set out to bring the two thinkers together in the same room. In 2007, when she'd crossed paths with Tenzin Dhonden, a Tibetan monk who was "special emissary for peace" to the Dalai Lama, Sara had proposed inviting the spiritual leader to Albany; Lama Tenzin had since arranged for her and her sister Clare to meet him in India.

After their initial meeting Sara hosted Lama Tenzin at one of her Albany-area properties, showing him all the tools for ethics and compassion NXIVM students were supposedly learning. Multiple former insiders say that the two developed a sexual relationship—despite the monk's vow of celibacy. The affair was an open secret, as the two shared a bedroom at times and were once interrupted while making out in a hot tub.

When the Dalai Lama event was finally announced in January 2009, it sparked a media frenzy that underlined Raniere's past as an alleged pyramid schemer and his company's aggressive stance against defectors and critics. Critics of NXIVM had started a letter-writing campaign warning the Dalai Lama that NXIVM was a cult. A March 29 op-ed in the Schenectady-based *Daily Gazette* claimed that Raniere's past wasn't in line with the World Ethical Foundations Consortium's peaceful mission and named high-profile critics, including Edgar Bronfman and actor Goldie Hawn, who'd rejected a speaking invite. "If Goldie Hawn has the sense not to appear at an event sponsored by Keith Raniere," the op-ed read, "then cancellation by the Dalai Lama, winner of the Nobel Peace Prize, should be a no-brainer."

THE DALAI LAMA was expected to make several NXIVM-sponsored appearances between April 18 and 22, at two college campuses and the Times Union Center. The panels were supposed to cover wide-ranging topics. An opening discussion was titled "Compassionate Ethics, Education and Active Non-Violence." Subsequent events were to tackle violence in Mexico, women as social icons, and the science of media.

But on April 6, days before the spiritual leader's first scheduled appearance, the Albany *Times Union* reported that the Dalai Lama had pulled out. "We had naively believed people would be excited about his visit and that our community would put their pettiness aside to unite for this momentous occasion. We were wrong," Sara Bronfman wrote on her blog. "His visit was met with fear and cynicism and some of our local media sources worked ardently to destroy the honor faster than we could build it."

Left: "Vanguard" Keith Raniere wore a long white sash to signal he's a lifelong student. Taken in 2002.

Below: Nancy Salzman and Keith Raniere formed Executive Success Programs in 1998, which became NXIVM in 2002. Seen here at V-Week in 2004.

Photo courtesy of Barbara Bouchey

Photo courtesy of Barbara Bouchey

Left: Beginning in 2000, financial planner Barbara Bouchey helped expand the organization across the United States.

Below: Seagram heirs Sara and Clare Bronfman took their first NXIVM classes in 2002 and 2003.

Photo courtesy of Barbara Bouchey

Photo courtesy of Barbara Bouchey

Above: An inner circle photo taken at V-Week in 2006. Back row: Barbara Bouchey, Keith Raniere, Lauren Salzman, Pam Cafritz. Middle row: Sara Bronfman (with the hat), Kathy Russell, Monica Duran, Karen Unterreiner, Linda Smith. Bottom row: faces have been blurred to protect identities.

Left: Barbara Bouchey became a top recruiter for NXIVM, while Kristin Keeffe (right) took on the role of legal liaison, battling perceived enemies in court.

Above: Vancouver actors started joining NXIVM's ranks in 2005. *Battlestar Galactica* actor Nicki Clyne (left) is seen with Seagram heir Sara Bronfman.

Left: Smallville actors Kristin Kreuk (left) and Allison Mack attend a red carpet event in May 2006.

Above: Loreta Garza (left) led NXIVM's language immersion experiments beginning in 2006. Clare Bronfman (right) became a top executive alongside president Nancy Salzman (center). Taken at Salzman's birthday party in 2007.

Left: Lauren Salzman became a cooperating witness at Raniere's trial, testifying about recruiting "slaves" and confining Daniela to a room. She pleaded guilty to racketeering and racketeering conspiracy.

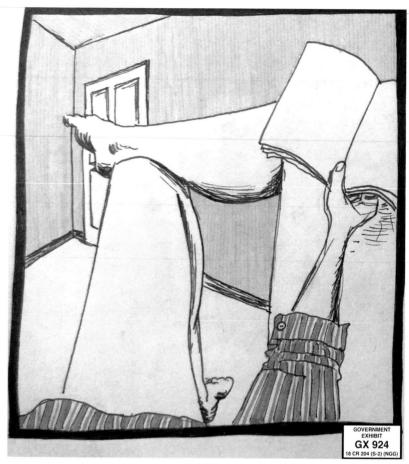

Presented as evidence at Keith Raniere's trial in 2019

Above: A drawing by Daniela while she was confined to a room from 2010 to 2012.

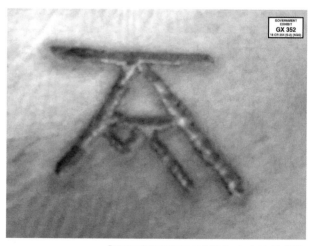

Right: A photo of a DOS brand submitted as evidence at Raniere's trial.

Presented as evidence at Keith Raniere's trial in 2019

© Drew Angerer/Getty

© Mark Lennihan – AP/Canadian Press

Above: Allison Mack was arrested for her role in DOS in April 2018. She admitted to forced labor and extortion as part of a racketeering conspiracy ahead of Raniere's 2019 trial.

Left: Clare Bronfman pleaded guilty to identity theft and harboring an illegal migrant for financial gain in April 2019. She was sentenced to six years and nine months in federal prison.

© Drew Angerer/Getty

© Mark Lennihan – AP/Canadian Press

Above left: Keith Raniere's defense attorney Marc Agnifilo.

Above right: The Eastern District of New York's lead prosecutor Moira Penza.

© Mark Lennihan – AP/Canadian Press

Above: Ex-girlfriend Toni Natalie (left) and mother of a DOS slave Catherine Oxenberg (right) speak to media following Raniere's conviction on June 19, 2019.

The sisters flew to India to negotiate with the Dalai Lama in person. Raniere and Nancy Salzman joined the mission on the Bronfmans' private jet, bringing back fantastical stories of monks not needing clothes to stay warm and beautiful moments shared with the Tibetan leader.

His Holiness eventually agreed to a lecture on May 6 at a smaller Albany venue. At the event, the Dalai Lama sat cross-legged on a brown armchair alongside the Bronfman sisters, each of them wearing a billowing white silk scarf. He used the platform to encourage investigation into any unethical allegations against NXIVM. "If you have done something wrong, you must accept, you must admit, change, make correction," he told the crowd.

Even though the talk brought another tidal wave of bad press, Clare and Sara considered it a victory. In the eyes of many NXIVM followers who'd been growing skeptical, the Dalai Lama's appearance secured newfound legitimacy for the company's leadership.

One former critic who remained notably silent throughout the drama was the Bronfmans' father. Edgar had made peace with his daughters' unwavering commitment to Raniere's mission, softening his stance as he neared the end of his life. "His relationship with his daughters is excellent and it continues to be and that's what's important to him," his spokesperson, Stephen Herbits, told *Maclean's* magazine and many other media outlets.

Almost a decade later, Tenzin Dhonden would be forced to step down from his emissary post when the press learned that the Bronfmans had allegedly made a $1 million donation to secure the Dalai Lama's appearance.

SUSAN DONES ALREADY had a plane ticket booked to visit Albany when she heard that the first scheduled Dalai Lama event had been cancelled, but Barbara Bouchey convinced her to get on the plane anyway. Bouchey explained that she was getting a group of women together to talk about their leadership concerns. She offered Dones and Woolhouse a place to stay while they were in Albany. "I said, 'Okay, as long as you're not going to try to manipulate me into staying,'" Dones says.

Bouchey wanted the women to "lay out all our cards on the table," as Dones puts it. When the group met, Kathy Ethier, a massage therapist and coach who attended, was shocked to learn that Raniere was sleeping with everyone on the executive board. "She really thought he was celibate," Dones recalls.

The "NXIVM Nine," as they became known, requested a meeting with Raniere, which lasted three days beginning on April 21. The confrontation did not go well. Over many tense hours, much of it recorded by Dones and Bouchey, cracks began to form in Raniere's usually serene demeanor.

"I saw him for the first time in such a flustered state," Bouchey told me. "He was scattered, fearful, swearing, angry, his face red, veins pulsating . . . and the entire time he tried to convince the other women I was full of crap, denying things, lying, and blaming me."

"We had him on the hot seat ten and a half hours," she adds, "something I never witnessed in my nine years there."

A leaked eight-minute video clip of the confrontation was posted to YouTube more than a year later. It shows Bouchey and Raniere facing off in mostly restrained tones. Bouchey said she knew of forty people in the company who wanted to see NXIVM address the issues it had been ignoring. "What I see are the effects," she told Raniere. "The effects are that our company is falling apart."

"You don't have the experience of leadership," Raniere countered. "You don't have the experience of preserving people's lives with what you say. And the truth of the matter is—"

"Neither do you," Bouchey interjected. Consumers' Buyline, she said, had crashed after only a few years.

Raniere lowered his voice to a barbed whisper. "Here's the thing. I've been shot at for my beliefs. I've had to make choices—should I have bodyguards? Should I have them armed or not? I've had people killed because of my beliefs, and because of their beliefs . . ." he said. "You might say . . . the brighter the light, the more the bugs."

For Bouchey and her allies, the meeting was the last straw. In that moment, they decided to resign from the company. The resignation letter, signed by all nine women, didn't mention Raniere's inappropriate sexual relationships explicitly, but it did allude to "inconsistencies in the leadership of the company" and "conflict of interest within the system."

The resignation letter included a list of unpaid invoices totalling over $2 million, most of it owed to Bouchey for her commodity trading loans. Susan Dones, her wife Kim Woolhouse, and six others cosigned

Bouchey's request for all outstanding commissions and loans to be paid by April 30, 2009. "If these requests are not met we will move forward by contacting the Press," the letter concluded.

The recording wouldn't go public for more than a year, but when it did, it became infamous for Raniere's apparent admission that he'd had people killed. On October 23, 2010, the *New York Post* covered the story under the headline "Creepy Cultist's Killing Confession."

NXIVM'S LAWYERS LEAPT into action in response to the women's demands. "The contents of this email constitute extortion and coercion in violation of the New York Penal Law," reads an email to Dones dated April 26, 2009. "As you know, NXIVM has notified the authorities regarding these threats. . . . We also demand that you refrain from any further contact with Mr. Raniere or Ms. Salzman until your personal differences have been resolved."

The company's lawyers later argued that Raniere's comment about having had people killed referred to a murder that occurred in Mexico during a months-long documentary project NXIVM produced about its anti-violence activism in the region. Raniere had advised a local Mormon family not to pay kidnappers a ransom for the return of their son. The family went along with Raniere's directive and the son was returned safely, but the father was later killed. It was this suspected retaliatory death that Raniere was talking about, according to his lawyer. NXIVM's critics disputed this claim, arguing that the murder didn't happen until July 2009, after Raniere had been recorded making his comment.

Within thirty-six hours of the NXIVM Nine confrontation, Raniere had to call a company-wide town hall to explain that he wasn't the celibate he'd claimed to be, that he'd had a secret relationship with Bouchey and others.

Mark Vicente, who took on a more central leadership role after Bouchey's exit, testified in Raniere's trial that retribution was swift. Raniere called the women socialists and supressives and said they'd never really worked through the personal issues they had identified in NXIVM classes. "He explained to me that there were a number of issues with these women. They were basically engaged in criminal behavior," Vicente said. "They were described as enemies. As being suppressive. As enemies of the company and enemies of Raniere as well."

Bouchey and the other women were immediately cut off from contact. "We were told not to engage with her, not to talk to her," Vicente said.

Lauren and Nancy Salzman characterized the request for $2 million in owed funds as an extortion attempt. They asked Vicente and others to tally up the financial losses that could be attributed to Bouchey's exit. With the Salzmans' help, Vicente went on to write a letter to the Saratoga County district attorney's office alleging that Bouchey had committed criminal extortion. He accused Bouchey of contacting NXIVM associates and discouraging them from doing business with NXIVM. Vicente wrote that he'd personally lost hundreds of thousands of dollars and that the company had lost millions as a result of Bouchey's extortion efforts. "Barbara Bouchey has flagrantly slandered Nancy Salzman and Keith Raniere," reads part of the letter. The Bronfmans fired Bouchey as their financial manager on May 1, 2009. A year later, Bouchey filed for bankruptcy.

Vicente was promoted to a green sash. "I was praised as being somebody who was very loyal and stood by the company and stood by Raniere," he testified.

SINCE 2009, BOUCHEY says, she's been dragged into fourteen legal cases by NXIVM and the Bronfman heirs, as either a defendant or a witness. She has stood before eight judges in four different states, accused of breaching fiduciary responsibility, breaching client confidentiality, and colluding with adversaries to wrongfully defame NXIVM.

The Bronfmans personally sued her three times, at one point seeking $10 million in damages. Clare Bronfman also went to five government agencies to file a criminal complaint of extortion based on Bouchey's resignation letter, in which she requested that Raniere return the $1.6 million of hers he lost on the commodities market.

"It was a very effective strategy," Bouchey says of the never-ending lawsuits. Her financial planning business struggled, her credibility was seemingly ruined, and NXIVM supporters actively spread false rumors of her guilt. Looking back, Bouchey says she thinks she was tormented in part because Raniere wanted to make an example out of her—to show what would happen to anyone who tried to blow the whistle.

"Anyone who left NXIVM was terrified to talk to me," she says.

CHAPTER SEVENTEEN

Spy Games

NXIVM's enemy list was getting longer.

When Nancy Salzman first asked Kristin Keeffe to coordinate the company's "legal" efforts in 2003, the organization was targeting only a handful of people. The case against cult deprogrammer Rick Ross was at the top of Raniere's priority list, and there were constant motions and filings to manage. But as Keeffe settled into that role, overseeing more lawsuits against critics and ex-members, the range of duties expanded along with the list of targets.

Keeffe has a pale, younger-than-her-age face and a slight voice to match. There's a certain anonymity to her appearance, with her gray-blue eyes and an in-between hair color that isn't quite dark but wouldn't be called light without some help from hair dye. In photos she shows a lot of teeth when she smiles, signaling ease and agreeability. She wasn't as tiny or striking as some of the women around her, and this was a point of shame Raniere leveraged. He set Keeffe's weight goal at 128 pounds, and would ask her to report her weight in front of colleagues. Like many NXIVM women, she developed an eating disorder.

As legal liaison Keeffe increasingly relied on private investigators to track NXIVM's perceived enemies covertly, and over time she

became a self-taught investigator herself. In the wake of the mysterious disappearance of NXIVM student Kristin Snyder, Keeffe began
amassing evidence that Snyder was alive and "resort hopping" in
another state. After Snyder was pronounced dead in 2005, Keeffe
ramped up the investigation. In emails produced as evidence at
Raniere's 2019 trial, one private investigator told Keeffe he'd carried
out searches at a guest house in Key West, Florida, and at a location
in Palm Springs, California. Keeffe provided leads on possible aliases
and post office locations that the missing woman might have used. By
2009 Keeffe had a drawer full of dirt, not just on ex-members but also
on journalists, judges, and politicians.

New York private investigator Juval Aviv, who'd first been hired
by NXIVM in 2003 to gather intel on Rick Ross, said of Keeffe in a July
2009 deposition, "She almost really lived in our office. She wanted to
be one of our investigators. She loved it."

ACTING FOR NXIVM, Juval Aviv reached out to Rick Ross in 2004 and
told him a fake story about a mother who had a twenty-seven-year-
old daughter in NXIVM. Aviv said the mother, Susan Zuckerman, was
a family friend who'd discovered that her daughter had sold family
heirlooms to pay for her classes. Aviv's company, Interfor, was apparently looking into the daughter's involvement in the cult and wanted
to bring Ross onto the case to do an intervention.

"He said repeatedly this mother is a wealthy woman," Ross told me.

Aviv secretly recorded a conversation that later became evidence.
He asked Ross for dirt on NXIVM to "impress" Zuckerman.

"How's this for impressive," Ross replied. "I have two hundred
photographs of Raniere at one of his functions. I have him in compromising poses with his girlfriends."

"Oh my god!" Aviv said.

"I have him in the nude," Ross continued. "I have one picture of
him standing in front of his girlfriend with a red ribbon tied around
his penis . . . which is erect."

In April 2005 Ross went to the Interfor office on Madison Avenue in
New York City to meet with the mother. As Ross recalls, there seemed
to be a plan in place in which the mother and daughter would meet
on a cruise ship, where it would be difficult for NXIVM to interfere by

phone. Ross would also board the ship and help the daughter begin to question her participation in NXIVM. Interfor was excited about the plan and had already paid Ross a retainer for his services.

"At one point I make it clear to [the mother]: at no time will I be alone with the daughter," Ross told me. He also requested that Aviv be present at the cruise ship intervention, since Aviv was personally invested in the case. "Once I made that clear, it was like it was abruptly dropped."

Aviv claimed that NXIVM couldn't come up with a woman to play the daughter. Aspiring double agent Kristin Keeffe wanted to play the role, according to Aviv, but Raniere and Salzman wouldn't allow it.

The cruise ship fiasco was far from NXIVM's only spy mission against Ross, and Interfor wasn't the only collaborator on the case. According to testimony at Raniere's trial, Keeffe brought on a second investigation firm, called Canaprobe, to dig into several enemies' bank records. Keeffe bragged about finding someone who was able to get Ross's phone records, according to Barbara Bouchey's 2009 deposition. Bouchey also admitted to having seen a Canaprobe invoice for $10,000 on which "Ross bank sweeps" was the only line item. "They wanted to know who he was speaking to, what he was doing, what he was spending his money on," Bouchey said.

IN THE END, Interfor didn't need to orchestrate an elaborate cruise ship sting to score plenty of info on Rick Ross. Interfor provided NXIVM with pages and pages of material on his medical background, tax returns, daily bank transactions, criminal record, business associates, and past civil lawsuits. One report alleged that Ross had been an informant during an attempted raid on the Branch Davidians' ranch in Waco, Texas, and might have even been somehow responsible for the fifty-one-day siege there in 1993 that ended with seventy-six deaths.

"I had no idea to what extent I was being surveilled," Ross told me for a *Vice* story in March 2019. It was the same week Nancy Salzman admitted that NXIVM had conspired to alter court records in the fourteen-year civil case against Ross.

Ross says it was a phone call from *Metroland* reporter Chet Hardin that first tipped him off about Keeffe's spy games.

"Did you know they have all your banking info and phone records?" Hardin asked, according to Ross. (Hardin confirmed that he made the phone call but declined an interview.)

"That's ridiculous," Ross replied.

Hardin said it was true, and that he had the dollar amounts to prove it. "He started reciting portions of a bank statement," Ross told me.

Ross says he later learned that NXIVM had paid to have his garbage searched. He lived on the twenty-second floor of a New Jersey high rise, where at one point he was told about a problem with the garbage chute. "One of the building attendants said to me, 'Would you please put your garbage bags outside your door? I'll take care of it.' I didn't think anything of it, I just thought, 'That's nice, I don't have to go to the garbage chute.'" Ross says he later believed the attendant was actually someone hired to go through his trash in search of personal information. Court records eventually confirmed this was true.

These so-called garbage runs, which are legal in New Jersey, still couldn't explain how NXIVM got detailed bank records over a long period of time. In a counterclaim Ross alleged that the company used illegal tactics to access his bank information, social security number, and other private data.

Even Aviv, a seasoned investigator, was apparently stunned when presented with the questionably sourced bank and phone records Keeffe had scored. "I said to her, 'Where did you get this? I need to know before I even work with it.' She said, 'Don't worry, it comes from a friend who is authorized to do certain things,'" Aviv said in a deposition.

According to court records, Keeffe told Aviv she had a relationship with a U.S. marshal or a deputy sheriff who allowed her to run plate numbers and telephone records. She'd developed these kinds of law enforcement contacts over years of spy work for NXIVM, which somehow led to her placement as a victim's advocate with the Albany County district attorney's office between October 2006 and February 2007. She then leveraged this cozy relationship with law enforcement to encourage criminal charges against Raniere's ex-girlfriends, NXIVM critics, and journalists.

Clare Bronfman made her own separate efforts to get Ross and his allies indicted. "The 'Ross camp' needs to be fearful, back down and look to fix the damage they have done; the thought of criminal charges may help inspire this," she wrote in a 2008 email to one of her father's closest personal and professional associates weeks before a mediation date on their civil claim against Ross. "I know you are incredibly resourceful and have the intelligence to figure this out. I don't need to know who is funding them, how you stop that from continuing, in fact I don't want to know—it just needs to be done quickly."

Stephen Herbits, a confidant of Edgar Bronfman since the 1970s, told Clare that her requests were inappropriate and lacked evidence.

Ross says he likely would have spent something in the range of $5 million defending himself in court had his defense team not waived the legal fees. His lawyer has estimated the full legal bill was more like $50 million. Ross adds that NXIVM's lawyers weren't helping by constantly delaying the process. "That's a very unusual scenario," he says of the interminable case. "The way that was done was changing legal teams repeatedly; NXIVM changed legal representation a half dozen or more times. They pleaded with the court that they needed to extend everything, to bring the next team up to speed."

NXIVM's inner circle didn't seem to understand why Ross wasn't crumbling under pressure and settling. Clare suspected that her own father might be funding their enemies' court fees.

"It seems obvious to me that you still think I am supporting RR [Rick Ross] in some way or another. That is simply not true," Edgar wrote in an email to his daughters in 2011. "In no shape or form would I do that and tell you that I am not. Whether or not you want to believe me, I do not lie, and I love you two very much. Someone is not telling you the truth. Why don't you try and figure out who that might be. Who has something to gain? Certainly not me."

NXIVM HAD BEEN carrying out intense surveillance schemes for years, something that wasn't widely known until the Ross lawsuit put much of it on the record between 2007 and 2009. The evidence compiled by Ross's lawyers gave credence to accusations from other long-time NXIVM enemies who said they'd been subjected to intimidation and harassment, often while being made to feel alone in their struggle.

Raniere's ex-girlfriend Toni Natalie claims the title of "patient zero" when it comes to spying and intimidation. In a *Vice* interview in 2017 she described break-ins, stalking, and threats made by Raniere's inner circle of women after she cut ties with him in 1999. As well as showing up at her work and surveilling her mail, they invaded her home upward of fifty times. "[Raniere] showed up one night with ten people and took everything that belonged to him," Natalie said. "They would unmake my bed, turn over my photographs. He just wanted me to know he could get in there."

Bouchey recalled Raniere's inner circle having open discussions of these break-ins around the time they were going on. "I believe it was Kristin that said that she had broken into [Natalie's] house to get back things that they believed were Keith's, or things that they believed would be good to take," she said. Stolen items included letters, photos, Consumers' Buyline records, and other personal items.

Joe O'Hara, the lawyer who'd done consulting work for Raniere and had introduced NXIVM to Interfor, told me that after he ended his contract, his cable and phone lines were cut and the words "You will die in seven days" were spray-painted on his property. Before he left, O'Hara had warned Raniere in writing that surveillance material gathered by NXIVM, which O'Hara had discovered by accident, was likely illegal.

Like Rick Ross, O'Hara and Natalie were both simultaneously fighting off "legal attacks" initiated by NXIVM. In a counter-lawsuit filed in 2012, O'Hara listed more of the bizarre and vengeful ways he believed NXIVM had retaliated against him over the years. They called up his consulting clients to accuse O'Hara of illegally practicing law in New York. They reported him to the District of Columbia bar association, where his practice was located. They filed "fictitious change-of-address cards" with the U.S. Post Office, apparently hoping to intercept important correspondence. According to O'Hara, they succeeded in turning his consulting enterprise upside down.

Joe O'Hara says he now regrets introducing NXIVM to powerful contacts that enabled them to abuse the legal system. "They used the tools that I gave them, and by that point they had Bronfman money," O'Hara told me. "They were hiring the best attorneys money could buy. They would have multiple firms working on each case." By one lawyer's estimate, Clare Bronfman employed as many as sixty attorneys at thirty firms.

AFTER BARBARA BOUCHEY staged her revolt in 2009, Kristin Keeffe and Raniere seemed to double down on their spying efforts. With nine more insiders now on the outside, all hanging on to potentially damaging information, full-blown paranoia set in and Keeffe began using bizarre coded language in her communications with Raniere.

According to emails presented as evidence at Raniere's trial, Keeffe became wary of passing cars and of house painters in the neighborhood, and stopped referring to Ross by name in emails about surveillance. She and Emiliano Salinas both created new Gmail accounts that they believed weren't linked to their real names.

In an August 2009 correspondence with Raniere, Keeffe vaguely refers to bank sweeps as "dishes" of food she intends to have made according to Raniere's "recipe." "I'm checking on the toppings," she wrote, apparently alluding to different methods of bank snooping. "I reminded Richard [from Canaprobe] yesterday to make us only one layer dishes if the topping is different than the layer; to do two layers only when the first topping is the same. He's erred so far and cooked two layers each time no matter what. It's turning out pretty tasty."

In response, Raniere requested more info on what went into the "dishes" and referred to Emiliano Salinas as "our Mexican chef," perhaps a reference to Salinas's role translating and delivering investigation reports through third parties in Mexico.

Keeffe's confusing new style of communication seemed to be part of a larger effort to remove any links between Raniere and NXIVM's spy missions. In one August 2009 email chain about private investigation reports, Keeffe wrote to Salinas, "NEVER SEND TO KEITH. EVER. PLEASE DON'T FORGET THIS AGAIN. XO."

DESPITE THE NEW layer of secrecy and the increasingly high price tag for surveillance, the information Keeffe and Salinas were getting seemed to be less and less credible. One set of search results claimed that Rick Ross had bank accounts in tax havens all over the Caribbean and Europe, but attempts to test activity in those accounts came back negative.

"I feel the information they sent us now is not high impact and not very credible," Salinas wrote.

As one of Keeffe's newest targets, Bouchey knew what was coming to some extent. She'd been present in the room when Keeffe and Raniere had discussed their investigations and legal cases. But it wasn't until after Keeffe left NXIVM in 2014 that she told Bouchey about many of the more insidious tactics used against her. (I made many attempts to reach Kristin Keeffe and go over these spying and intimidation allegations with her but was not successful.)

In Bouchey's case, much of the campaign against her was more heavy-handed than it was with Ross. Private investigator Steve Rambam, who was first hired to investigate Kristin Snyder's disappearance, began showing up at the homes and workplaces of Bouchey's friends and coworkers, suggesting she was in trouble with the law. He led people to believe that Bouchey had stolen money from the Bronfmans, and that she was a jilted ex-girlfriend trying to extort Raniere.

Rambam spooked Bouchey's personal assistant in a parking garage in December 2009, according to court statements. "She was parking her car when a silver SUV pulled up very close to her car. A man got out with a woman. He identified himself as Mr. Rambam and demanded to speak to her," reads an affidavit describing the incident. "When she refused to converse he made threats saying he would see her in court. He was very intimidating and she was frightened."

In another incident, a woman blocked the personal assistant's car and proceeded to bang on her hood and car window in an effort to serve subpoena papers. And according to court documents, Rambam lurked outside of homes and took photos of residences and cars.

When I called Rambam in July 2019, he denied ever working for NXIVM. "I have nothing useful to tell you," he said. "I can say unequivocally, if I was aware of women being taken advantage of, or abused against their will, I would have stepped in pretty quickly."

In 2012, *Times Union* investigative reporter Jim Odato found that Rambam had been investigated for professional misconduct related to alleged witness intimidation leading up to one of NXIVM's civil lawsuits. The complaint also revealed that his legal name was Steven Rombom, not Rambam. He got off with a $6,500 fine and was allowed to keep his private investigator license.

Bouchey said she began wondering whether new clients coming to her were actually moles sent by NXIVM to gather information. She believes that NXIVM's inner circle filed complaints with several government agencies, including the U.S. federal finance watchdog, claiming she stole money. Then her passport was suspended. She also got a voicemail message saying her pet bird was going to die. Later, she says, she learned from Keeffe that they'd been looking at all her credit card charges in real time.

Emails between Keeffe and Salinas in July 2009 reveal their attempts to sue Bouchey for blackmail in Mexico as well as in the United States. To this day, Bouchey told me, she has trouble when she leaves the country due to some kind of flag on her file. Because of NXIVM, she says, she went for years without disclosing which state she lived in to most of her friends and colleagues. Her own employees didn't know her home address.

"Raniere's manipulation of the courts and law enforcement . . . to scare and silence people—hoping to keep damaging information about him from coming out—has been an extremely effective strategy so far," Bouchey wrote in a 2010 court statement.

After a decade of working the legal system to wage NXIVM's battles, Keeffe had become a near unstoppable force. But she was also kept on a shorter and shorter leash. Keeffe told a judge she accepted an enormous pay cut out of fear that she would otherwise be shunned from the community. She lived off $13,000 a year with no benefits, and at times had to ask Clare Bronfman for permission to buy food. Before she escaped NXIVM in 2014, Keeffe clocked one last achievement for Raniere: bringing indictments against Toni Natalie, Joe O'Hara, and Barbara Bouchey.

CHAPTER EIGHTEEN

Room

It's now a matter of court record that beginning on March 9, 2010, Daniela was illegally confined to a room for close to two years. But the conditions of her captivity began to take shape much earlier—on the day in October 2006 when she confronted Keith Raniere about her romantic feelings for Ben Myers. From that moment on, Daniela felt her grasp on the world begin to slip.

Raniere wasn't speaking to her face to face, but email records show that Daniela was still the focus of much of his thinking, feeling, and strategizing. And although on some days Daniela accepted that this focus was a good thing—meant to help her learn and become a better person—she had a growing suspicion that Raniere's obsessive attention was slowly chipping away at her freedom.

Immediately following their blowout confrontation, Daniela was coached on how to overcome the prideful and destructive tendencies that Raniere said had gotten her into that mess. Nancy Salzman and her coach Karen Unterreiner made regular stops to help Daniela understand the extent of the damage she'd caused and the exhaustive "program" she'd need to undertake to fix it.

At first Daniela resisted this coaching and continued her romantic relationship with Myers in secret, which only seemed to embolden her handlers, who were directed by Raniere.

"I knew that it was from Keith because I had been around for three years in his life, and I knew how he worked on women," Daniela told the jury. "I knew that people were coming to me not because they were concerned and they wanted to know what was going on. They were being sent to me to work on specific things and to get me to do specific things. Namely, go back to Keith, apologize."

Though Daniela was certain that her reason for confronting Raniere was innocent and well-meaning, her grasp of what had happened and why became foggy over time. "It was no longer as clean as 'I no longer want to be with you, I want to be with him,'" she said. Her coaches told her that committing to weight loss and writing book reports were also part of her program, and that she owed the whole community a massive debt for her many, still-accumulating transgressions.

AT TIMES DANIELA threw herself headfirst into her self-improvement program, fasting for forty days at one point and recording her weight as it dropped from 154.8 to 134.8 pounds. "I became ridiculously attuned to when I drank water, how much I would gain weight, when I went to the bathroom how much I would lose," she testified.

Daniela was eventually encouraged to reach out to Raniere by email, though her coach said he might not respond. At trial she estimated that she went on to exchange thousands of emails with Raniere about Ben Myers, her pride, and the "ethical breach" she was now wholeheartedly trying to fix.

The emails show a young woman writing around and around in circles, trying to anticipate subtle interpersonal dynamics three to twelve steps ahead. In one, she laid out plans to address Myers's perception of Raniere, Myers's perception of Daniela, and Myers's perception of Raniere and Daniela as an "us."

"It is my perception he thinks extremely highly of you," she wrote to Raniere on June 10, 2008. "I have been making a very conscious effort to make sure he has the right idea about you for a long time now. If he is weird around you, the only reason I can think of, and I doubt it is a real reason, is if he thought you were competition." (At trial, Daniela explained that the "competition" concept was one drilled into her by Unterreiner.)

In her email, Daniela proposed that she pull back on all "indulgent" interaction with Myers. She wrote that he already knew about her character flaws, listing anger, lying, pride, entitlement, and "sneaking behavior." She suggested that stopping all interaction might be necessary at some point, but that it could be interpreted as "an order coming from elsewhere (possibly you) not me."

In later emails, Raniere riffed on this theme some more: "Part of the problem is a perception that consequences had to be imposed or suggested to you. It should never be a consequence has to be suggested or imposed," he wrote. "Because you allowed this, any changes are likely to be seen as imposed."

On the witness stand Daniela called this "absurd dissection" typical of Raniere's paranoid, impossible demands. "Part of my breach is that people saw me as a victim," Daniela explained. "There was a very intense focus on precisely making it look like it wasn't that way."

Raniere responded to Daniela's self-flagellation with more crude judgment. "I think you have missed a lot. I think you are still trying to balance things," he wrote. "Do you understand what you have destroyed? What sort of hurt is this? Was/is this in the name of not hurting Ben? Although this might seem disjoint [sic], when was the last time you were with Ben kissing? More? Have you ever had an orgasm with him?"

Daniela testified that extreme disclosure was a theme throughout her exchanges with Raniere and could be requested of her at any moment, often seeming to come out of nowhere. The interrogation style resembles that of a "security check" in Scientology. In response she would give highly detailed play-by-play accounts of her makeout sessions. She felt shame in having to recount her most intimate moments, but at the time, she thought Raniere was trying to help her untangle her own neuroses in a "clinical," if unconventional, way. "These are a little hard to read," Daniela said in court, looking back with a decade of perspective. "In that mindset and just going back there—it's a little upsetting. This is just a perverted curiosity, or I don't know what other type of manipulation and control."

Raniere reminded Daniela that she wasn't "pure" anymore—a concept that would come up again with at least one of his other young victims. "I had been a virgin and I had never been with anybody

before, so he always acted very proud of that, and when my relationship with Ben started, took place, that was one of the main things that
he brought up—that I was no longer pure," she testified.

Shaming worked. Raniere succeeded in making Daniela believe
she'd caused a lot of damage, and that fixing it would be an enormous, difficult task. She also believed that her complete cooperation
was necessary because her being in the country was a liability for
NXIVM. But the more Daniela conceded that she'd acted unethi-
cally, the more outlandish and punishing Raniere's vision of justice
became. If she was really committed to healing her ethical breach, he
told her, she'd want to live in "speechless, monk-like seclusion" until
the task was done.

Throughout this time, Daniela's family didn't know the real reason
why she was reluctantly swearing off all "entertainment" and worldly
connection under Raniere and her coaches' direction. They wanted
her to be a part of the community, to share meals and spend time with
them. "It's like my world closed in on me," Daniela testified. "I felt like
my life was becoming extremely isolated."

Daniela was living with her parents and younger sister Camila in
a boxy townhouse with pastel yellow siding at the end of a crowded
Clifton Park court. It was just a five-minute walk from the Flintlock
house and a five-minute drive from the gym where the NXIVM community played volleyball—but Daniela was expected to stay away
from both.

In January 2009, Daniela discovered she'd made a grave mistake
by appearing briefly at a party. In unanswered emails to Raniere in
which she'd asked permission to attend, she said that people were
starting to worry about her and that a short visit would help them
understand she was alive and well and busy working toward her
goals. Afterward Raniere wrote that she'd caused irreparable damage by reinforcing a "captive" narrative about her breach-healing
program.

"During volleyball, Fluffy [Daniela's brother] kept on implying I
needed to give you permission to go," Raniere wrote about the party.
"I told him it was up to you in a puzzled fashion. This belief of your
imprisonment is your direct doing. If you said or had said something
like 'I can't stand anything until I fixed myself,' no one would bother

you. What you do promote is 'I love the social life, I love parties, I love the limelight . . . but I can't go, I just can't.' The translation: the evil ogre Keith is keeping me in the castle."

Though Raniere seemed able to will his own version of events into existence by repeating it over and over, his command over Daniela faltered at times. In March 2009 she wrote to him that the "illusion has been shattered" and that she didn't have the "ethical strength" to do what Raniere insisted was right. "I have been thinking more and more about creating a life for myself, one that does not necessitate your presence," she wrote. "I feel very trapped/cornered by the way things are right now. I would like to be able to at least sustain myself, pay my rent, pay for my food, pay for my health, etc, but with the restraints imposed on me, I can't work on anything else."

Daniela anticipated that Raniere would attempt to break her "prideful" line of thinking with further punishment and coaching, just as he'd done hundreds of times before. She knew that expressing desire for anything other than Raniere was grounds for more discipline, and yet she repeated that she wanted to leave Albany and start an independent life.

RANIERE'S NEXT MOVE was to get Daniela's family to sign on as disciplinarians. Raniere and his inner circle stressed that Daniela's parents were part of her upbringing and therefore bore some responsibility for her ethical breach.

Daniela's family still didn't know about her sexual relationship with Raniere, so they couldn't understand what had actually caused the conflict in the first place. They still believed him to be one of the world's most ethical thinkers, able to spot honor and injustice where others couldn't. With the help of his inner circle, Raniere convinced them that it was Daniela who had lied, manipulated, stolen, destroyed, and played mind games with them by pretending to be a victim.

"I remember getting really angry all the time," Daniela testified, "and telling everybody, 'You don't understand.' Telling my parents, 'You don't understand anything. You don't understand anything about this.' . . . There were a few things that happened that made it very clear for me that anything I told my parents, they were not gonna believe me. . . . Now they were on Keith's team."

With Daniela's parents involving themselves, the situation escalated quickly. They took away her phone, computer, books, personal documents, and even her bed. "They told me I need a consequence because I spent my entire life being very indulgent and destructive without consequences, so it was winter and they locked me out of the house."

Daniela said she was in shock. She wrestled with the door handle, certain the door couldn't actually be locked. "I couldn't believe it, so I kept knocking on the door because it was cold outside. I didn't have anything on me. I had no money, I had no food."

For days, as she went without basic necessities, Daniela was left with her own thoughts. She thought about how her own parents were acting out Raniere's cruel instructions and not listening to her. But before she could think about how to repair her relationship with her family, she had to find food and shelter. "I went to a laundromat and a man thought that I was a homeless person and he gave me a five-dollar bill," Daniela recalled. "With that I bought the cheapest snacks that I could find so they would last a long time. I just kept walking and checking back into the house to see if they would let me in."

Daniela checked back repeatedly over multiple days before her parents finally allowed her inside again. She was grateful just to be home once more and told her parents she was sorry. At trial she said she couldn't recall her exact words, but that they were "all the right things."

Karen Unterreiner and Daniela's mother began coaching her on how to apologize to Raniere. "I remember my mom saying, 'If it's an apology and it's a sincere one, that's healing your breach because that's where it starts,'" she testified. She was instructed to visit Raniere at his executive library to apologize.

Daniela was allowed to walk over unsupervised, which she recalls was unusual given how closely she was being monitored at the time. "I knocked on the door and Keith opened the door," she said. He was expecting her. "I knew what I had to do." She looked at Raniere, but she couldn't find the words. "I just could not apologize. I just had nothing to apologize about," she recalled. "So he closed the door and I left."

FROM THEN ON, Daniela's punishment seemed inescapable. It was hard to imagine how it could get any worse, but Daniela suspected she would soon find out. "I was begging to go back to Mexico. I had given up," she said. "I told my parents I just want a simple life."

Her mother, Adriana, seemed to think Daniela had a point. Maybe it would be good for her to return to their home country and earn a living for herself. Daniela would need some help from the family to get there. Because she was undocumented, she couldn't board a plane, and she'd need her Mexican documents to apply for jobs in her home country. A ride south, her birth certificate, and maybe some cash to get settled—that was all Daniela wanted, more than anything else in the world.

But Raniere talked Adriana out of assisting her daughter with this plan. In a recorded conversation on March 3, 2010, he compared Daniela's ethical breach to hitting a toddler with a car. Adriana's English comprehension wasn't as good as that of her bilingual daughters—"She doesn't have an extensive vocabulary," Daniela testified—and so Marianna, the only other person there when Raniere spoke with Adriana, translated for her mother. Raniere said that Daniela asking for help leaving the country was equivalent to a child killer asking to go on a vacation. He said she was acting without any conscience or care. It's not clear whether Adriana understood that Raniere was repeatedly using the dead toddler as an analogy. She had no idea what Daniela's ethical breach actually entailed, and it seems possible that she believed her daughter had hurt or killed someone. The conversation ended when Daniela's father, Hector, arrived and reminded the family about a meeting they had to attend with Nancy Salzman and Karen Unterreiner.

Nancy's daughter, Lauren, was also brought in to help deal with the "Dani problem." Raniere called Lauren and told her about Daniela's misbehavior—that she was stealing food from her family, wasn't doing work she'd committed to, and had gone off her weight-loss program and gained forty pounds. "What he proposed," Lauren testified, "was that Dani be given an ultimatum that she go in her room with no distractions and come up with a plan for how to fix this or be sent back to Mexico."

Lauren asked Raniere why he wanted her to take on this project. Raniere framed it as an essential growth opportunity, a way to learn how to deal with a manipulative and sociopathic personality. The project, he said, would prepare her for future high-stakes parenting situations—for instance if a kidnapper called asking for a ransom. Lauren was still hanging on to her belief that Raniere would be the one to make her a mother. As she understood it, she had to take on the Dani project to prove herself as a worthy parent.

"I thought that Keith understood everything about people's psychodynamics," Lauren Salzman said of her belief in Raniere at the time. "If Keith observed something and I couldn't see it, it was because I didn't understand and needed to learn something." Raniere told Salzman that Daniela's family felt responsible for her out-of-control behavior and that they saw seclusion in a room as the best option. "He said the family was concerned that she might extend the time in the room or view it as a type of vacation," Lauren recalled. "And so in order to make it less comfortable and to inspire her to want to get out of the room quickly, they were going to remove anything comfortable from the room."

ABOUT A WEEK later, Daniela's family sat her down with Lauren Salzman and Karen Unterreiner. Lauren recalled that the family appeared sad and ashamed. Daniela testified that they presented her with a "horrifying" idea.

"Listen, you can't go back to Mexico. If you go back to Mexico it's on our terms," Daniela said she was told. She had only one other option: stay in her bedroom with only a pen and some paper until her ethical breach was healed. "If you are not willing to do that, then you go back to Mexico but not on your terms," they said, according to Daniela. "You lose your family, you go with nothing."

Though her family would remain under the same roof if she chose to isolate, Daniela was terrified by the uncertain end date. Her room had already been stripped of furniture, photos, books, and everything else that reminded her she was home. "No way," Daniela said. "There's no way I was going into that room, because I had no idea what I had to do to heal my ethical breach. I had been trying to heal my ethical breach for years."

She was given one day to think about it. She didn't want to lose her family, because, she said, they were the only link she had to anything in the world. She tried desperately to think of a third option.

"I remember I walked to Walmart with a few cents, and from a pay phone, I called Ben," she testified. "They had taken my phone, they had taken my computer. I didn't have anybody in the world except my family. I thought Ben, Ben will get me out of here."

She hadn't talked to him for a long time, but Daniela knew Ben's number by heart. When she dialed it, he didn't pick up. "I waited and I waited and I tried again and he did not pick up," she said. "I went back home and I slept on it and the next day, I realized I had no choice."

THE RULES OF the room were not negotiable. The door wasn't locked and the family brought her three meals a day, but Daniela wasn't allowed to talk to anyone. She had no books or reading material, no music, and her parents and siblings made every effort not to show their faces. At mealtimes Daniela would hear a knock at the door, but by the time she opened it there was just a plate on the floor. She shared a bathroom with her family and was allowed to write them notes, but they agreed not to respond.

Lauren Salzman was the only person permitted to speak with Daniela face to face. She showed up on the second day and reminded Daniela about the commitment she'd made and the consequences she'd encounter if she didn't follow through. Daniela asked questions and listened for clues about how to fix her ethical breach. She thought that if she wrote down the right combination of words, either an apology or an ethical breach plan, that would be the key to her freedom.

Over time Salzman's coaching visits grew less and less frequent. Daniela described not wanting Salzman to ever leave, and then "hating" her when she did. "Sometimes she would take three days to come. . . . [Then it was] a whole week of seeing no one. Not a human being, not a face, not a nothing. . . . And then time passed and there was a point where I didn't see her for up to three months."

In a notebook she kept at the time, Daniela drew the view from her foam mattress on the floor. The yellow walls are bare, the door is closed in front of her, and there are no windows in sight; she testified that the only window was papered over for much of her time in confinement. Daniela also spent time translating the labels on salad containers and shampoo bottles. "I would take all of these materials and I would write all the words in English and all the translations into French, and I would make a dictionary," she testified. "I was just trying to keep myself busy and I was trying to have a schedule." To keep her mind occupied, Daniela fantasized about the simple task of walking to Walmart. She imagined opening the door, stepping out of the house, counting her steps down the street. "'Remember, the first aisle has this,' and I would try to think of the music," she said. "I would try to construct something inside my head so I wouldn't go crazy, because sometimes I would go crazy."

She experienced wild mood swings, sometimes feeling panicked and destructive, and after that numb for days. "I would just lose control of myself," she said. "There were times where I just remember, like, laying on the carpet and scratching my arms and wanting to scream, but I knew I wasn't allowed to. . . . There were entire days where I would just sit against the wall."

In emails presented as evidence, Salzman described a note Daniela wrote on November 8, 2010, that signaled her deteriorating mental state. "Let me out. I'm coming undone," it read. Daniela's sister Camila found it, and she texted Lauren asking permission to speak with Daniela. Camila didn't want to show it to her parents, because they would be alarmed and might take "reactionary" action.

Salzman relayed the message to Raniere and pledged to visit Daniela early the next morning to explain that resisting the project this way was a major setback. "This focus of 'letting me out of the room' is totally in the opposite direction of healing the breach," Salzman wrote in an email to Raniere. If the family spoke to Daniela, or let her out of the room, she would learn she could throw a tantrum and get what she wanted.

DANIELA STARTED a newsletter she called the *Wilton Times*, named after the keyhole-shaped street outside the family townhouse. In a cheery, tongue-in-cheek tabloid voice, Daniela logged daily activities of "the resident" (and sometimes Lauren, "the visitor") in neatly printed Spanish. "Our editors? Unqualified and just barely passable, but eager! Our reporters? The most daring and reliable! Our sources? There are none more exclusive!" she wrote in a signed editor's note on November 11, 2010.

In one entry, more than eight months into her confinement, Daniela announced an "exclusive!": the resident had impulsively cut her hair. Included with the report was a "before" drawing of waist-long hair and an "after" sketch of a bob reaching just below her ears. "The breaking news on a totally unexpected makeover," reads a subheading styled with precise serif touches. Daniela "transitioned from looking like a Disney princess to a hybrid of Prince Valiant and Mafalda," she wrote, referring to a popular Argentine comic strip about a six-year-old girl with an oversized peanut-shaped head. "The sources also report that her head looks about twice as big!!"

"I remember it was something I could control, something I could do—cut my hair because it's mine," Daniela recalled at Raniere's trial. She knew Raniere liked long hair and that he wouldn't have allowed her to cut it if she'd asked. "I remember I made a braid. I was wearing a blue shirt," she said. "I remember looking in the mirror and looking at my short hair and being satisfied."

In the same two-page issue of the *Wilton Times*, Daniela listed her weight at 120 pounds and her daily calorie intake at 940. She reported that after some back pain, she'd returned to doing fifteen hundred jumping jacks per day: five hundred before breakfast, five hundred before lunch, and five hundred before dinner. She expressed excitement at reaching sixty days of writing a daily letter, and pledged to swear off naps. "Today I have squeezed the most I possibly could out of the day, the maximum of what I have been able to imagine," she wrote. "No more naps or long moments staring into space. I have a purpose in mind and it is to heal my broken pieces."

Daniela's excitement dissipated after Raniere found out about her hair. He told Salzman that Daniela's haircut violated an important agreement between them. He asked Salzman to take a photo of Daniela so that she'd know he'd seen the result of her reckless behavior. Salzman said, "He told me that she should come up with a way to fix that, and that a way to fix that was staying in the room until the hair grew back. He thought that she would feel bad if he saw it and that would somehow inspire her to change something."

In a November 15 entry of the *Wilton Times*, Daniela wrote about the "harmful act" of cutting her hair and the consequences she'd been asked to impose on herself. She acknowledged that it was a "blunder" and agreed to let it grow back, but resisted the idea of staying in the room for the duration. "This seems really unreasonable to me and I'm still in shock about it," she wrote.

"The hair thing was so ridiculous, to me it seemed like a game," Daniela testified. "Like, tomorrow I'll do something else and they're gonna extend it eight years."

For the first time since she'd entered the room, Daniela had seen a possible endpoint to her confinement, and it was a terrifyingly long time away. She suggested alternative consequences, including spending a week living outside in the cold, water fasting for ten days, and sleeping only four hours a night for a month. All of these were preferred to staying in the room for the years it would take her hair to grow back.

"The action of cutting my hair is much more serious than I wanted to see or think," Daniela wrote, seemingly coming to grips with her lack of control over the situation. "Decisions like this one are a great part of the way I have lived until now, which has been so indulgent and harmful, and it is precisely this life and this decision process that I came to this room to heal."

Only weeks after it began, Daniela's newsletter was deemed an indulgence and an ethical breach. The *Wilton Times* was discontinued.

LAUREN SALZMAN WANTED to let Daniela guide her own healing program, but Raniere was against it. "I would spend time with her and I thought that we had made progress, and he told me that she had just been manipulating me for hours and I couldn't see it," Salzman said. Raniere told her that Daniela was having temper tantrums, or playing games, and that she was creating more work for him by not being able to negotiate the situation properly on her own. "I felt that somehow I was screwing it up in my ineptitude and my failure to be able to see what was going on, which he seemed to think was so obvious."

Raniere always had an explanation for why Daniela wasn't progressing or was possibly getting worse. "I was really mad at her for not figuring out whatever she was supposed to be doing to end this for herself and for all of us," Salzman testified, her voice wavering with emotion. "I thought she was playing games and being manipulative with me and I couldn't figure that out."

Adriana felt deep responsibility and guilt about her daughter's situation. She'd been caught leaving notes for her in the bathroom, which Raniere said was interfering with the project. He told Salzman that Adriana had agreed to go into a second room and experience the same discomfort until Daniela healed her breach. The arrangement was aimed at motivating Daniela to make progress quickly. She needed to know that her actions were hurting somebody else, too.

In theory Adriana was supposed to experience exactly the same conditions as Daniela, but in practice this wasn't the case. "Adriana within a short period of time had many things in the room, like exercise equipment or art supplies," Salzman testified. "At one point she had a pet fish, and she was making kombucha and sprouting vegetables." Family members ate meals in Adriana's room and kept her company while Daniela was still cut off from all communication. After a few months, Adriana left the room to attend a funeral in Mexico and never returned.

On the witness stand Lauren Salzman expressed deep guilt and shame over her role in confining Daniela and splitting apart her family. "Of all the things that I did in this case and the crimes that I committed," she said, breaking into sobs, "I think that this is the worst."

Daniela wasn't supposed to suffer in the room; she was supposed to focus on what she was learning through the experience. But she did suffer, sometimes physically. For months she wrote to Salzman about tooth pain, and eventually part of her tooth broke off before she was taken to a dentist.

Around V-Week in 2011, Daniela heard her brother and another NXIVM member talking about installing security cameras outside her room. "I thought I was helping her," Adrian, her brother, told a judge.

It's hard to imagine how so many people in Daniela's life went along with such cruelty, why they didn't stand up for her. This question weighed on Daniela, too. She often fell into a disorienting despair when she wondered why her own family wasn't putting an end to her confinement.

There's no satisfying answer for why Daniela's family didn't stand up for her. Lauren Salzman suggested they thought that above all else they needed to maintain their relationship with Raniere. "All of our perspectives were highly influenced by Keith's perspectives," she said. "We wanted him to think that we would do the hard thing, the ethical thing, and wanted him to see us as people who were willing to do that."

Salzman and both of Daniela's sisters were in sexual relationships with Raniere and wanted to prove to him their own commitment to and worthiness of motherhood. He knew their most unflattering secrets. Precarious immigration status weighed on the whole family. They were caught up in the same fear-based tunnel vision that later propelled women inside the secret NXIVM sorority known as DOS to do unspeakable things.

MORE THAN a year and a half into Daniela's confinement, she made some attempts to reach the outside world. "I was desperate to just be able to read something," she said. One day, when nobody was in the house, she snuck down the stairs and used her mother's PlayStation to scan the internet. She also managed to look at photos of her family by guessing her father's Facebook password. She said that seeing the fullness of their lives overwhelmed her with emotion.

"It was the saddest thing, because I remember I was able to check my email, from that PSP, and I remember nobody had written me.

"There was one email from Ben on my birthday the year prior, with like, 'Happy birthday!' But I was gone from the world and nobody noticed," she said. "I remember I cried for days and days.

"Nobody came and got me. My own family didn't come," she testified. "They didn't say, 'Enough, it's our daughter.' My mom didn't say, 'Hey, I made her, maybe she deserves to live her life.' They didn't come. They didn't get me."

DANIELA HIT HER lowest moment in winter 2012. "I started accumulating cleaning supplies and I thought, 'As soon as I have enough, I'll just drink everything and it will be over soon,'" she testified. "It was gonna be over, you know. I wasn't afraid. I was just gonna do it.

"I looked out the window and there was a bird that I'd been watching. I had seen this family of birds over a few years. And it was a red bird, and I later identified it as a cardinal. It had babies. It had nested in front of my window. I had seen it. And I think like for the winter he had disappeared for a while and this day he came back—it was a he, according to me.

"I don't know what it was about that bird, but in that moment I remember thinking, 'I want to live.'"

Daniela had reached a tipping point. She had accepted that she might never see her family again, and might soon find herself destitute in an unfamiliar Mexican city. It didn't matter to her anymore; she was determined to leave the room. "I remember thinking ridiculous things. I remember thinking I can be a drug addict, I can be a prostitute, I can do anything because I'm gonna die anyway, and there was a sense of freedom."

Daniela opened the door and walked past the security camera, out of the house, and onto the street. Later she headed for the volleyball court where she knew Raniere would be. "I wanted to go tell Keith because he was the one who put me there," she testified. "I wanted to know why."

A game was already underway when Daniela arrived. She was overwhelmed by the sight of so many familiar faces, all of them surprised to see her.

"I remember Keith running to hide," Daniela said. A crowd formed around her, and Raniere faded into the background. "I could not get through those people. Someone pulled me aside and Keith was out of reach."

Almost two years had passed since Daniela had first heard Raniere's ultimatum, but she knew the stakes were just as high as the day she went into the room. By appearing at volleyball that day, she had publicly broken her commitment to resolve her ethical breach. She knew it meant she'd be sent back to Mexico under the harshest imaginable circumstances: no money, no documents, no family contact. She would still need to settle her conflict with Raniere if she ever wanted to see her siblings and parents.

Daniela testified that she was able to pack a few days' worth of clothes, a journal, and some gold earrings she planned to pawn once she crossed the border. She also took about fifty dollars' worth of pesos from her father's wallet before getting into the back seat of a car headed for Laredo, Texas, where she would cross the border by foot.

Her father and NXIVM fixer Kristin Keeffe sat in the front seat. Keeffe supervised Daniela's interactions with her dad. When they arrived for an overnight stay at a hotel, Daniela learned she was not allowed to stay in the same room as her father. She recalled finding some alone time in the hotel gym, watching television news for the first time in years from a treadmill. In 2012, violence breaking out at Mexico's northern border was a global story.

"Please do everything you need to do to get back to us," Hector told his daughter when the time came to part ways. Both of them cried, Daniela testified. "It's going to be hard," he said, "but you can do it."

PART THREE

A Place of Survival

CHAPTER NINETEEN

The Act

M aja Miljkovic's introduction to NXIVM began with a flirtation in an acting class.

"As happens with ridiculous scenes in acting class, you work together and then you go, 'Oh hey, maybe I like you,'" she says.

The flirtation with her scene partner led to a date, and about a week into their relationship, Miljkovic's new man friend asked if she'd ever heard of NXIVM. She knew of a few actors in town who'd mentioned the name, but she didn't know what the classes were about. He said it was a group of actors helping each other set goals and stick to them. Some of them were kind of famous. The classes would help her connect with her emotions, face fears, and deal with rejection.

To Miljkovic, it sounded social, challenging, fun. The next week she went to an open house hosted by Sarah Edmondson and immediately saw the vision of success she wanted.

"For an up-and-coming actor it was like getting invited to an Oscar party," she told me. "I signed up on the spot. I didn't think twice."

I MET MILJKOVIC for the first time in July 2018. She picked me up from a bus stop on the outskirts of Vancouver and drove me to her suburban home perched on Burnaby Mountain, where the grid of

East Vancouver stretched out like a mostly green, slightly dirty crocheted blanket. She gestured with a bottle of pink wine she'd picked up, joking that we were going to need it.

In 2013 Miljkovic became part of an in-crowd of Vancouver actors who attended NXIVM classes on evenings and weekends. She was captivated by the "aha!" moments the classes seemed to inspire in people and wanted to learn to recreate those feelings in a performance or script. Edmondson and Miljkovic's boyfriend both urged her to take upper-level courses as a way to encourage that creative path.

In level two classes like "Mobius," students did a lot more feeling and exploring. Mobius was known as the "self-love intensive." In a typical exercise, people would think of a time when they felt angry with someone and then ask themselves, Why were you angry with them? What were they doing? Why were they doing it? After some reflection on each of these questions, the exercise would flip. What about when someone was angry with you? Why were they angry? What did you do? Why did you do it? The process would then be repeated, but with a new emotion, like love, replacing anger.

At the end of a Mobius intensive, all students would make a vow. One might declare they'd never eat red meat again, another might promise to never text a certain ex. The point was to say it out loud, confirm it, and get some peer accountability going. At the end of "Human Pain," another intensive that often followed Mobius, students would form a "penance group," where failures would be punished with cold showers or plank exercises—something hard or uncomfortable to serve as a deterrent. DOS wouldn't be created for another two years, but some of the elements that would define it were already taking shape.

WHEN MAJA MILJKOVIC started climbing the course ladder, NXIVM was going through a period of rapid expansion and innovation. Vancouver's community was especially vibrant, well on its way to two hundred regularly attending students. The inner circle in Albany could see there was a new cohort of young people primed and eager to help expand the curriculum into the realms of fitness, ethical media, and creative arts.

As Edmondson's self-help classes filled up with more local actors, conversation turned to the possibility that NXIVM would one day offer formal acting classes. Miljkovic was particularly keen on the idea, pursuing it with Edmondson in the summer of 2013. If the company was developing an acting curriculum, she wanted to be part of it.

Miljkovic was twenty-six when she first visited Albany for V-Week in August 2013. There she met Raniere, who didn't fit the vision of the wise, nurturing teacher she'd had in her head. Other students had gushed about his "magnetic" presence, but standing in front of her, he appeared unimpressive and a bit robotic. "I was like, You're kind of weird. Why do people think you're cute?" she says.

But Miljkovic quickly came around to thinking Raniere was at least "deep." He invited her to share whatever she was struggling with and listened carefully while she tried to articulate whatever was on her mind. His advice sounded philosophical and tinged with an urgency that suggested NXIVM really needed her to succeed.

Raniere seemed to know already that Miljkovic was interested in a NXIVM program that catered to actors. One night, during a gathering at Allison Mack's house in Clifton Park, he told her that he could use her help in testing out a new program called "Ultima."

It was a big deal to be invited to Ultima. The "tech" was supposed to apply to all the creative and athletic fields Miljkovic and her peers were excited about. Miljkovic said she'd love to be a part of it but that she had to go back to Canada.

"Keith was like, 'Why? Why don't you want to stay?'" she recalls.

Raniere wouldn't let her say no. He was pulling out the "specify, isolate, overcome" routine.

"What would you need to stay?" he asked. "Money, a visa, a house— what if we could get you all of that?"

Miljkovic looked around the room and for a second felt star-struck. Here she was at Allison Mack's house, with Mark Hildreth and Kristanna Loken, two actors with exceedingly long IMDb pages, being asked to help start a new acting class. By the end of the night, Raniere had convinced her to stay in Albany to help make the NXIVM acting curriculum a reality.

The aim of Ultima was to "put your emotions, thoughts, and physical body on a slider scale," Miljkovic explains. It was like being a sound engineer, turning your own feelings, thoughts, and physicality up and down on command. Richard Bandler, founder of neuro-linguistic programming, told audiences they could access a similar "control panel" in their brains. "That meant, if you were an athlete, you could turn down your emotions all the way—have zero feelings—and have your body be all the way up to 100 percent physicality," she says. An actor, on the other hand, might want to dial physicality to 80 percent, thinking to 5 percent, and emotions to 90 percent.

Miljkovic learned that the Ultima curriculum testing would start up in December and run for six months. She called her boyfriend in Vancouver and told him she was going to remain in Albany. "He was not supportive of the fact that I had made the decision by myself to stay in Albany without him," she says. They broke up, which gave her one less reason to return to Vancouver.

MAJA MILJKOVIC MOVED in with Allison Mack and Mark Vicente and was enlisted to help shoot interviews for a few of Vicente's film projects. Since 2007 Vicente had been working on a documentary that aimed to debunk so-called lies about Raniere; he'd already amassed thousands of hours of footage. Miljkovic drew up questions for on-camera sessions with Sara and Clare Bronfman, Pamela Cafritz, and other high-ranking execs. She was paid $15 an hour, usually in credit toward her next class.

Miljkovic grew close to Mack, Vicente, and his new partner, actor Bonnie Piesse, whom he married in 2011. On Miljkovic's twenty-seventh birthday, Mack threw a party for her. "She was like, 'I know you like to drink, so for this one time we'll have booze in the house,'" Miljkovic recalls.

Though Miljkovic had arrived in the United States on a tourist visa, everyone around her seemed confident that Clare Bronfman would help sort out her work status. (NXIVM's proposed visa strategy would later result in Miljkovic's short-lived marriage to motivational speaker Marc Elliot. The marriage ended soon after a U.S. customs investigation in 2014.) The company seemed to have a number of new causes on the go, from peacekeeping in Mexico to research about Tourette's syndrome. The important thing for the time being was to keep busy and focused—doing the kind of creative work she actually wanted to do full time.

But despite her early enthusiasm, she couldn't help noticing signs that the NXIVM community wasn't as forward-thinking as it seemed on paper. One of the first glimpses of this came during one of Raniere's signature late-night volleyball games. Going to watch Keith play volleyball was a big deal for many, but not for Miljkovic. Allison Mack roped her into attending, and she immediately recoiled at the scene. "It was just women sitting on the sidelines in their little cliques, and only men playing volleyball," she says. It was a cartoonish performance of masculinity and femininity, with young women seemingly losing their minds in excitement every time Raniere connected with the ball. "I was like, *Eww.* There's nothing I hate more than all-male sport with all the women cheering for them."

Miljkovic liked volleyball well enough, if she was able to play it. But in Raniere's universe, apparently women just weren't good enough players to compete on his court. Miljkovic knew of just one woman, a former high school volleyball star, who was allowed to break the unspoken gender divide and play with Keith's "pros." If enough "amateurs" showed up, women would sometimes join a second game off to the side. But the real game people came to watch was between Keith and his regular dude competitors. This was accepted by nearly everyone who attended.

When Miljkovic asked why it was only men on the court one night, Raniere said it was men who always showed up. They brought the equipment, set up the nets, and took everything down at the end of the night. Women were less consistent in their attendance and skill, he told her. That's why they didn't get to play.

Miljkovic pushed back. She said she had the same level of skill as the rest of them and wasn't interested in the "amateur" side of the gym. So, as the game continued, she was made to prove herself in a series of drills. A friend named Mike spiked the ball at her on the sidelines and she hustled to return it, not exactly eager to jump through more hoops or be the target of more doubts. The strange side spectacle lasted until Raniere deemed her capable enough to join the real game.

The gameplay itself was anticlimactic; Miljkovic remembers virtually nothing about the teams or the score. "He let me play for two games," she says, "and then Keith was like, 'You should work on this, and next time do this.'" Raniere wasn't the best athlete—far from it, according to Miljkovic—but he was quick to enforce the rules. His coaching felt like being publicly berated, which made her fume in silence. "I was like, Fuck that. You missed half of your own shots, buddy."

It seemed straight-up sexist to exclude women from a recreational game of volleyball, but it wasn't enough to make her question NXIVM's world-changing credentials.

BY THE TIME Ultima got started, another fifty students had paid their own way to Albany just to be part of the teaching experiment that would spawn acting, journalism, and personal training spinoffs. Many of these students were from Vancouver with a specific interest in writing and acting. Some of the women would stay in Albany permanently, anchored by secret relationships with Raniere.

The acting group consisted of about ten people, including Mack. The group would meet up at a Clifton Park clubhouse called Apropos and test out acting exercises one by one. Then they'd report back on how they felt, what they found useful, what they thought should become a core part of what was then called "Ultima Acting." All the sessions were recorded on video, Miljkovic says.

One of the exercises she remembers was called "Masks," in which students would usually pair up and face each other, then one actor would mirror the other's facial expressions as closely as they could. "From imitating their face," Miljkovic explains, "you would try to feel what they may be feeling." The theory behind this went against the grain of contemporary acting: if an actor has an emotional scene to get through, many acting coaches will advise them to call up a memory that evokes those strong emotions and let their inner feelings animate their face and body. And yet "Keith argued you could do the opposite," she says. His students began with face and body language, then attempted to feel it on the inside. It was an "outside in" way of feeling emotion rather than "inside out."

When Miljkovic wasn't with the actors, she often joined a group of about twenty in Nancy Salzman's basement for "Ultima Ethical Media" sessions, where they discussed journalism, media spin, and how to counter it. The downstairs space, outfitted with a cluster of chairs around a table, was sometimes called the "war room." Many NXIVM students from the acting and fitness groups attended these sessions, which were also captured on video. Raniere lectured on writing techniques and the separation of "data" and "emotion."

NXIVM's flagship classes already taught the separation of different classes of data, categorizing most traditional reporting as "hearsay" or "once removed." The strongest source of data, according to Raniere's teaching, was firsthand experience that was consistent and verified by others. By this measure, the journalists who wrote about NXIVM were failing at their jobs because they lacked the firsthand experience of taking courses. They were just circulating secondhand information.

In 2014, Rosa Laura Junco, whose family owned a media empire in Mexico, became the CEO of a NXIVM-inspired media criticism website called The Knife of Aristotle, later shortened to The Knife. Raniere said a knife could be a life-saving instrument or a murder weapon, and that the media could be harnessed as a similar tool. He encouraged Miljkovic and others to cut through the noise and separate truth from fiction. Actor Nicki Clyne became one of the site's main coordinators, teaching new writers to dissect articles appearing in the Albany *Times Union* and other news outlets.

Leading up to the site's launch, Miljkovic practiced highlighting spin words, separating data, and rating the reliability of various news sources. She also helped prepare a script to enroll new contributors, who were asked to pay $2,000 for four weeks of training. "Who here would like access to news which reflects the truth of what is happening in your world? News that adheres to ethical standards?" read the presentation script. "Currently whatever is published by media is forever stored as human history. But media does not have strong standards. It's subjective, skewed, and being spun a certain way. . . . When we consume this skewed media it distorts our perception of reality."

The pitch went on to say that Keith Raniere had guided the development of a news analysis "product" that would raise media standards "forever." "What we need is scientific media. Media with high standards and a code of ethics which goes through a rigorous, verifiable analysis to ensure it really is what it says it is."

WHEN THE ETHICAL media group wasn't talking about news or data collection, the lectures turned to creative writing.

"We have to indoctrinate readers," Raniere told a room of aspiring writers, including Clyne, Mack, and Miljkovic. He talked about using conditioning techniques to play with associations in readers' heads, claiming that someone with the right indoctrination skills could invoke a specific voice or accent just by typing in italics or a different font color. At one point he launched into a monologue about hypnosis and neuro-linguistic programming, adding that a skilled hypnotist could communicate messages "totally outside the person's awareness."

When we met in 2018, Miljkovic didn't immediately recall Raniere's lecturing about the power of hypnosis and neuro-linguistic programming. She'd attended and filmed what seemed like hundreds of hours of sessions, but the closest thing she could remember was Raniere making a party trick out of putting senior counselor Barbara Jeske's Maltese puppy to sleep using a sleepy expression in his eyes. He then turned his "magical sleep eyes" on his students. "He was trying to do that to a bunch of us, and I was behind the camera," Miljkovic says. "Like when I yawn, you want to yawn—that's what he's trying to do."

There was good reason to yawn. Students like Miljkovic were staying up late doing "ethical media" prep for what would become The Knife and then getting up at five a.m. to attend yoga sessions that would eventually become the basis of yet another new NXIVM curriculum. Many women were also going on late-night, one-on-one walks with Raniere to talk about their own business ideas. There was so much overlap between the acting, journalism, fitness, and creative projects that students would often sacrifice sleep to absorb as much of it as humanly possible.

EACH NEW CURRICULUM and company was an opportunity to bring in more money and people. All the successful ones followed a similar recruitment and pay structure, with 10 percent of dues going back to their "philosophical founder." This was the case for Jness, the women's group Raniere founded, and a men's group called the Society of Protectors. Both groups charged a $50 monthly membership in exchange for guided discussions about femininity and masculinity, plus extra for intensives. These organizations were seen as successful, long-lasting expansions of the NXIVM universe, following a familiar multi-level marketing blueprint. Like all recruitment-based businesses, they were not profitable for most members. Studies have found fewer than one percent of multi-level marketing participants make any money.

But Raniere had a more ambitious plan for Ultima and reserved the biggest potential price tag for special acting classes led by a real Hollywood actor. After six months of class development, Allison Mack became the de facto leader of Ultima Acting—eventually renamed the Source—but not without a power struggle. At the time, Mack, who'd advanced only to a yellow sash, had taken to regularly meeting in private with Raniere. Higher-ranking students who'd put in years of work recruiting and funding new projects didn't necessarily have the same access to Vanguard.

Looking back on those classes, one participant remembers that there wasn't actually a lot of acting going on. Raniere, who would lecture the group on the importance of theater throughout history, openly acknowledged his limited knowledge of acting in a half-hour conversation with Mack meant to advertise the program, posted to YouTube in 2017.

"I come from a non-acting background. You could say I don't know what I'm talking about," he tells Mack across a round table. "It comes from a behaviorist, humanist sort of practical philosophical background dealing with communication, dealing with all sorts of things relating to the psychodynamics of people." In this video, shot in front of a stone fireplace, Raniere stresses that the key to "authentic" acting lies in unlocking the parts of oneself that are usually locked away in a "dungeon."

In the classes, former students told me, this dungeon was also called "the box"—where we hide aspects of ourselves we don't want to examine. It was a concept that took some actors to very dark places. Students were told they should be able to find it within themselves to embody the worst human traits they could imagine. One former student says this included trying to feel the lust of a child rapist. "Like you need to come to a place where you could play that character—the thing you hate most in the world—including pedophiles," Amy (not her real name) told me.

It took me a couple of tries to actually process what Amy was telling me. Somehow it was worse than I imagined. "We spent a whole day on how you should be able to rape a baby," she said. "So put yourself in a place where you could identify with a pedophile who rapes babies. If you can't, it means something is 'in the box' for you. It means it hits too close to home, so you won't go there. If it's in the box, it's because you know that trait well, meaning you have that trait within you."

Amy had a sibling who was abused by a grandparent, so she was immediately horrified by the exercise, but she didn't want to say anything for fear that the group would accuse her of being a pedophile herself. She withdrew after class to try sorting out her feelings privately. Facing typical audition fears this was not.

The acting classes were another forum in which Raniere suggested that love was something that could be measured only by pain and sacrifice. "It's not that love doesn't contain moments of happiness or moments of joy," he says to Mack in the same 2017 video, as her eyes well up with emotion, "but the way we have a weight to our love, or understand love itself or the magnitude, is through pain. When we feel love, we feel pain. And the depth of pain we feel measures that love."

People who knew Mack saw that as her devotion to Raniere grew, she was suffering. She became consumed with calorie restriction and was quick to snap. Colleagues said she was becoming cruel and unhinged. It became increasingly clear that her devotion to Raniere wasn't an act; it was urgent, seemingly impossible to hold back. This was on public display at a V-Week performance in 2016, when she sang on stage about turning her own flesh and blood into "anything you demand." With her eyes closed, tears welling in the corners, she appeared to be in a state of smiling desperation.

NXIVM'S BRAND OF progressivism often seemed to emerge from highlighting the reality of gendered experiences. Raniere taught that in order to understand the roles of men and women, students needed to live them—to feel all the societal pressures and confines firsthand. This was especially prevalent in the Jness and Society of Protectors organizations, which were aimed at uncovering and harnessing innate "female" and "male" ways of being.

Unsurprisingly, the search for innate qualities meant riffing on some very tired gender stereotypes. Women had "princessy," "oblivious," and "caretaker" tendencies, while men deep down were "big beasties" ready to either fight or have sex. Mark Vicente testified that it was the men's program that first introduced "readiness" drills—a practice where members would receive a text message and have to respond to it within a minute. Later this became a source of relentless sleep deprivation and punishment for women in DOS.

In an eight-day Jness intensive, Miljkovic didn't see herself reflected at all. Women were protected from the real world and were allowed more space to be emotional, coaches suggested. They withheld sex because there wasn't much else in women's control. Breakout groups made distinctions between how women and men handled sex or child-rearing, which left Miljkovic with a lingering impression that women were supposed to be quiet and thankful "as long as you weren't being raped every day."

In Vancouver, monthly Jness meetups aimed to tackle big questions about what "womanhood" really was, but at the end a group facilitator would read out a "disquisition" that served as the final word. These debriefs claimed to be culled from psychological, sociological, and anthropological studies, but of course it was Raniere behind the rulings. This was how Raniere's "primitive hypothesis" was disseminated to the NXIVM community. "The primitive hypothesis is the thing in Jness that says men are designed to spread their seed and women are designed to be monogamous," Sarah Edmondson told me. This thinking became a shorthand used throughout the NXIVM curriculum, and a quiet point of contention for women who identified as polyamorous. Men needed sex with many partners—it was in their genes, Raniere claimed—while women were best suited to stay with one person for life.

Any woman who challenged this was viewed as a troublemaker. "If you have a problem with it, it's because you think you're special. It's the woman's problem," a former member told me.

SINCE THE JNESS intensive left Miljkovic with more questions than answers, she joined other women in signing up for the Society of Protectors sessions as well. This was encouraged as a way to build empathy for the societal roles the opposite gender had to live up to. She hoped that seeing the other side would help her put it all together.

The intensive was framed as a way for men to show women the dark and difficult parts of their own experience—to expose what it really took to excel in a male-dominated world. In this session, a NXIVM-associated doctor asked Miljkovic to wear a "brain cap"—a net of EEG electrodes that supposedly measured activity in the brain while "integrations" were happening. She agreed, which meant reluctantly becoming the focus of everyone else's attention. Participants did extended wall sits and plank exercises at the mercy of coaches instructed not to hold back any judgment, no matter how demeaning or cruel. This culminated in an aggressive reenactment of schoolyard bullying, complete with name-calling, body shaming, and other abuse Miljkovic did not see coming.

"They were being really misogynistic" toward the women in the session, she says. One woman accused of cutting in line had to wear a tiara and tutu. Any woman who acted at all assertively was told to wear a jockstrap for the rest of the day. The name Esther became "Breaster," and Bibiana became "Boobiana." In a later session, the men revealed they had surreptitiously taken photos of women's bodies and then presented a "best in show" slideshow for maximum embarrassment.

With gel in her hair and a net of electrodes on her head, Miljkovic was an easy target for childish taunts. At one point she asked the doctor if she could stop wearing the EEG monitors for the remainder of the class. She was told to keep the cap on; otherwise, the experiment would be ruined. "That's when I was like, This is not cool," she says. The same doctor lost his medical license in 2019 for conducting unsanctioned human experiments.

IT REQUIRED EXTENDED exposure to NXIVM logic to appreciate how these strange sexist and traumatizing rituals lined up with the organization's core principle of making the world a better place. NXIVM wasn't concerned with "equality" per se; it was about harnessing an individual's "potential" and showing them that growth was a hard-earned, painful process. The world was a tough place, the logic went, but NXIVM could teach you how to punish yourself for your laziness, weight gain, self-indulgence, and whatever else you deemed a personal moral failing, so that succeeding felt less tough by comparison.

Creating a mental association between physical discomfort and failure to meet a goal was simply building character and discipline—two traits that Jness coincidentally concluded were often lacking in women. But somewhere along this line, more themes of male dominance and female submission were introduced into the equation. Maja Miljkovic says that an ex-boyfriend of hers was all but convinced Raniere was trying to groom her as a "sub."

"I just want to ask you, Did anything happen between you guys?" she recalls her boyfriend saying. She was firm that Raniere favored her, and even hit on her at times, but she never saw him as a viable romantic interest. Even the suggestion that they could have hooked up made her gag.

"Are you sure?" her boyfriend said. "Because the way he's speaking to you . . . he's talking to you like a dom."

MILJKOVIC HADN'T CONSIDERED that Raniere's strange demands on her time might be part of some sexual power move. In fact, she thought the idea was pretty far-fetched. When Raniere made her wait hours in the middle of the night just to go for a walk, to her that only meant he was busy, not that he was testing how much boundary pushing she would accommodate. It was only after she learned of other women's experiences with Raniere that she started to see how she might have been groomed after all.

Raniere would occasionally summon her to his side at social gatherings. Miljkovic remembers one evening when, at an Apropos community night, where many tables of people were chatting and eating dinner, Clare Bronfman came to get her and bring her to Raniere.

"Keith would like to talk to you," Bronfman told her.

After some resistance, Miljkovic says, she agreed to leave her gluten-free pizza and go join Raniere's table. Marianna stood up from her place beside Raniere to work the crowd, leaving the two of them to chat privately. Miljkovic remembers it all feeling very *Godfather*-esque in the way Raniere commanded a room, always giving special attention to the pretty ones. Whenever he entered Apropos at the end of a day, the kitchen knew to bring pizza to his table as soon as he sat down.

Raniere seemed to test his rapport with the women he favored by applying mirroring techniques. "If he talked to you, he'd stare deeply into your eyes," Miljkovic said. "He'd physically try to get you to go where he was going. I remember he would reach out his arm—not quite touch you yet—then maybe on the third time, you'd respond in kind. Eventually you'd just be touching hands. And then he would smile, so you would smile back. He openly talked about that as something he did."

Miljkovic says she was usually quite aware of the games Raniere was playing, and that she wouldn't play along if she didn't feel like it. "I'm a great flirt, and I know how to close myself out," she told me.

But when she didn't mirror Raniere's movements the way he liked, he'd sometimes call her out on it. "Why are you so closed off?" he'd ask. Raniere told her she was sexually repressed and that it showed in the way she hugged. He said that for her sex was in "the box," the NXIVM term for something that hit too close to home, often causing a repressed or overly sensitive reaction. ("I don't tend to hug people with my crotch," Miljkovic told me wryly.) Raniere also suggested that she didn't like people thinking she was slutty. He went "on and on about it."

This constant physical boundary testing became more intense once you were part of Raniere's circle of girlfriends. Lauren Salzman testified that he would touch vaginas or breasts openly with lots of women around and then comment on how women reacted. "The reactions that we were having . . . were things we needed to get through," she said. "So we stayed and participated in things that in any other circumstance we wouldn't have."

Only a select few saw this side of Raniere, where boundaries and privacy were stripped to nothing. Many women existed on Miljkovic's side of the spectrum, where nothing Raniere did escalated beyond an unexpectedly touchy greeting. (Yes, he habitually said hello with a kiss on the lips.)

But given how many young women were receiving this escalating attention from Raniere, it seemed only a matter of time until things went too far.

CHAPTER TWENTY

Slave Number One

K eith Raniere had a lot of secret girlfriends. But the level of secrecy varied widely, depending on the girlfriend, and this had an inter-esting effect. If anyone in NXIVM dared to speak in hushed tones about Raniere's treatment of women, his least concealed relationships provided enough scandal to occupy the rumor mill. But underneath this chatter, obscured by dozens of more likely and age-appropriate affairs, was his most closely guarded secret: Camila. (As a victim of child sexual exploitation, Camila's identity is protected by court order.)

By 2014, most of the NXIVM community knew that Raniere had a relationship with Camila's oldest sister, Marianna, who'd lived with Raniere and Pam Cafritz since her early twenties. The three of them would be spotted strolling through the neighborhood as an unbreakable unit, sometimes holding hands and laughing together. And a select few—the ones who were allowed to drop in on Raniere's Flintlock home unannounced—also knew that Raniere had had a rela-tionship with the middle sister, Daniela.

Camila was the youngest sister, and almost nobody suspected she was involved with Raniere. At fifteen years old, she was well under New York's age of consent when he first sexually exploited her in 2005.

She'd lived separately from her parents and siblings when she first arrived in Albany. They didn't know he'd secretly given her his private phone number and was meeting her in the middle of the night. By the time Daniela caught on to what was happening, in 2006, Camila was already sexually frustrated, self-harming, and intent on having Raniere's baby. Raniere would justify his actions by telling Daniela that some girls were more emotionally mature than their age.

In photos shown in court, Camila has an oval face and long dark hair like her sisters, but with apple cheeks and a sleepy, mischievous look in her eyes. Well into her twenties she had the petite, rectangular frame of a teenage track athlete. Raniere nicknamed her Virgin Camila. He became increasingly demanding and volatile as Camila reached her mid-twenties.

In WhatsApp messages presented as evidence at his trial in 2019, Raniere appeared excited by the secrecy that this forbidden relationship required. At V-Week in 2014, he attempted to arrange a secret cabin meetup with Camila on the messaging app. He wanted to collect his birthday present (to "taste" her, is how he phrased it). Camila was only twenty-four, but Raniere had been her secret boyfriend for nearly nine years.

"Go to our cabin!" Raniere messaged Camila around one a.m. on the night of his fifty-fourth birthday. "Be careful, sneak in, stay there."

Raniere had already warned Camila that she couldn't be discovered on her way in or out of the cabin, which was some distance from the other accommodations where each of them was expected to sleep during the weeklong retreat at Silver Bay, New York. He advised against turning on the lights while inside.

Camila was unsure about this plan. She was sharing a room, and she didn't want her bunkmates asking questions about where she was going or telling her sister Marianna that she was running around in the middle of the night. "I'd have to pack. I'm afraid it would look too suspicious," she replied. "Love, I don't know when or if I can sneak out."

By two-fifty a.m. Raniere was rapid-fire texting through his disappointment. "Today and tonight was so important for me. . . . At times I wish you desired me so much you resourcefully found the way to make these things happen no matter what . . . and have our meeting be the most important thing. . . . Tonight I really needed you. I am very sad and alone." Camila didn't reply until morning.

Camila was among a growing cohort of young women at V-Week who restricted calories as a way to build discipline. Raniere's goal weight for Camila was one hundred pounds or less, and she reported her weight to him every day.

"Thinking of you while reviewing my shopping cart," Maja Miljkovic messaged Allison Mack during the same V-Week, attaching a photo of a sparse-looking grocery haul consisting of two heads of cauliflower, two squashes, a tub of greens, sweet corn, yogurt, and soy milk.

"Aw!!" Mack wrote back.

V-Week was in full swing, and Miljkovic wasn't there for that year's mix of poetry classes, nature walks, TED Talk–like lectures, and a cappella performances. The two women traded "I miss yous" charged with exclamations and terms of endearment: love, baby, muffin, *amiga*. "Wish wish wish you were here!!!"

Like Camila and many others, Mack was becoming obsessed with setting and achieving food and exercise goals. Miljkovic's shopping cart was an example of the extra-low-calorie vegetarian diet that all of Raniere's harem adhered to. Squash was one of Mack's favorite ways to feel full—a low-calorie vegetable dressed up as pasta. She ate so much of it that her palms once turned orange.

Miljkovic had mostly given up on severe dietary restriction after falling into a destructive binge/purge pattern one too many times. Both Camila and her older sister Marianna had a history of similar eating disorders.

"There are definitely cognitive impacts to someone who is being calorie restricted," nutritionist Ali Eberhardt, who specializes in eating disorders, told me. "When my clients are able to improve their nutritional intake, they'll say, 'I felt like I was walking in a fog. I didn't realize until now that I'm in this place of clarity where I can see, and I feel very detached from who that person was.' Because you're essentially in this place of survival."

By the summer of 2014, Camila had been living for the last four years in a secret Clifton Park apartment outfitted with dark velvet curtains blocking out any view inside. This allowed Raniere and Camila to stay out of sight of her parents and the NXIVM community. In messages

Raniere called it "our home," but it could also reasonably be described as a hiding place for an undocumented migrant. Even Camila's close friends and family didn't know where she lived.

This secrecy came at a cost. NXIVM's bookkeeper, Kathy Russell, paid a full year of Camila's rent in cash each summer, according to testimony at Raniere's trial. Russell used a pseudonym and handed the bills to the landlord in a paper bag at a Starbucks. All of this was arranged to keep Camila in the country without legal status and to hide her and Raniere's relationship.

Behind the thick velvet curtains, Camila was struggling. As her sister Daniela had done before her, Camila was, by 2014, starting to realize the drawbacks of the commitment she'd apparently made to Raniere when she was still a child. And, like her sister, she'd hooked up with someone else.

Camila slept with Robbie Chiappone, a bushy-browed twenty-something with a light brown crew cut and wide jaw. He was one of four kids who'd moved to Albany with their mom from Alaska in NXIVM's early days. He'd come of age surrounded by the same talk of self-help and personal growth familiar to Camila.

Camila had hoped the affair would end their secret relationship, but it didn't free her from Raniere. When he found out, he told her to forget breaking up—she should first seek to repair all the damage she'd caused.

Raniere had a "program" for women he deemed guilty of betrayal, and the demands were near impossible. In addition to convincing Robbie that their encounter had been nonconsensual and traumatizing, Camila had to prove her repentance through more calorie restriction and a tougher ban on "indulgences."

Raniere demanded that she prove her desperation to please him in absurd, self-flagellating ways. "What have you done today that was difficult in the name of love for me?" he wrote on October 10, 2014.

"I have not eaten and am dedicating all my free time to you . . . either reading or communicating to figure it out. I have not indulged in anger," Camila replied.

Sarah Edmondson told me about Raniere's ideas around "penance" as it related to eating, especially if you were a woman. If you ever broke a commitment to yourself—say you slept through a workout or didn't meet a writing goal—you were encouraged to cut calories as a penalty for bad behavior. "There was a woman I saw once on a three-hundred-calorie diet because of some ethical breach she did," Edmondson says. "She was eating mashed frozen zucchini and tomato stew. Just nothing."

Raniere repeatedly asked Camila to report her weight but became upset when she admitted bingeing and purging.

"How much do you weigh?" he asked on November 28.

"I don't know," Camila replied. "I think 120."

"Why did you gain? You were 113?"

"Lack of exercise during intensives."

"You then need to eat less," Raniere wrote. "The extra weight hurts my heart physically when I am with you."

These WhatsApp messages are a rare record of a turbulent, coercive relationship hidden from public view. At times Camila alluded to the pain she felt in having been ignored by Raniere in front of the NXIVM community for years—something he claimed was a test of their true love.

At Raniere's trial, prosecutor Tanya Hajjar read Raniere's messages for the court, with FBI agent Maegan Rees reading the part of Camila. They read out Camila's requests for permission to text her friends and parents or shave her pubic hair. They read Raniere's many ultimatums: fix the damage or leave the country. They read Camila's messages about her depression, her eating disorder, her suicidal ideation. They read Raniere's warnings that Camila was not to reveal to anyone who she was texting, especially not Marianna.

After many demands that Camila pack up her stuff and prepare to leave Albany forever, Raniere offered her another option. He told her to write down "a specific vow of obedience." This language would be repeated to seven other women in an escalating scheme to secure lifelong indentured servants.

"The vow doesn't have to be that long," he wrote.

"I get fearful because I project you will abuse that power," Camila replied. "But I understand it is my own horrible projection."

"There will be times it will seem like I am," Raniere wrote. "I won't. But it is part of proving trust. If it never seemed questionable, then it wouldn't be trust. I've earned trust. Do it now please . . . text it now."

"I vow to do as u say," Camila wrote.

"100% obedience?" Raniere replied.

"100% obedience. I don't know why I'm scared shitless."

"You are scared because you are serious. That is good," wrote Raniere. "You must be the model of restraint. No alcohol of any sort, not a sip and eat very little. You must build yourself to be a new woman, one that is serious about her future."

"Shit," she responded. "I'm already questioning because I don't understand why I have to do that since I don't want to be that type of woman. Never have."

"Do you want honor, dignity, respect or love?" Raniere wrote back. "What I said serves many purposes. You actually do want to be that type of woman. You react to terms such as slut and whore. As you age you will be . . . more and more like that if you don't change."

Though much of the transcript is crowded with Raniere telling Camila what to think and say and feel, there are many places where she pushes back, or tries to express a sense of injustice. She tells Raniere that he's more like a parent or god to her, that she feels powerless to change her situation—as if there were a gun pointed to her head and she's constantly trying to say the right thing to avoid being killed. In some cases she explicitly states that Raniere's actions seem "controlling and abusive." But she doesn't appear to have any meaningful leverage, and Raniere doesn't give an inch.

"I feel like a prisoner," she wrote on December 8, 2014. "This is your world and your rules, if you suddenly decide to change the rules (which you have) it is fine because this is YOUR kingdom. I can either abide by your ruling or leave. Unfortunately, I promised I wouldn't so I am in your kingdom, under your rules. It doesn't mean I agree."

Raniere then flipped the script, describing himself as the victim. He said he was physically damaged and did not receive any support, while Camila received plenty of it.

Raniere's victimhood story evolved over the next few months. He revealed that he was in great pain and might possibly die soon, because Camila's unfaithfulness meant she could no longer be his "spiritual successor." Though Camila said she had "no idea" that this was a thing, Raniere insisted she was chosen as a "pure" vessel for his spiritual teachings.

"My lineage is not supposed to end with my death," Raniere wrote on March 12, 2015, adding that he'd been transferring knowledge and "energy" to Camila that would have allowed him to live on through her. But because she'd had sexual contact with somebody else, this was no longer possible, he said, and would leave him mortally weakened.

"I can't even breathe when you say that, much less say anything," Camila replied. "It is beyond heartbreaking."

AT RANIERE'S TRIAL, psychologist and expert witness Dawn Hughes named threats, isolation, gaslighting, surveillance, subjugation, and economic control as forms of nonphysical violence that can take away someone's ability to freely give consent.

I kept this in mind when reviewing Camila's contradictory replies: at one moment she'd vow to trust and obey Raniere forever, and at another she'd say that this commitment made her feel dead inside. There were times when she was interested in sex and wanted to be tied up, and other times when she explicitly said she didn't want to be touched.

Hughes's testimony was a reminder that threats and gaslighting can create a state of terror in which the need to placate an abuser comes before personal safety. "I had to become good at figuring out how to stay in his good graces," Camila later recounted in court. "He had made himself my only lifeline and I was not going to mess with that."

After a blowout argument in April 2015, the WhatsApp conversation with Raniere turned to Camila's safety. Camila had stopped replying for several hours, and when she returned to the chat, Raniere asked about a self-inflicted wrist wound.

"How's the injury feel?" he asked.

"Deeper than I thought. I put a butterfly thingy on it. It hurts."

Raniere suggested that Camila tell Nancy Salzman about what had happened and ask her to examine it. "I think it's best she knows you cut yourself," he wrote. "She is very caring and could help you. And would keep it a secret."

Camila wrote that she didn't want Salzman or anybody else to know.

"I think we should get a medical person, but one who won't force a psych evaluation and suicide watch," Raniere countered. He later claimed that Camila's suicide attempt was part of the reason he created the secret sorority known as DOS—to help her build discipline and character.

JUST OVER a week later, Camila was preparing "collateral" to cement her vow of obedience to Raniere for life. She eventually pledged that if she ever broke her vow, she would resign from her job at Rainbow, give up all her belongings—including two computers, a hard drive, treadmill, bike, passport, and her email passwords—and deliver a letter that would ruin her relationship with Gaelyn, Raniere's son. She also wrote up a statement alleging that her father, Hector, was gay.

Raniere had referred to Camila as his "slave" before, but he used the term more frequently after she submitted her collateral. In September she went to New York City to pick out a "slave necklace" that would symbolize her vow—a chain she would never take off.

"I'm so used to hiding our relationship that it feels like it goes against everything to say those words: my boyfriend," she wrote. "When I was in nyc I went to macy's to look for a slave necklace and I got to say 'my boyfriend' and I couldn't say it without feeling like I was doing something wrong . . . but part of me liked it."

Raniere and Camila had an apparent history with bondage themes. In emails to Raniere as far back as 2009, when Camila was nineteen, she eagerly signed off as "slavey slave." But in 2015 things with Raniere were different, given the collateral on the line. BDSM educator Carlyle Jansen is quick to point out that consent isn't something you can give if someone is threatening to hurt you. "There should never be something hanging over your head, where you have to do something—or else," she told me. "That totally violates free will and consent."

This bears mentioning, given what Raniere wrote to Camila next: "I think it would be good for you to own a fuck toy slave for me, that you could groom, and use as a tool, to pleasure me."

Camila replied, "huh? not disagreeing, just don't understand."

"Get a slave . . . you're her master."

Camila questioned why Raniere would even want that. "I am not as turned on by owning," she said.

IN EARLY OCTOBER 2015, Camila discovered that Nicki Clyne was wearing a chain collar like her own. "I have her right next to me and it looks like she has one," Camila texted to Raniere.

Raniere deflected. "If you knew how I loved you, you would not care even if it were true!"

Camila had to leave the room to catch herself. "I feel extremely betrayed. I feel insignificant. Worthless and disposable to you. I am wondering what else have you not told me."

"Your pride is over the top," Raniere shot back. "Unless you can somehow make me believe you get it and are truly sorry this is very bad. If you are humble you can't be betrayed by me. Only ugly pride does that."

On October 9, Raniere revealed more to Camila about the secret organization of women he was building. He claimed that Camila's suicide attempt had "set off a chain reaction" that led to Nicki's and others' participation.

"It caused there to be other slaves, all who want to be branded with my monogram plus a number," Raniere wrote. "Your number is reserved . . . it is number 1. It is now a secret growing organization. I don't know well some of the other people involved but I command them ultimately. They are not who you might think."

Camila was not happy about the branding. "Branded like cattle?" she asked. "You want to burn me?"

"You don't want to burn for me?" Raniere responded.

CHAPTER TWENTY-ONE

The Call

Barbara Bouchey was speechless.

It had been more than five years since she'd left her boyfriend and business partner Keith Raniere behind—though he continued to chase her with lawsuits in several states. NXIVM had accused Bouchey of defamation and breach of client confidentiality, and she was still fighting low-level felony charges for allegedly accessing their computer servers using a former client's login credentials. (All those charges would eventually be dismissed.)

So the last person she was expecting to call was Kristin Keeffe, one of Raniere's most loyal girlfriends, mother to his child, and longtime overseer of the very lawsuits that had intimidated and silenced perceived enemies like Bouchey.

"For five years I had sat across from her in all those lawsuits. She was their legal liaison, commanding seven law firms in four states," Bouchey told me. When she took Keeffe's call, in March 2015, she could in that moment have accused Kristin of ruining her life. But she was also kept in line with threats and group influence, so Bouchey decided to listen to whatever it was she had to say.

Keeffe told her she'd left Raniere and NXIVM and was in hiding with her eight-year-old son, Gaelyn. This was an inconceivable development, and not just for Bouchey. Most people assumed Keeffe to be so committed to Raniere that she'd be prepared to go down with the ship—even to die for the cause.

"I didn't know if it was real. She said I was the first person she called," Bouchey says of the phone call that would change the lives of both women. "The whole time I thought she was trying to set me up or frame me, maybe hoping I would slip up."

Despite her suspicions, Bouchey earnestly hoped she was telling the truth. Because if Keeffe really had defected from NXIVM, it meant that anyone could wake up and leave.

"He's not trying to succeed, he's trying to enslave," Keeffe told her.

FOR NEARLY TWO hours Keeffe unloaded her knowledge of what she described as crimes and conspiracies committed by Keith Raniere, Nancy Salzman, Emiliano Salinas, and Clare Bronfman. This included an alleged plot to get Bouchey and others thrown in jail in Mexico.

Keeffe asked whether Bouchey remembered being invited to an anti-cult conference in Mexico. Bouchey said she'd gotten a few calls from a Mexican journalist, but that she'd never picked up. (Another one of Raniere's exes, Toni Natalie, had told Bouchey about similar calls.) Then Keeffe alleged that Raniere and Salinas had bribed a judge in Mexico to issue an indictment against Bouchey. "You were going to be lured into Mexico, and when you got to Mexico, they were going to put you in fucking prison. You should see the emails!"

"Were they really?" Bouchey replied, shocked. "How serious were they?"

"They were as serious as a fucking heart attack. I saw the judge's decision. Keith helped write it, and there were issues about Emiliano translating it. He worked on this for years. Fucking years."

All Bouchey could say was "Wow."

At this point, in 2015, Raniere was still at the height of his power. In Vancouver the NXIVM community was celebrating new enrollment milestones, and recruitment in Mexico City was now outpacing every other center. NXIVM critics had their electronics seized and were losing in court. Bouchey, who'd been accused of computer trespassing, was still struggling to bring her new attorney up to speed and would later represent herself in court. Anyone who turned against Raniere could expect an onslaught of intimidating phone calls and spying. Given how much Keeffe knew, Bouchey thought even worse might happen to her.

But now, after being sworn enemies for the last five years, Keeffe and Bouchey were suddenly going into battle on the same side once more. Bouchey says she felt a wave of forgiveness. For the first time in a long time, she thought they stood a chance against Raniere.

"Do you have a prediction of what you think, how this will go down for Keith? Do you think that we'll be able to hold him accountable?" Bouchey asked.

"Yes, I do," said Keeffe. "I think he will be thoroughly and utterly destroyed."

FOR BOTH WOMEN it felt like a game-changing moment. No one had had the means to take Raniere down before, and now Keeffe was giving Bouchey hope that it was possible. Most former members didn't know the extent of what was going on behind the scenes, but Keeffe had more dirt than anyone who'd ever left.

And yet, even with Keeffe's inside knowledge of alleged fraud, tax evasion, hacking, obstruction of justice, and other crimes, the two women probably understood that the path ahead wouldn't be easy. Keeffe said she knew Clare Bronfman was socking away an "off the grid" fund for Raniere. "There was $2.5 million in it," she told Bouchey. "Now I'm sure it's ten times that."

This recorded conversation would eventually become evidence presented in court, but it wasn't the allegations of tax evasion, fraud, or even the plot to have enemies thrown in prison in Mexico that would finally catch law enforcement's attention. It was an even larger conspiracy, involving sex slaves and branding, that pushed federal agents to arrest Raniere, Allison Mack, Lauren Salzman, Nancy Salzman, Clare Bronfman, and bookkeeper Kathy Russell in 2018.

Some former members suspect it was Keeffe's exit in 2014 that tipped Raniere into the dark, vengeful headspace that birthed the secret society called DOS. Others view Dominus Obsequious Sororium as a culmination of discipline and control practices he'd been developing since before NXIVM existed. By the time of his arrest, at least 102 women had been initiated into Raniere's secret society. Not all of them had been branded, and not all of them had been coerced into sex, but court records and testimony would show that he considered all of them to be his slaves.

CHAPTER TWENTY-TWO

The Vow

Nicole's dream was a simple one: become a great actor. Not just a good or competent actor, but a great actor—one who'd be appreciated for her range and skills as well as her beauty.

"I think the first time that I was ever on stage I was four, and that was in like a Hans Christian Andersen story," Nicole said at Raniere's trial. (By court order, Nicole can be identified only by her first name.)

It was through an acting class that Nicole met Mark Hildreth, a Canadian actor with a square jaw and vast collection of unsmiling headshots that undoubtedly helped him land acting roles in fantasy and action flicks. They worked with the same beloved acting coach in 2013, and they started dating soon after that. It wasn't long into their relationship that Hildreth brought up NXIVM and other actors who were part of it. "I think we were talking about character work or something of that sort, which then got into a deeper conversation," Nicole said. Hildreth told her he was working on becoming a better person through this program that taught business and psychology mixed together.

"It kinda sounded like something that I had done when I was a kid, called Landmark," she testified. Nicole thought some discipline and life coaching would be good for her. "Acting is tough, and sometimes your own fears get in the way of being in the audition room," she said. "I was always trying to better myself in any way."

Of course, there were downsides she had to consider. She knew that one of Mark's previous girlfriends, *Smallville* actor Kristin Kreuk, was associated in some way. Nicole, as the new girlfriend in a group of friends that went back nearly a decade, thought that could be a source of discomfort. And Hildreth also warned her not to read anything about the program online, as there were some naysayers who had apparently written some negative things.

"Mark said that was the best way to go into the five-day . . . to go in completely open-minded, and to really not have any expectations," Nicole recalled of her boyfriend's pitch. He name-dropped Seagram heir Clare Bronfman and Emiliano Salinas, son of Carlos Salinas de Gortari, the former Mexican president, as powerful, smart people who were moving mountains in the NXIVM community.

In the end, Hildreth offered to lend Nicole the money so that she could take her first five-day intensive in 2013. "He said that he believed in it so much that he would pay—pay for me and I could pay him back as I could," she said.

Nicole was mostly impressed by her first NXIVM experience. She liked to explore her own personality and patterns; she equated it with character work in acting class. "I like to learn, and I can kind of get something out of anything," she said.

THOUGH SHE HAD a good time, Nicole wasn't smitten with the program the way some of her acting peers were. The secrecy and ritualistic aspects left her feeling a bit confused and uncomfortable. "When I learn something cool, I like to call my little brother and I'm like, 'Guess what I learned today?'" she testified. "They were basically saying you can't do that, which seemed really weird to me." All things considered, she thought the classes were just "okay."

But Nicole's lukewarm feelings about NXIVM didn't stop Hildreth from suggesting more courses. Even after they broke up, he suggested that Nicole would benefit from taking classes on ethics or emotions or communication.

"He used to drive me nuts," she told jurors with audible exasperation. "We weren't even dating anymore, but we were still in acting class together, and I'd be struggling with something and he'd been like, 'You know, the ongoing ESP [Executive Success Programs] would really fix this problem.'"

Hildreth was ahead of Nicole in his acting career, but Nicole still wasn't convinced he knew what was best for her. She didn't want to take more NXIVM classes, no matter how good Hildreth was at selling it. She was getting more comfortable with auditions and commercials, and she had a better idea of what she needed in order to level up: she wanted to move to New York City to try her hand at stage acting. "There's something about being on stage that I just really loved and I found it easier," she told the jury. "You can take a character through the whole story. Every night you're taking this character through the whole story and you're kind of like living it, and it's a little bit different each night because you don't know how the audience will react to things."

Hildreth and Nicole were still taking acting classes with each other. On a day when the two were paired together, Hildreth told her about another acting program she could try in upstate New York. "I think he actually said, 'It doesn't have to do with ESP, so like don't get mad at me,'" Nicole testified. "There's another course that they were working on that was about psychology and acting. . . . And they had been working on this program for a while, and it was supposed to be really cool and tailored to artists."

If she signed up right away, Nicole could do the five-week acting program for a discounted $6,000 instead of $8,000. "The timing was perfect," Nicole said. "It was supposed to be a five-week course. And I was moving out of my apartment in L.A. and I hadn't gotten a job yet in New York and I hadn't found an apartment yet in New York. So, like, when in your life do you have five weeks where you don't have to also pay rent, you know?"

IT WAS THROUGH the Source, the NXIVM acting program developed in 2014, that Nicole finally spent time with Allison Mack. It quickly became obvious that the program was heavily influenced by NXIVM concepts. But unlike the fourteen-hour-plus days Nicole had experienced in a NXIVM intensive, the Source teaching schedule was spare. Classes happened only in the afternoon, which left her to fill her time with exercise and self-reflection.

"I didn't realize quite how isolated it would be," Nicole said of her first impressions of Albany. "Like, there wasn't a grocery store you could walk to." Though their time together was limited, Nicole developed a reverence for Mack, who was clearly committed to improving herself. "I think I looked up to her because, you know, she had a lot of discipline and she had gotten to a certain level in her career and had a certain amount of success, but was also very serious about becoming a great actress. And that was what I cared so much about," Nicole testified.

For her part, Mack showed obvious devotion to her own mentor, Keith Raniere. Students recall that he was constantly cited as the source of Mack's inspiration and discipline. Raniere appeared in many of the videos Nicole watched as part of her Source training, and Mack elaborated on what they'd worked on together.

Nicole began to place a lot of hope in the Source program as a way to both improve her acting chops and make money. The idea was to take the skills and exercises from the program and go on to mentor others.

But she found that she was mostly removed from other actors in the program and rarely spoke with Mack. "Allison and Mark were really big on that when I first moved. Like, 'You're so lucky because now you have a built-in community when you get to New York . . . we're going to introduce you to people in the New York center,'" she explained. "I met, like, a few other people in Albany, but I didn't really hang out with Allison outside of class."

AFTER THE FIVE weeks were up, Nicole tried to keep connected to the Source program by attending weekly classes via video conference. But a thriving acting community and starting her own teaching practice still seemed out of reach. She later learned that she'd need to retake the whole five-week course plus a "teachers in training" program to advance toward becoming a certified acting coach.

Mack invited Nicole to attend V-Week that August, and they slept in the same bed to save money on an extra room. "One day she brought up that she was part of this really cool women's mentorship," Nicole said on the witness stand. "It was this really cool thing for women who wanted to be serious about being strong women, and she thought that I might be interested in it."

"'I'm just going to plant this seed in your mind, but that's all I'm going to say for now,'" Nicole said Mack told her.

She eventually did retake The Source program that October. The second run was supposed to be half price, as well as the cost of the teacher training, but she ended up paying the same amount she had the first time. "I thought it was going to be $3,000, then maybe plus the extra thousand. But they had raised the prices [to $10,000], so now it ended up that it was going to be $6,000."

Nicole had only $2,000, but Allison Mack lent her the rest. Nicole learned that as soon as she had her teacher certification, she could be making a 50 percent commission on new acting students she brought in, which at $10,000 per course sounded like a very lucrative way to teach acting. So she took on the $4,000 debt and went up to Albany for more acting mentorship with Mack.

"She asked me how much my family meant to me, which is obviously a lot," Nicole said, recalling a walk she had with Mack while taking the course for the second time. "She asked me if I was willing to—I don't remember how she phrased it exactly—but willing to let go of my attachment to my family or push hard enough to let go of my attachment to having a family."

Nicole was confused. She replied, "Why? Like, why would I need to do that?"

By February the next year, Nicole's insecurities about her move to New York City had grown into aching existential anxieties. "I was just feeling really lonely and unsure of how to move forward with my career in New York," she said. "I was really depressed."

She reached out to Mack, who replied almost immediately. "I'm sorry I have not been there for you," Mack wrote. She said she was coming to New York City for an audition the next day and would make time to check in with Nicole. "I will prioritize you."

THE TWO ACTORS met in the lobby of Manhattan's Ace Hotel, where hulking white columns support an impossibly high ceiling and bare light bulbs hang from spare, industrial-style chandeliers.

"She said that she had something that she thought would fix how I was feeling," Nicole testified.

Mack told Nicole about a women's mentorship organization she'd mentioned at V-Week the previous year. She said it was exactly what Nicole needed to get out of the rough patch she'd described. The details of the organization were top secret, but once Nicole had proven her commitment to secrecy, Mack would mentor her and Nicole would be able to mentor others.

In that moment, Nicole felt hopeful. "I really enjoy working with people, and if someone helps me get somewhere, I absolutely would want to repay that and help somebody else," she said. But with the benefit of hindsight, Nicole would realize that she'd been desperate for support and wasn't thinking rationally. Mack was one of the few people she trusted enough to show her most vulnerable self to, and she was ready to lean into that in whatever way was necessary.

Mack explained that she'd provided "collateral" to back her own vow of secrecy, and that Nicole would need to do the same. In fact, Nicole would need to "collateralize" several dimensions of her life, including her family, her career, and all her important personal relationships.

Nicole hadn't kept up with the higher-level NXIVM classes, so the concept of collateral—at least the way Mack was using the word—sounded foreign to her. In Mack's universe, giving collateral was a powerful way to show your commitment. It added weight to your word, assurance that you'd never renege on your personal decisions. It felt good to be locked in this way, Mack said, because it built trust and took ambivalence out of the equation.

Mack told Nicole she'd need to write a letter that would hurt her family if it was ever made public. Nicole told her she couldn't think of anything that her family would want to keep hidden—none of them had broken the law to her knowledge. Mack herself had written a letter claiming her father had molested her as a child, and she suggested Nicole do the same.

"She said, 'You could lie,' and she said she had written that—her father had sexually abused her," Nicole said, her voice steeped in remorse.

On the witness stand, Nicole held her head in her hands and sobbed when she recalled what she'd written about her family. She accused her father of sexual misconduct and put the statement in an envelope addressed to the local newspaper in her California hometown. She wrote similarly horrific things about her mother and an actor ex-boyfriend, addressing one envelope to her mom's workplace and the other to the *Los Angeles Times*. Mack assured Nicole that no one would ever see what she'd written.

By comparison, Nicole thought providing career collateral was an easier task. She made a solo sex tape that Mack promised to keep in an underground vault where no one could look at it. "The letters were so much, so much harder for me," Nicole testified. "Making the video was kind of freeing, again, under the circumstances that I thought no one was ever going to see it, ever."

NICOLE MET MACK again at the Ace Hotel to deliver her collateral, then the two actors headed to a vegetarian restaurant in Manhattan's East Village, where Mack told Nicole about the secret women's empowerment group, which Mack called the "Vow."

Mack told her about the incredible women who were already part of this growing network. She said that women who joined were pushing each other to be stronger in all facets of their lives. The program would make Nicole physically, emotionally, and intellectually stronger so that she could build the life she wanted for herself. The Vow was a lifetime commitment, Mack said, and all the women who joined would get "a small brand, like a tattoo." Nicole would have to decide if she was ready within twenty-four hours.

Nicole wasn't sure about the lifetime commitment, but the opportunity itself sounded exciting. "As an actor, you always want to be physically, mentally, and intellectually stronger. You want to play those kind of characters, you want to be that kind of woman," she said. "I wanted to be like Wonder Woman, I wanted to play that role. So it sounded—compared to where I was at mentally—yeah, it sounded pretty good."

IT WASN'T UNTIL after Nicole confirmed her life commitment to the Vow that she began learning what practices she'd apparently signed up for. Mack explained that the "mentorship" was actually a master–slave relationship, and that every day Nicole would have to text her "Good morning, Master" when she woke up and "Good night, Master" when she went to bed. "There were so many things that were added on later once you were sealed into this situation," Nicole said.

Mack came down to the city again to have lunch and go to a museum with Nicole. "She set up my first off-Broadway audition for a really great play, and also set me up with a meeting with her agency," Nicole recalled.

Nicole began a new job serving tables at a rooftop nightclub. Her shifts would last from nine-thirty p.m. until after the bar closed at five a.m. "I could pay all my bills myself at this new job," she said on the witness stand. "I wasn't as stressed about money, and I started to meet other girls in New York City." With a new job, new friends, and free time during the day for auditions, Nicole was already feeling as if she'd moved past her seasonal mental health struggles. And when her mom came to visit New York, she decided it would be better for her to renegotiate her "lifetime commitment."

But when she told Mack she wanted to leave the secret mentorship group, Mack said that wasn't an option. She repeated that it was a lifetime commitment, like an arranged marriage, Nicole testified. "I started crying, and she seemed upset, too. But she said she couldn't let me out no matter how hard I cried because it would show me that . . . if I cried hard enough I could get out of anything," she said.

Nicole had been in the secret group for only about a month, and yet she was growing more and more uncomfortable with it the more she discovered. She got the sense that Mack was in a similarly frightening double bind when Mack talked about the possibility of her own collateral being released. "We were driving in her car to find a parking spot in the city, and she said she had been really struggling with something, and her master had said they were going to release her collateral—or her sex tape, that particular piece of collateral—if she didn't get her act together," Nicole recalled. "She said she got her act together real quick."

DURING THE FIRST week of April 2016, Nicole got a new assignment. Her job was now to reach out to Keith Raniere. "I think she said it was my first secret spy assignment, to reach out to him," Nicole said.

Nicole had never had a face-to-face conversation with Raniere. What she knew about him she'd mostly learned secondhand, either through Mack and others praising him or by watching videos where he talked about concepts.

Part of the challenge was figuring out a way to get in touch, since Mack refused to give Nicole Raniere's email address—and except for Mack and her ex-boyfriend Mark Hildreth, Nicole didn't have much contact with NXIVM's insiders. It was Hildreth who eventually supplied Raniere's contact information, after consulting Vanguard for permission. Nicole then wrote to Raniere to thank him for creating the Source. She said she felt awkward about it and didn't know exactly what to say.

Afterward, Mack grew impatient waiting to hear from Nicole about whether Raniere had responded, at one point saying she was "slow as molasses." Then, on April 16, Mack texted Nicole about stage two of her assignment. "If you haven't heard back from Keith before the end of the night you may wanna reach out again—continue to pursue until he responds," she wrote, adding, "How do you get the attention of the smartest man in the world??"

Mack told her that if Raniere didn't respond by three a.m. that night, Mack would have to take a cold shower. Feeling pressured, Nicole laid out all her feelings and insecurities about the bizarre situation in an email to Raniere. Without mentioning the Vow, she pointed out a contradiction she was struggling with: the goal of constantly challenging fears seemed at odds with leading a "joyful" life.

"In all the videos I've seen and things I've heard about you, you're very joyful and playful," she told Raniere, "but for me, thinking about pushing on my fears for the rest of my life doesn't make me feel playful. It makes me feel scared and heavy hearted. It makes me want to run away. Allison told me to be honest with you and the truth is that Allison is trying to push me, or I assume push against my fears, and is going to stand in a cold shower if I don't figure out how to hear back from you by three a.m. Yeah, that's happening."

Finally, Raniere responded. "The thing with Allison and the shower is not a good lever for me, but more on ethics later," he wrote. "It is a scary difficult journey to experience existence with the lightness of true freedom with the depth of love."

When asked in court how she'd interpreted this impenetrable phrase about experiencing existence, Nicole admitted she'd had no idea what it meant. But she thanked Raniere for the feedback anyway and elaborated on her struggle in solving the joy versus fear equation. She'd noticed that many NXIVM students seemed caught up in pain as a means of growing. "I just didn't want to live my life constantly needing to struggle and feel bad or find something to struggle against," she testified. "Life gives you enough struggles."

Raniere had yet more lessons for Nicole in his next email, dated April 19, 2016. "True freedom in the physical world comes from absolute commitment to a principle with no tolerance for excuses," he wrote. "Only then do we find freedom does not depend on being able to do what we want; it depends on not being able to do what we want yet still experiencing self. Love is only measured through pain. Our ability to feel human pain determines the depth and strength of our love."

WHILE NICOLE WAS continuing to have these exchanges with Raniere, Mack requested that she come up to spend time in Albany on her days off. Nicole got into a habit of working Tuesdays to Sundays—arriving home each morning at six a.m.—and then on Sunday nights taking a bus or train up to Albany until Tuesday morning. She slept in Mack's bed during these visits, as she had during V-Week in 2015.

Later that April, Nicole spotted Raniere in the flesh one night while she was waiting for Mack to come home. It was the first time she remembered seeing him. "I saw Keith walk by and I thought, 'Oh, that's the person I've been emailing back and forth with, I should go say hi,'" she testified. "So I went outside and I said hi."

Raniere finished up a conversation, made his way over to Nicole, and asked her if she'd like to go for a walk with him. She was well aware of the significance of being asked to take a walk with Raniere. "People waited around awhile to go on these walks," Nicole testified. "He said that I had earned—because we had been going back and forth on email—that I had earned a walk."

Raniere asked Nicole what she knew about him and his lifestyle—"which was not a lot," Nicole testified. He explained that he wasn't married and had more than one partner.

It began to rain, and Raniere asked Nicole if she knew how to get back to Mack's place. Nicole replied that she did, even though most days she found the neighborhood confusing.

Then Raniere threw her a curveball: "He said, 'Isn't this funny that this is our first date?'" Nicole recalled. "I just remember not quite being able to wrap my head around it. Because I thought, 'What? Like, *what*?'"

Raniere asked if she was okay. She had zoned out for a beat, but she jumped back in. "I said, 'Yeah, I'm just feeling overwhelmed.'"

Nicole ran back to Mack's house feeling oddly uneasy. "I wasn't really thinking. I didn't know what to think, but I remember that my body really did not feel okay."

Mack was home. Nicole told her about the walk and that she sensed something was off, that there seemed to be a plot to bring her and Raniere together in Albany. "That's what it felt like," she testified. "I wasn't accusing her, because I was so out of my element, but I was like, 'This feels like a plot to get me up here for Keith.'"

"Oh, sweetie, I'm so glad you told me that," Mack replied. "That's not true, that's not what's happening, but that's such a good sign that you can trust me enough to tell me that."

BEFORE LONG NICOLE was going on regular walks with Raniere, all arranged through Mack. Except now they were happening between two and five a.m. While sleeping in Mack's bed, Nicole would hear the special ringtone Mack had assigned to Raniere's phone number and immediately feel her body go into fight-or-flight mode.

She thought it was suspicious that Raniere seemed to know exactly what she was struggling with, things she hadn't confided in him. "It drove me nuts," she testified. "It just seemed too weird for him not to know [about DOS], yet I had no reason to believe that he was part of this women's organization." Even when Nicole brought up these coincidences, Mack would flatly deny that Raniere knew about their secret group.

On their walks, Raniere would ask Nicole the kinds of personal questions that often appeared on NXIVM worksheets: What's the worst thing you've ever done? What are you afraid of? What would be the hardest thing for you to tell me right now?

Nicole's next assignment truly frightened her. Mack told her that on her next walk with Raniere, she had to tell him she would do anything he wanted. Before the walk, Nicole recalled, Mack said, "Now go be a good slave."

"I went outside and he was waiting outside, out the back door of Allison's house, and we started walking. And I was too nervous to say it," Nicole testified. "We walked a little ways and then I just kind of blurted it out, like, 'I'll do whatever you want me to do.'

"I was just saying it because I had to," Nicole added. "I didn't want to say it."

Raniere may have sensed this. "I don't think you mean that," he replied.

"I don't," Nicole admitted.

Later in the walk, Raniere asked what would be the worst thing he could ask Nicole to do. Her mind raced with dark possibilities. "I remember looking up at the roof of a house that we were walking past and thinking, 'Oh my god, he could ask me to jump off that roof.'" Sexual humiliation was one of the first horrible scenarios she imagined, but she told Raniere that wasn't the worst.

"The worst thing that you could ask me to do would be to ask me to hurt someone in my family," she told him. "I was like, 'What if he asked me to never speak to my family again?'"

"Do you really think that I would ask you to do those things?" Raniere responded.

Nicole didn't know at this point what anyone around her was capable of. Mack had repeatedly surprised her with the intensity of her orders and the consequences she claimed would follow failure. But Raniere's question still cut through some of the tension between them. She felt calmer as they continued walking back toward Mack's house.

Before they parted, Raniere told Nicole to come back out only when she really meant it when she said she'd do anything he wanted.

CHAPTER TWENTY-THREE

"This Is Not the Army"

When Nicole returned to Allison Mack's house, Nicole told her she'd said exactly what she was supposed to say but that Raniere hadn't believed it and told her to try again.

"Okay, so you'll go back tomorrow," Mack replied.

Just as she had many times before, Nicole sensed she didn't have a choice. She would have to say it and mean it.

The following night, "I was sleeping in Allison's bed," Nicole recalled on the witness stand. "He called Allison and Allison told me to go outside."

Nicole walked out the back door and locked eyes with Raniere. "I was like, Okay, you can do this, you can do this," she testified. "And I said, 'I will do anything you ask me to do.'"

"Do you mean it?" Raniere asked.

Nicole said she did.

"He took my hand and took me across the street, directly across from Allison's house into another house," Nicole testified.

Raniere asked Nicole to trust him, no matter what was about to happen. "I said yes. I mean, I already said I would do anything he asked, so I said yes," Nicole recalled. "Then he asked me to take off my clothes."

Nicole undressed as Raniere sat and watched. He made comments about whatever he noticed, from her belly button piercing that had grown in to the fact that she hadn't recently shaved or waxed her pubic hair. "He was surprised because it didn't seem like my nature," Nicole testified.

"I responded, 'Yeah, I've been celibate for three months. Sorry, it's not the first thing on my mind.' Or something like that."

Raniere replied that that was okay, he liked a woman with a bush, which set off a series of realizations in Nicole's head. While staying in such close quarters with Mack, Nicole had seen her master's pubic hair situation and guessed that she'd grown it out for Raniere. "I was like, 'Oh, he has a sexual relationship with Allison. I was right about that.'"

Nicole thought it was safe to assume that sex was about to happen next, but Raniere steered left of that expectation. "He told me to put my clothes back on and he said that there are two blindfolds to put on."

The first blindfold pressed so tight into Nicole's eye sockets that it left marks under her eyes. Raniere tied the second blindfold over top and told Nicole they were leaving the house. "He took my hand and took me to the car, put me in the car, and then we drove somewhere."

After ten minutes of driving, Nicole said she was led out of the car and through some bushes. "I just remember feeling things crash under my feet, like branches breaking," she said.

She couldn't see anything, but she could feel a doorstep with her foot. She stepped up, trying not to trip, and was led through a front door. "In my imagination it was a little cabin," she said. "But I don't really know."

Raniere told Nicole to get undressed again and to lie down on a table. He then tied down her wrists and feet.

When asked in court how she felt being tied, Nicole replied, "Super vulnerable and exposed. And I was hoping that maybe that was it," she said, her voice starting to crack, "maybe that was the whole thing, you know, just that I had to be super vulnerable and exposed."

She testified that she suddenly felt a tongue nudging its way between her legs. She assumed it was Raniere's, but then she heard his voice coming from somewhere near her head.

"I was like, 'Holy shit, there's somebody else in the room.'"

She tried to stay calm. Raniere was moving around the room while an unknown person performed oral sex on her. Raniere was asking Nicole questions about her sex life: Had she ever been in a three-some? How many people had she been with at once?

"I'm trying to process what's going on," Nicole recalled. "There is somebody else in the room. Okay, so now there's two people in the room. *Are there three people in the room?* Like, how many people are in this room right now?"

NICOLE DIDN'T KNOW how long this went on for. At some point Raniere asked her if she was okay. "I didn't think that there was an option, so I just said, 'Yes, I'm okay.'"

Raniere untied Nicole but left her blindfolds on. He helped her get dressed and took her back to the house across from Allison Mack's place.

"He said he wanted me to know that nothing bad had just happened, and that I was a young woman who was allowed to be sexual," Nicole recalled. "I was not in a relationship, so what happened was not bad."

Nicole thought about how she wasn't in a relationship because Mack had specifically ordered it. Raniere went on about trust and bravery. "He was just kind of talking, and eventually I just felt like, Can I go?" she testified. "And finally I said that out loud. I said, 'Can I go?' And he told me not to tell anyone what happened."

Nicole asked if she could tell Mack, and he agreed. By the time Nicole made her way outside, the sun had already risen. "I just remember it being really bright when I walked out," she said.

Outside, Nicole saw Clare Bronfman and Emiliano Salinas out for an early morning run. "I ran to Emi and I just hugged him, because, you know, I always felt safe with Emi."

She went back to Mack's house and took a shower. Then she sat Mack down to tell her what had happened. "She seemed a bit freaked out," Nicole said. "I don't think she knew exactly what was going to happen, but she also said I was really brave."

Nicole didn't have time to consider whether what had been done to her was a crime, and anyway she placed nearly all the blame squarely on her own shoulders. She left Albany with only a short time to rest before another all-night shift at the club. Raniere texted her later that day, repeating that he thought she was "very courageous."

LESS THAN TWENTY-FOUR hours after it happened, Nicole had already pushed the incident to the back of her mind. She didn't want to talk about it or even think about it—and even if she had wanted to talk about it, she wasn't allowed. Allison Mack was the only person she had permission to tell, and for security reasons she wasn't allowed to discuss it by email.

Though she kept her vow of secrecy, Nicole seemed to redirect some unfocused anger into a journal entry about her messy apartment the following day. "Coming back every week to an unorganized home and hectic life here feels awful. Words can't even express how stressful and bad it feels," she wrote on June 1, 2016. "It fills my whole body with this raged up anger and pain."

At Raniere's trial, Nicole explained that she hadn't absorbed what had been done to her. "I don't think I processed what had actually happened for a really long time, but I was emotionally upset," she said.

Nicole emailed the journal entry to Mack, and Mack wrote back that Nicole was choosing to be angry rather than choosing the calm that was in the eye of any storm. "I feel sad, I thought you were through this but OK," she wrote. "You are very attached to your physical comforts. It's weak, spoiled and entitled." Mack signed off with "I miss you. I love you. XO."

Nicole knew she was expected to continue "working" with Raniere. Mack said she'd "earned" his time, which NXIVM students and coaches generally thought was a rare privilege. Nicole reasoned that the worst was likely behind her. She even held out some hope that she could learn something from their weekly scheduled walks in the middle of the night.

The following week, Raniere took Nicole to a location she'd never visited before. It was Raniere's "executive library," which included a sleeping loft accessed through a trapdoor that prevented others from coming up behind. Nicole looked at Raniere's collection of books and his scribbles on a massive whiteboard. The windows were blacked out, and Raniere warned that Nicole wasn't permitted to touch or move anything. "Everything had to be left exactly how I found it," she said.

Nicole learned this when she peeked out one of the windows to see if the townhouse had a yard. "I moved the curtain over a little bit and Keith got really freaked out," she said. "I don't know if he thought that someone was spying on him or something, but he said, 'You moved the curtain, right?'"

It was on this day that Nicole learned Raniere had actually created the secret women's group Allison Mack had asked her to join. Raniere told her that he was Mack's master, which made him Nicole's grandmaster. Nicole felt a small amount of relief hearing this news, because it explained so many of her confounding experiences over the last several weeks. "I thought, 'Oh, thank god, people can stop lying and talking around things to me,'" she testified. "Someone can finally explain to me what's going on."

The revelation explained why Raniere had been able to describe internal struggles that Nicole had shared only with Mack. Until that moment, Nicole had guessed that Mack's master was one of the older women in the community.

WHATEVER RELIEF NICOLE felt in knowing this, it was short-lived. "The next walk we went on he said that because of the nature of the master–grandmaster situation, that he could have commanded me to have sex with him that morning, but he didn't because he wanted it to be . . . he didn't want me to think that that was all it was about," she recalled.

In WhatsApp messages, Raniere repeated this to other women he considered his slaves: he could command sex from any one of them at any time, but that wasn't the "purpose" of DOS.

Nicole didn't know how to take Raniere's offhand claim that he now had unhindered access to her on request. On the one hand it was outrageous, but on the other hand she didn't feel she had room to object. What could she say? Mack was constantly monitoring her mental state, coaching her not to be angry. After every walk, Mack would ask Nicole about her mood and remind her that emotions were a choice. "How I acted reflected on her, so I needed to be well behaved," Nicole said.

Perhaps Raniere sensed he was in dangerous territory, or perhaps he really did want Nicole to think she was more than just a sex slave. Either way, Nicole testified, he waited a month before he tried to touch her again, when, on one of her weekly visits in July 2016, he asked to kiss her. The kiss marked the beginning of a new phase in which Nicole was regularly expected to submit to oral sex, and sometimes intercourse, as a way to face her fears and grow.

AS THE WEEKS passed, Nicole said, she grew less resistant to her weekly Albany visits. She tried to get comfortable with the idea that she was bound to Mack and Raniere for the rest of her life.

"Sometimes I would get into just being, 'Okay, if this is my future, then I'm going to try to make the best of it.' So I tried to get to know him," Nicole testified. "I tried to figure out what his life had been about and who he was."

Nicole could text Raniere and ask to stay at his library instead of Mack's place, and if he agreed, she would have more space to herself. She grew less resistant to Raniere's sexual advances, too, though she still told him when she felt uncomfortable. Raniere usually replied that discomfort was good for her and that in time she would "learn to like it."

"Like I would learn to love him, just like I would learn to love Allison," she testified. He seemed to prefer blow jobs, she said, and so she would oblige. She preferred not having to worry about being disciplined or told she had to work on her "issue."

On the last day of V-Week 2016, held at the same Silver Bay retreat center, Nicole met Raniere at his cabin for a walk. He led her to a kids' cabin with bunk beds and began kissing her. "He saw that I was very uncomfortable," she testified. "He said, 'Well, you can choose. Do you want to be intimate and have sex here, or do you want to go on a walk?' I said I wanted to go on a walk."

Later, according to Nicole, Raniere lectured her about choosing an interesting life over one with a white picket fence. He said he was disappointed that she'd chosen a walk.

AFTER V-WEEK, NICOLE flew back to California to spend time with her family and best friend. Raniere told her to stay in touch during the trip. While out for a hike, Nicole tried to tell her friend about some of her struggles and asked for advice.

Nicole couldn't say anything about the collateral and how she was being sexually coerced. "I kind of talked around things," she recalled. Her friend told her, "I don't care how special this guy thinks you are or how much potential he thinks you have. . . . If you're not comfortable, you don't have to do anything you don't want to do."

Her friend couldn't understand the secret pressures that were preventing Nicole from saying no. But Nicole took her friend's advice to heart and felt more comfortable expressing her feelings to Raniere.

She texted Raniere that she was overwhelmed and would like to put aside the sexual aspect of their relationship. She wanted a teacher, and maybe a friend, not a master.

Raniere replied with a long message explaining that Nicole didn't have enough life experience to understand what she was asking. He was offering her a shortcut to experience and wisdom. Because of her lack of experience, she had to relate to him on a sexual level. They couldn't just be friends.

Lectures like these popped up anytime Nicole pushed back against Raniere's control. When she protested, he would talk about the levels of obedience required in the military. "He said in the army sometimes they will have you scrub an entire tank with a toothbrush and then when you finish, put the tank in the mud, bring it back out, and make you do it again," she recalled.

"I remember being like, 'Well, that doesn't sound like very much fun, and also I'm not in the army. This is not the army.'"

RANIERE DIDN'T SEE Nicole as just his personal sex slave it seemed; he also saw her as his personal spy. After Kristin Keeffe's surprise exit from NXIVM in 2014, there was a gap to fill in the company's euphemistically titled "legal" department, one that specialized in uncovering dirt on perceived enemies. Raniere was apparently still boiling with jealousy over Camila's fling with Robbie Chiappone, and so Nicole's latest spying assignment was to seduce him.

Nicole heard about it initially from Allison Mack, who said Raniere had a "really cool" task for her. It was like an acting job, but better.

Then, on one of their late-night walks through Clifton Park, Raniere told Nicole that she needed to seduce Chiappone as part of a bigger plan to track him.

"We talked about it," Nicole testified. "He told me where Robbie worked out and that they were going to arrange for me to kind of run into him and, like, start up a conversation." The spying assignment went smoothly at first. She initiated an innocent conversation, stuck to a well-practiced backstory, and continued texting from a fake identity. She even met Robbie and a friend for a drink. But as the months went by, the sting grew unwieldy and absurd, with Raniere demanding that Nicole use her sway to pressure Robbie into visiting a dominatrix. He went away to a U.S. Navy boot camp instead.

BY OCTOBER 2016, Nicole had learned that Mack had other slaves. Among them were Michele, a nanny with Rainbow Cultural Garden; Danielle, a doctor leading a fitness program; and India Oxenberg, who wanted to start her own catering company but was overseeing odd jobs in the NXIVM community.

Nicole grew to be close friends with India, daughter of the *Dynasty* actor Catherine Oxenberg. "She was really good at talking me off the ledge," Nicole testified. "So if I was going into one of my moods or getting very upset and worked up . . . she was very good at calming me down."

Once Mack's other slaves had been introduced to each other, discipline started to take on a group function with the DOS sorority. "When India and I became close, they used her to help me behave," Nicole testified. "If I didn't do something, then it would make things harder on India." Oxenberg seemed to take more punishment than the rest, especially when it came to calorie restriction. Her goal weight was 107 pounds, and she had to stay on five hundred calories per day until she reached it. "It was just really hard to watch sometimes," Nicole said. "She would get really tired. You could just tell, like, she was just all over the place and hungry."

Mack told Nicole that her own goal weight was around 102 or 103 pounds. Nicole testified that "[Mack] said sometimes she felt like Keith wouldn't care about her if she gained weight, and she knew that wasn't true, but that's how it felt."

Mack and her slaves began meeting Monday evenings for a session that Mack started calling "church." "The four of us would sit on the floor and Allison would sit on a chair or on the couch, and we would talk about the week and where we failed and what we were trying to work on for the next week," Nicole said.

Next, Mack introduced something called a "family photo." "Whenever we all got together, we all had to take off our clothes and take a picture," Nicole testified. "I absolutely hated it."

Nicole had become accustomed to having her personal boundaries constantly challenged. She knew that resisting would only cause her more trouble, but she tried to fight it anyway. Mack would push back, either by telling Nicole she didn't have a choice or by pointing out how her "tantrum" would only hold up everyone else.

In the "family photos," slaves were required to appear happy and uniform. "Sometimes it was fun and I could have fun doing it," Lauren Salzman testified about the photos. "But a lot of times, it was just very painful and hard to put on a happy face for that."

"It made you feel really unsafe . . . because anytime you were together with all the girls, that could happen," Nicole told the court, her voice becoming pained and breathless. "It feels really horrible to not be able to say no to that. Sometimes it felt like the very worst— like one of the worst parts of everything happening because you have no control when you were just told you have to take your clothes off."

THAT OCTOBER, THE five women—Nicole, Allison, Michele, Danielle, and India—drove to Massachusetts for a weekend getaway. "It was supposed to be a bonding trip, and some of it was nice," Nicole testified. "We went on a hike . . . and we kind of explored one of the small towns."

After dinner, Mack made another announcement. "As much as I would like this to be just a bonding trip, it's not," she said, according to Nicole. "I have another assignment for you guys." It was like a family photo, but different. "I am going to take a close-up photo of all of your pussies."

Nicole testified that she said no, absolutely not, but it didn't matter. Her anger was her own problem; it wasn't going to get her off the hook.

After some argument, they each took turns sitting on the couch with legs spread while Mack took photos.

"Beautiful cunt," Mack said, looking at one of the images on her phone.

Nicole said she refused to speak after the assignment. She knew the photos were sent to Raniere; she testified that she'd seen him text Mack a purple devil face emoji after receiving nudes. Mack chided Nicole for making such a big deal out of it. "Are you still throwing a fit over there?" she teased.

Behind the scenes, Mack was working with Raniere and other "founding" masters on a plan to expand DOS and brand its members with a cauterizing pen. Raniere wanted more women, more pain. More regimentation. One DOS master testified that Raniere envisioned thousands or maybe even a million members one day. They talked about hosting high-powered meetings wearing masks and using pseudonyms. They even hatched plans to place a DOS candidate in high-level political office.

Raniere and the founding DOS masters were working on a book, later submitted as trial evidence, which contained NXIVM-style modules on submission and surrender. The lessons aimed to program DOS slaves to endure greater encroachments on their freedom.

"Practice bringing up a high state of joy when being given a command," reads one lesson. "The more distasteful, the greater the joy. It is a gift, it is an opportunity to receive a command from your master." Slaves were encouraged to imagine that a loved one was going to die if they didn't complete their assigned tasks.

By late November 2016, Mack was demanding more collateral from Nicole and the others. They all had to submit fresh collateral by the first of each month or face punishment and risk having their other collateral released. Nicole offered her credit card numbers in December and her grandmother's wedding ring in the new year.

"I just felt like I was getting more and more trapped," she said.

At different times Nicole considered suicide and the witness protection program as means of escape. Suicide wasn't a good option, because she thought it would hurt her family just as much as if her collateral were released. "I don't know that I was thinking incredibly rationally," Nicole said, "but I thought that maybe if I just disappeared, that they wouldn't have any reason to release my collateral."

IT WASN'T UNTIL late 2016 that Nicole and her sorority sisters were branded. The ceremony took place at Allison Mack's house in Clifton Park. Nicole was instructed to think of her master through the initiation, and to show her love through the pain. "I didn't want to say that. I wasn't having that," she said on the witness stand. "I thought about my little brother, I thought about my mom, and I just thought, 'I can do this.'"

By the new year, "readiness" had become a more central practice in DOS, which meant waking up at all hours of the night to respond to drills. "Allison would text me and I had to respond within sixty seconds and it would be any time, day or night," Nicole said. If Nicole didn't answer, Mack might call her coworkers, friends, or manager to track her. Failure to respond was punished.

Nicole testified that she often felt she was on the edge of giving in completely but that a voice in her head always stopped her from total surrender. She put up the strongest fight when she felt herself falling in love with someone around March 2017.

Just as Daniela had done a decade earlier, Nicole told Raniere about her romantic feelings. She wanted a normal relationship with someone she'd chosen and the freedom to act on her own feelings.

"He said, 'Okay, fine, just give me one year. Just trust me for one year and then I will help you find a partner,'" Nicole recalled. "For me that was really good news. One year felt like, 'Okay, I can do that. I can get through one year.'" Nicole eased up on her protests after that. She'd still have to remain committed to DOS for the rest of her life, but she had a light to look forward to at the end of a one-year tunnel.

Nicole wouldn't have to wait that long to be free of Raniere's trap, as it turned out. Within two months, most of DOS was disbanded. Within a year, Raniere was in jail.

CHAPTER TWENTY-FOUR

"Master, Please Brand Me"

When I first met Sarah Edmondson, I had only a superficial understanding of her relationship with Lauren Salzman and why she might choose to formally bind that relationship with a "collateralized vow of obedience."

Before DOS, Edmondson and Salzman had talked about a lifetime of closeness ahead of them. They looked forward to wearing matching tracksuits and leading self-help seminars together well into retirement.

So how was Salzman able to lie to her best friend? She lied about Raniere's involvement in DOS and denied that his initials had been scarred into her flesh. And she used her deep knowledge of Edmondson's inner life to manipulate her into compliance.

It wasn't until Salzman testified at Raniere's trial in 2019 that a whole new side of her story emerged. Back in early 2017, over only a few short weeks, she'd become the most prolific recruiter in DOS in part because she, too, had been lied to.

On New Year's Eve, 2017, Salzman told Raniere that she was unhappy about his being surrounded by a new inner circle of women. After spending half her life near the center of his world, she'd found herself on the outside looking in. Raniere's response was to tell her he wanted to re-establish their relationship and bring them closer again, Salzman testified. "He asked me what I was willing to do for my growth and for my commitment to him."

"Anything," Salzman replied. "I'm fully committed to my growth and fully committed to you." She believed she was being evaluated for her fitness as a parent. She knew she was under a microscope because years earlier, in 2011, Raniere had challenged her eligibility as a mother when he accused her of "roughhousing" with another man at a volleyball game. Salzman had dropped all her commitments and written a ten-page "ethical breach plan" to regain her position on Raniere's waiting list of would-be mothers. She single-mindedly pursued this outcome with Raniere, even as he slowly became more public about his relationship with Marianna.

Pam Cafritz died of cancer in October 2016, after which Raniere turned more of his attention to Marianna, who had recently become pregnant with his child. Marianna was not sworn to a life of obedience, and with Cafritz no longer around to facilitate abortions, she had more leverage than ever to start a family. Raniere knew Marianna was pregnant in early January but he kept this from Salzman, knowing it could wake her up from her dream of starting a family with him, which was what had kept her so closely bound. As her mentor in all areas of her life, including her medical decisions, Raniere knew that Salzman valued him and family above everything else.

Rosa Laura Junco, a wealthy proctor overseeing NXIVM's "ethical media" projects, then approached Salzman about a very important secret. But first, Junco told her, she needed to submit collateral—something very damaging to her life and relationships—to hear what the secret was. Salzman testified that Junco's invitation was significant, since she was the one who'd convinced her not to be discouraged by Raniere's increasingly public relationship with Marianna a year earlier, reminding her that if she left NXIVM, she'd never get to be with him.

Salzman's aspiration to have Raniere's baby didn't come up during the conversation with Junco, but she still linked Junco's offer with the possibility of working through her issues and fulfilling that dream. She walked away from the meeting with her mind racing. It was only after Raniere approached her again, this time revealing that he'd created a secret "sorority," that the pieces started falling into place.

Raniere asked her to become one of eight founding members of the women's group, even though DOS had secretly been operating for well over a year already. He asked her to guess who the other founding members might be. "Once I knew Rosa Laura, I guessed the others," Salzman testified. It was the same group of women, including Nicki Clyne and Allison Mack, that she'd admitted made her feel like an outsider on New Year's Eve. After years of feeling neglected, Salzman was becoming an insider once again. She wrote a letter of support for Mack and Clyne's marriage application—an arrangement that allowed Clyne, a Canadian, to stay in the country. Clyne posed for their wedding photos in the same black suit jacket she'd later wear to see Raniere in court.

RANIERE WAS SELECTIVE about what he told Salzman. He didn't reveal the master–slave part, or that she'd need to submit more and more collateral until her life was "fully collateralized." He made it sound like a women-led support group. "He told me that the sorority had started because of a personal struggle that Camila had surrounding a suicide attempt," Salzman testified.

As collateral, Salzman provided an account of an actual crime involving not only herself but her parents and Raniere as well. She wrote that, at a volleyball game in the fall of 2002, a NXIVM student from Mexico had had a psychotic break and become agitated. Instead of taking the woman to hospital, Salzman and others drove her around, physically restrained her, and put Valium in scrambled eggs to make her sleep. Salzman had borrowed the meds from her mother, who got the prescription from her father. Raniere was the one who suggested that, rather than taking the woman to the emergency room, a drive might calm her down.

This was the most damaging thing Salzman could think of, but Junco wouldn't accept it as collateral. "She told me that she rejected it because it would be a conflict of interest for Keith to release the collateral, because he would be implicated in the collateral," Salzman testified. "I needed to submit something that wouldn't hurt him so he would be sure to feel good releasing it, if I ever break my vow."

Junco suggested that Salzman submit naked photos, which she eventually agreed to do. Salzman testified that she was comforted by the fact that Junco had submitted similar photos as part of her own collateral. Salzman put the photos on a USB drive and gave them to Junco. That's when she found out she would be Raniere's slave.

"She explained the concept that he would be my master and I would be his slave, and the idea that having a master in your life is to help you learn to become a master in your own life," Salzman testified. Raniere taught that everyone was a slave to impulses—to eat, to have sex. But this was an opportunity to serve something bigger, something rooted in Salzman's highest values and principles, as defined by NXIVM.

JUNCO THEN TOLD Salzman about the branding. "The idea of the brand was to memorialize on our body our promise to ourselves that we made this lifetime commitment to our growth and our master," Salzman recalled at Raniere's trial. NXIVM defined greatness in the context of overcoming great adversity. Receiving the brand would test Salzman's readiness to face pain in pursuit of her goals.

"I was very familiar with the concept," Salzman testified. "I was very enrolled in that idea of doing hard things to become somebody who would do hard things when it was most important."

Junco showed Salzman her own scar. It was a kind of monogram, with a *K*, *A*, and *R* representing Raniere's initials. Salzman was more than ready to do the hard thing for Raniere. She "collateralized" everything she owned—her investments, her two homes, her two cars, all her art, and signed letters resigning from all her positions if she ever broke her vow.

Like a few of the other "founding" slaves, Junco and Allison Mack had received their brands months earlier from a professional body modification artist. But now, after one of Mack's slaves had been trained to use the cauterizing pen, Raniere wanted to change the atmosphere of the initiation. The day before Salzman was branded, Raniere and Mack went on a walk and discussed how future branding ceremonies would be carried out. A recording of their chat would later become evidence at Raniere's trial.

Raniere suggested "a certain ritualization" for each of the seven lines of the brand. "Maybe each of the strokes has something that's said with them, and maybe repeated after the stroke is done," he said. He asked what rituals would be most meaningful and encouraging of surrender, and suggested that recording the branding on video from different angles would provide another layer of "collateral." This became an important detail at his trial two years later.

"Probably should be a more vulnerable position," Raniere continued. "Legs spread straight, feet being held to the side of the table, hands probably above the head, almost like tied down like a sacrificial whatever."

After a pause, he added, "And the person should ask to be branded."

"Okay," Mack replied.

"Should say, 'Please brand me, it would be my honor,' or something like that. 'An honor I want to wear for the rest of my life,'" Raniere said. "And they should probably say that before they're held down, so it doesn't seem like they're being coerced."

This became the script for Lauren Salzman's branding ceremony the next day.

ON JANUARY 10, 2017, Salzman arrived at Allison Mack's house and was asked to take a naked photo. She lay on a massage table and helped place a stencil on her bikini line. NXIVM senior proctor Loreta Garza recorded the procedure as Salzman's other new "sisters" surrounded her, holding her limbs in place as if she were a human sacrifice.

"Master, please brand me, it would be an honor," Salzman said. She braced for the most painful moments of her life.

The ceremony fell on the same day as a memorial for Pam Cafritz. Salzman thought it was strange to see Raniere talking with giddy excitement about this new sorority in the wake of Cafritz's recent death. According to Salzman, DOS seemed crafted to fill the gap left in the absence of Cafritz, who'd functioned as a kind of procurer for

Raniere. "Pam facilitated all Keith's objectives, whatever Keith wanted in many of his personal relationships," she testified. "Especially my relationship with Keith was facilitated by Pam." Salzman hadn't realized it yet, but she and the other slaves were already filling Cafritz's shoes.

FIVE DAYS AFTER submitting her collateral, Salzman flew to Vancouver to tell Sarah Edmondson about the sorority. She wanted more than anything to prove to Raniere that she was loyal and capable. She also wanted to prove to herself that she believed in DOS and could make it transformative.

Salzman would put her powers of persuasion to work and bring in more slaves faster than all seven of the other "founding" masters. "I think I have good capacity to enroll other people in my ideas," Salzman explained in her testimony. "I had the least experience and the least objections at the time."

Ten days after Salzman submitted her collateral, Raniere told her that Marianna was pregnant. He'd known for three months but had waited until after Salzman had put her whole life on the line in a vow to never disobey him. It was a personal betrayal, but it was also a betrayal of the ethics Raniere taught, according to Salzman.

"He got me to stay because he thought I would leave if Marianna was pregnant," Salzman testified. "He stole from me and himself the ability to know if I would have stayed no matter what, without being in a 100 percent collateralized vow."

Salzman learned that Mack and Daniella Padilla, another first-line DOS recruiter, both believed they would raise Keith's babies, too. Mack was particularly excited about having new sister wives, which left Salzman feeling alienated and confused. "I was like, number one, I've had sister wives for twenty years; number two . . . it's been something that's been incredibly difficult for me," Salzman testified. "This was just a lot to learn."

Out of self-preservation, Salzman had to turn off the part of her brain that was hurting and questioning. Bound by collateral that made every moment an emergency situation, she didn't have time to second-guess herself. Not with her job, home, and family on the line. "I stuffed it, I compartmentalized it, and 100 percent went full force forward with my conviction that DOS was not bad, that it was a growth program, that it was amazing, that this was for women and for me to get through my issues," Salzman told the court. Later, she would discover that Allison Mack and Nicki Clyne were giving "seduction" assignments to their slaves—ordering them to seduce Raniere, take a photo, and enjoy it.

When initiating the group of women she'd recruited into DOS, including Sarah Edmondson, Salzman did a lot of work to soften the strangeness of it all. She wasn't allowed to reveal Raniere's involvement anyway, so she presented the best version of what she thought a women's group building discipline and character could be. She lit candles, made dinner arrangements, and broke the evening up into small, escalating reveals. She led each of the five women to different rooms in her house, timing their arrivals so that they wouldn't see each other until the ceremony was underway. She asked them to take their clothes off and put on a blindfold before they were led into the living room together. Sitting cross-legged in a circle on the floor, they all took off their blindfolds at once.

"Guys, get over it—get over your body issues," Salzman told them. "We're a sisterhood, relax."

Then they all got dressed.

IT WASN'T UNTIL later, at Allison Mack's house, that the brand stencil came out and the clothes came off again. Salzman said the brand represented the four elements: earth, wind, fire, and water. Each woman was held down on a massage table and video recorded. Nudity was easier the second time around, but there was no avoiding the blinding pain of the cauterizing pen. Some of the women thrashed and squealed and asked for a cloth to bite down on.

It takes a twisted imagination to come up with such a scenario, but its basic premise has been studied by scientist Stanley Milgram. His obedience experiments of the 1960s found that most study participants were willing to cause harm to another person despite their own conscience if doing so was presented as mandatory by an authority figure. Instead of branding, the Milgram experiments instructed participants to read out memory tests to an unseen student and administer what they thought were electric shocks of increasing voltage when the student answered incorrectly. (In reality, no student was electrocuted.) The study's findings suggest that more than half of us are capable of inflicting traumatizing, potentially lethal pain if we believe we don't have a choice.

Sarah Edmondson told me that the trauma actually bonded the women together. There were fart jokes, yogic breathing lessons, and words of gentle encouragement. Edmondson disassociated, which oddly earned her praise. "She did her yoga breathing," Salzman testified. "She handled it, comparatively, much better than the other girls did and I was very proud of her at the time."

After Edmondson spotted the text on Salzman's phone from "KAR," her first guess was Karen Unterreiner, but she did consider that it could have come from Raniere. She thought Raniere might even be proud of how well she'd done. Days after the painful ceremony, Edmondson wanted the brand to be a good thing—it was hers and she'd survived it. According to the research kept in Raniere's library, severe initiation rituals actually increase the commitment of new members. It took time and soul-searching for her to realize that she'd never freely given consent.

Lauren Salzman testified, "At the time I thought it was consensual and they wanted to do it, but even if they didn't, I was their master and I told them to."

CHAPTER TWENTY-FIVE

Reckoning

In March 2017, Mark Vicente was reaching a point where he had to choose between Keith Raniere and his wife, actor and former NXIVM member Bonnie Piesse.

Piesse had decided in January to resign from all things NXIVM over conflicts she was having with the upper ranks. She thought NXIVM had turned against her. She was constantly getting critical "feedback" from Lauren Salzman and Clare Bronfman on what she was told were her defiance issues.

NXIVM had been encouraging her to move up the ranks, but to get there, Piesse had to show a concerning amount of obedience. "Bonnie's this little firecracker who doesn't really care what you say," actor Maja Miljkovic told me. "They were trying to make her just into another woman who will do whatever."

That wasn't the only reason Piesse had backed away. She'd watched some of the other women in NXIVM become unhealthily skinny, tired, and stressed. Allison Mack was wearing a belly chain and India Oxenberg was wearing a similar chain around her neck. Both of them were wasting away, becoming increasingly frail-looking.

Vicente wanted to follow Piesse back to Los Angeles and escape whatever it was that was happening under his watch, but he still felt committed to his friend Raniere and his responsibilities as a senior proctor and NXIVM board member. The organization was also a steady source of income at a time when his filmmaking projects had stalled.

AT TRIAL, VICENTE recalled a conversation he had with Raniere during a springtime walk around Albany. The exchange planted seeds of doubt that would soon upend his life completely.

"We were walking and I was beginning to have very distant, at that point, doubts about him," Vicente testified in May 2019. "And he said something to me that sounded, you know, one of the usual things that sounded very 'principle.' And I said to him, 'Well, you could be a psychopath and say those exact same words.'

"He seemed to me to get very excited. And he said, 'Well, I could be. Let's say I am.' And the whole discussion continued. To me it was a strange response, his what I perceived as excitement about it."

Vicente told the court that his apprehension grew as his conversations with Raniere continued. "'I don't know what is going on with you and all these women, but I have deep concerns about this all blowing up in some way that is bad,'" Vicente told Raniere. "He said to me, 'Well, I don't think this will blow up; maybe other things will, but not this.' I thought, 'I don't know where to go from here. He's not engaging me on what I'm concerned about.'"

Vicente received a worrying phone call from an L.A. student who'd been propositioned about submitting collateral for entrance into a secret society. Around the same time, he was called to participate in a Jness intensive that solidified his suspicion that something sinister was happening. The program riffed on familiar NXIVM themes geared for women around not choosing victimhood, but it also went a few steps further.

"My general understanding of that intensive was, in essence, if somebody complains about abuse, they are, in fact, the abuser," Vicente testified. "So if somebody says, 'There's abuse going on and so-and-so person is doing it,' the whole idea is, 'Well, actually you're the abuser.'"

Vicente took Lauren Salzman aside and told her about his concerns. On top of the bizarre lessons, he was worried for Lauren's health, as she was looking fatigued and experiencing bouts of vertigo.

"'You know,'" he told her, "'all these skinny women and all these things that are happening, why don't we start talking about that?'"

According to Vicente's testimony, Salzman went pale and replied, "'I don't know what you're talking about.'"

"'You absolutely do know what I'm talking about,'" he said. "'This stuff doesn't happen without you knowing.'"

Vicente began to suspect that Raniere had wanted the amped-up Jness course to influence him and drive an ideological wedge between himself and Piesse. Raniere had reason to suspect that Piesse was exhibiting "suppressive behavior" behind the scenes and likely wanted her removed. "I began to piece together that this intensive was designed for me," Vicente testified. "It was designed for me to turn against my wife."

Sarah Edmondson was having her own doubts. An episode of *Black Mirror* sent her into a worried spiral of questions. In the TV show, a kid is blackmailed by text into escalating crimes—all because a hacker discovers his porn-watching history.

"I actually wrote to Lauren and I was like, 'Who has my photo?' I didn't freak out, but all of a sudden I was just like, 'What am I involved in?'" Edmondson asked Salzman who her master was and where all the photos were stored. The answer she kept getting in return was "You don't need to know."

In April 2017, Vicente learned about a "vow" found on Allison Mack's computer. "The vow was to Raniere, vowing in essence that she would never leave. And that if she ever did, she would give up any children she had to him and all her possessions," he testified. Vows were already a part of NXIVM's curriculum, but this was more extreme and disturbing than anything Vicente had encountered before.

"I had finally asked myself the question, the most terrifying question, which is, What if he is not who he represents himself to be, but what if he's the exact opposite? What if he is in fact evil? What if all of this is a mask to do heinous things to other people?"

Vicente told Sarah Edmondson what he knew: that there was a secret society involving "collateral" and lifelong vows. "Her response I recall was something along the lines of, 'Well, if something like this existed, then a person that was involved probably couldn't talk about it.'"

Edmondson was trying to signal to her friend that she was already branded and had given collateral. But it would take another few weeks for Vicente to catch on.

AT ANOTHER INTENSIVE in L.A., Vicente warned two coaches about the secret society he had discovered. "I believed that their girlfriends had been approached for the secret society. And I said to both of them, individually, I said, 'You need to get your girlfriends away from Albany. You need to get them away from these women that are trying to enroll them in something. You need to protect them, they are in danger.'"

Finally, on May 20, Vicente told Sarah Edmondson that he was going to resign. "'I think that something is going on that could be illegal,'" he recounted telling her. "'I think it's a huge problem.'"

Edmondson had been playing along with assignments simply to avoid punishment. She felt thankful she wasn't in Albany with the other women, who were punished with a studded leather paddle if they went against orders texted to them or failed to respond in under a minute.

Still, she gave Vicente the same answer she'd given the previous month: if somebody was involved in something like what Vicente was describing, she probably couldn't say anything about it. "That's when the light bulb went off," Vicente said. He asked Edmondson if she'd been invited to the secret society and her demeanor changed.

"They have too much on me," Edmondson said after a stressful silence. "They have confessions, recorded confessions, they have naked material, and I'm trapped."

"And I said, 'Well, if the consequence of you leaving is that all these things end up on the internet, then you better leave, because what you're involved in is illegal and you're complicit in this if you continue.'

"'You have to make peace with it,'" Vicente recalled telling Edmondson. "'So maybe your naked body is going on the internet, fine. *Make peace with it.*'"

Finally, Edmondson revealed that she'd been branded. She told Vicente about everything: the video recording, the punishment, the readiness drills keeping them up at all hours of the night.

That conversation spurred the first of many phone calls to the U.S. Federal Bureau of Investigation. The agency would eventually open a file on NXIVM that led to Raniere's trial and conviction in 2019.

"I was horrified," Vicente testified, his voice breaking. "I just—in essence, the walls just came tumbling down. Oh, my god, this is what is really going on."

JENN KOBELT USED to celebrate each May 31. It was the day she'd joined NXIVM, and it became an anniversary that represented a turning point in her life.

But May 31, 2017, was a different kind of turning point. After a roller-coaster four years in which she'd left a yoga studio job, launched an acting career, and become Sarah Edmondson's assistant as a way to fund her NXIVM education, she had begun to think the company had some terrible secrets.

"That was the day it all fell apart," she told me.

Kobelt had just finished a training session with the women's group Jness when she noticed that Edmondson's husband, Anthony Ames, had left all the NXIVM group chats almost simultaneously. Then her phone rang.

It was Edmondson. She had only cryptic things to say. "I'm sorry, we've been horribly misled," she told Kobelt. Edmondson said they could still be friends, but not in the context of NXIVM. She and her husband were quitting, effective immediately.

Kobelt knew from Edmondson's tone that something bad was happening, but Edmondson couldn't, or wouldn't, say what it was. "That freaked me out a lot," Kobelt says. If there was a good reason Edmondson was fleeing, she wanted to know about it, and likely flee with her.

After pacing around her apartment for two days, Kobelt decided to reach out to Edmondson using the secret chat function on the messaging app Telegram. She hoped Edmondson would feel safer answering her nagging questions there, not realizing that DOS slaves used Telegram to communicate with their masters. Edmondson instantly called her with a barrage of her own questions, apparently thinking Kobelt was in DOS.

"She was grilling me on whether I'd ever been in a secret group, and I'm just like so confused," Kobelt recalls. "I remember saying to her, 'You mean like ESP? That's kind of secret.' And she was like, 'Yes, but different.'"

Kobelt grew more disoriented by Edmondson's line of questioning: Had Kobelt ever wondered why ESP was so expensive? Or why asking questions was so strongly discouraged? At one point, when Edmondson burst into tears and yelled "Motherfucker!" Kobelt thought she might be listening to her friend unravel in real time.

"She was helping lead me down my own rabbit hole," Kobelt told me. "I decided I needed to resign and figure this out."

Edmondson had spent the better part of a ten-hour train ride making many similar calls, trying to figure out who was in DOS and to warn the women she knew without giving away too many details. If Lauren Salzman found out that Edmondson had broken her vow of secrecy, there was a chance her collateral could be released. So Edmondson had everyone swear not to tell. She told Kobelt that even her live-in boyfriend couldn't know about their conversation.

While Edmondson headed to Toronto to visit family, her husband took a noisier approach. He confronted NXIVM's leadership, including Lauren Salzman, at a gathering of more than a hundred coaches. Portions of a secret audio recording of the meeting were first published by the CBC podcast *Uncover: Escaping NXIVM*.

"Sarah tells me she got fucking branded," Ames told the gathering. His voice was icy, as if he was holding back stronger words. "This is criminal shit. . . . Don't even try to wrap your head around how this is okay. I'm out."

On his way out the door, he added, "You're branding my fucking *wife*!"

Causing a scene was part of Edmondson and Ames's plan to leave without setting off alarm bells. Ames was known for his "anger" issues, and Edmondson had spent plenty of exploration-of-meaning (EM) sessions working through her "dependency" issues. Ames's "tantrum" was intended to frame their exit as a spontaneous attempt to save their marriage, not a move to get the authorities involved. They were afraid of intimidation, lawsuits, and worse.

Lauren Salzman immediately jumped into damage-control mode. She texted Raniere "911." When she finally spoke with him, he acted as though he were learning about the branding for the first time. "How do you think I feel learning that this wife branded my initials next to her vagina?" he said. Salzman took this as an instruction that she needed to lie to protect Raniere. If anyone asked, she stuck to the story that he didn't know anything; he wasn't involved; he was as shocked as anyone that women went around branding themselves.

In the weeks after she'd been branded, Edmondson had showed the scar to a close friend, who pointed out that she could see a downward-facing *K*. But there also looked to be a small zigzagged *M* tucked under a letter *A*—possibly a reference to Allison Mack.

Edmondson called Salzman to say she had to leave in order to stop Ames from divorcing her. She asked about her naked photos and confessions, and if it was really Raniere's initials on her body. She wanted answers, but she was also testing how much Salzman knew and what she was willing to reveal.

Salzman admitted that Raniere knew about DOS and had given permission to use concepts of collateral and penance. She defended the initiation ceremony, saying, "It wasn't supposed to be a horrible experience. . . . I don't believe it's bad for women to build honor and character." This was a message Salzman would repeat many times over the next year as she spearheaded a wider damage-control plan within the NXIVM community.

THOUGH EDMONDSON'S EXIT was quiet at first, one week later an all-out war erupted in Vancouver. The branding allegations appeared on *Frank Report*, former NXIVM publicist Frank Parlato's tabloid-style blog. Kobelt remembers that she and her boyfriend were driving over a bridge when she first read the details. "I read the article out loud," she told me. "I was flabbergasted."

The only names mentioned in the June 5 post were Keith Raniere and Allison Mack, but the post described the nude photos collected as "collateral," the hours-long branding process that was recorded on cell phone video, and the vow of slavery taken by each recruit.

Not long after the post went live, Edmondson got a phone call from one of her coaches. "I heard about the *Frank Report* and I'm supposed to move to Albany," the Vancouver coach told Edmondson. Though she can't recall her exact words, Edmondson replied with some variation of "Please don't move to Albany."

"Why, it can't be true, can it?" the coach asked.

"Do you need to see my brand?" Edmondson fired back.

The woman on the other end of the call sounded concerned and confused, so Edmondson kept going. "I said, 'I got branded, please don't move to Albany,' and I hung up."

Later that day, Edmondson found out the call had been a trap. The coach was already in DOS and already branded. "She was taping me, to prove that I was breaking my vow of secrecy."

NXIVM leadership had discovered that Edmondson was warning Vancouver students about the branding ceremony and helping people cancel their memberships, and Salzman had quickly mounted a campaign to stop supporters from leaving. "That's when shit really started to hit the fan," Kobelt said.

KOBELT CONFRONTED ONE of her closest Vancouver allies, Lucas Roberts. Roberts ran a local computer support and repair business, and as one of the city's few NXIVM proctors, he often played the role of personal assistant to Lauren Salzman when she visited town. Kobelt said, "What would it take for you to leave NXIVM? What would you need to know?"

Roberts paused to think about it. He said he needed to know that they were really hurting people, and that they weren't doing anything to try to make it better. It seemed to him that Sarah Edmondson was lashing out because of her own marital problems, not because of any real injustice.

Kobelt says she nearly convinced Roberts to leave. He told her he was 80 percent of the way there but that first he wanted to talk to Salzman. Kobelt didn't yet know that Salzman was one of the first-line DOS masters, responsible for having recruited Sarah Edmondson and several others into a vow of lifelong obedience.

Apparently Salzman "ninja minded" Roberts into staying and taking on a bigger role within NXIVM. He immediately dropped all contact with NXIVM's critics and would later pick up the responsibilities that Edmondson had left behind.

This kicked off a period of elevated paranoia, where former members couldn't be sure who to trust. Innocuous messages of concern and wanting to help would often escalate to strong-arming manipulation.

Edmondson discovered that most of the women working as coaches in Vancouver had either joined DOS or had submitted first-round collateral to hear the DOS pitch. She guessed that fourteen of the eighteen women coaches had been propositioned, and that many had accepted. "There were women at different stages of their commitment to DOS. Many of them weren't branded yet," she said. "When I left, a ton of women left."

Jenn Kobelt was still coming to terms with the fact that DOS was very, very real. She discovered that some of her close friends were part of the secret slave group and had been subjected to disturbing punishments and threats. There was much more beyond what was said on Frank Parlato's blog. She didn't yet know about the dungeon the sorority had been building in the weeks leading up to Edmondson's departure. At Raniere's trial, prosecutors would show an itemized list of purchases from the website ExtremeRestraints.com, including ankle shackles, a hanging rubber strap cage, a studded paddle, a suspension kit, an electrified dog collar, and two human-sized cages. Punishments that DOS slaves may have received from these instruments of torture were apparently filmed, and probably on a hard drive somewhere.

There was another solid two weeks of constant phone calls. It wasn't easy for Kobelt and Edmondson to determine everyone's allegiances. Some members went totally silent, which was usually an indication that they were sticking with Salzman's version of events. But it became clear that some of the people calling in were essentially spying on enemies, trying to get whatever information they could to use against defectors in court.

NXIVM later accused Kobelt and Edmondson of accessing their servers and canceling over $100,000 in credit payments.

CHAPTER TWENTY-SIX

"Me Too"

On Monday, October 16, 2017, Sarah Edmondson looked at her phone, scrolled through a stream of #MeToo posts on social media, and cried.

Overnight those two words had echoed to the far corners of the internet. The slogan was first coined by civil rights activist Tarana Burke in 2006 as a way to break through the silence that hid pervasive sexual abuse. It persisted on the cutting edge of feminist thought for a decade. Then, on the heels of a *New York Times* exposé that recounted the unrelenting abuses of film producer Harvey Weinstein, the hashtag suddenly became a near-universal cry for women seeking solidarity.

It made sense that Hollywood actresses were the catalyst that sent the movement into unstoppable, viral territory. Not only were they Weinstein's alleged victims; they were finally acknowledging an unspoken industry-wide delusion that unwanted advances were just part of the job description and somehow unavoidable. Women like Edmondson were expected to grit their teeth or preferably smile through harassment at any personal cost. But all at once, women realized the absurdity and misogyny of this unfair tax on women's bodies and psyches.

Actor Alyssa Milano tweeted, "If all the women who have been sexually harassed or assaulted wrote 'Me too' as a status, we might give people a sense of the magnitude of the problem." She invited anyone with firsthand experience of sexual abuse of any kind to simply reply "me too." Tens of thousands of people responded, and many more posted their own harrowing stories.

EDMONDSON WAS STILL trying to process what she'd been a part of. She knew she'd been coerced. She knew she would not have consented to any part of DOS if she'd known its design and purpose. But it didn't easily slot into one category. Harassment? Assault? Her experience didn't quite fit with the accounts of unreported rape or workplace groping she was reading. NXIVM was way out in left field in many ways, and yet the silence, the shame, and the systemic enabling were all there.

"I can't be quiet anymore," she wrote in her own #MeToo Facebook status.

Edmondson wrote that she used to think sexual assault and harassment had never really happened to her; it was something other women experienced. She never saw herself as a victim. NXIVM had trained her to take responsibility for everything that happened in her life, and that pretty much included unwanted touching.

She had been violated before, her post explained: once at a rave in England, and again in a bathroom in Israel. But most recently she'd been sexually abused at Allison Mack's house near Albany. "Naked, pinned down, mutilated and videotaped," she wrote. "After the humiliation, disassociation, dehumanization and pain, the worst part was my closest male friend not believing me."

The next day, October 17, 2017, *The New York Times* published an investigation into Keith Raniere, another man who, like Harvey Weinstein, stood accused of feeling entitled to the bodies of women he encountered. Edmondson was featured on the front page of the next morning's print edition, carefully exposing her scar for photographer Ruth Fremson.

Actor Maja Miljkovic was overjoyed to see Raniere's story aligned with Weinstein's. "It was one of the best things to have happen—to have the Harvey thing come out first, then the thing about Keith right after. It primed everyone to go, 'I see, there's a pattern of abusing piles of women using their position of authority,'" she said. "I thought that was just brilliant."

I SAT DOWN with Edmondson just over a week later, as more allegations against powerful men circulated on social media, in private Google spreadsheets, and on the front pages of news sites. She told me that the #MeToo movement had given her a powerful collective consciousness to tap into. "All of a sudden my whole body was overcome with *I have to talk about this*," she said. "I had been silent. I was trying to get people out without even telling them what had happened."

Edmondson didn't want to let shame and the threat of retaliation stand in her way anymore. "I didn't ever see myself doing this sort of thing, but I'm feeling a really strong pull to expose this kind of stuff," she said.

For decades the many abuses of Keith Raniere had existed in plain sight—somehow too absurd and sensational to ever be taken seriously. Part of the reason those abuses went unchallenged for so long had to do with our cultural understanding of his victims, the majority of whom were young women.

It's true that young, beautiful women are often perceived as sympathetic victims—though this applies only to unambiguous crimes. Their abusers must jump out of bushes, or at the very least the abused must rush straight to the authorities—no negotiation or continued contact with abusers permitted—to secure their status as a good, "credible" victim.

Edmondson, too, had thought she was complicit and therefore not a good victim. To further complicate things, in NXIVM there were other women, branded as slaves just like Edmondson, who did not consider themselves victims at all.

Most of the women who would later testify against Raniere were wrapped up in his projects, his social life, and in some cases his other crimes. And, like the actors who kept silent about abuse by disgraced film producer Harvey Weinstein, they didn't want to invite the kind of scandal into their lives that comes with betraying a powerful man.

It has taken the #MeToo movement, and with it a paradigm shift in our understanding of sexual abuse, to even begin to realize that this kind of "complicity" does not disqualify women like Edmondson from seeking justice.

If Weinstein was an oversized jungle predator carelessly terrorizing whoever crossed his path, Raniere was a smaller but no less dangerous creature, a spider who meticulously lured women into his web. The power dynamic in the NXIVM case is arguably even more skewed than it was with Weinstein. These women weren't just working for Raniere's company; he held the keys to everything they owned and had the power to destroy all their important relationships. He was their therapist, their spiritual teacher, their second dad, their abusive lover. It was this power, fueled by the unlimited financial resources of heirs to the Seagram liquor fortune, that enabled Raniere to act above the law for so long.

As I met with Edmondson, NXIVM's inner circle was still working on a campaign to discredit her. The top ranks of DOS were planning for a public relations battle and had hired a firm to help them secure favorable media coverage.

Raniere prepared a "position statement" claiming that the branding ceremony was a consensual symbol of mutual commitment, drawing parallels to fraternities where men brand themselves. Raniere grandiosely compared the DOS vow of secrecy to the U.S. Declaration of Independence. He denied his involvement and called Edmondson a "vow breaker" and a liar.

"Any story based on the few liars who seek to shame their sisters because of their own dishonor is regretful," Raniere wrote. "Imagine if our forefathers had done the same the moment times got difficult." The statement was never released.

In meetings with Raniere and the other founding members of DOS, Lauren Salzman helped come up with new explanations for its most shocking practices. The seduction assignments were just a "dare," not meant to be carried out, Raniere suggested. The brand represented the four elements, or seven chakras, or a Greek symbol/letter combination, *bar alpha mu*. Salzman sketched out new versions of the brand on graph paper, highlighting the different symbols for reporters; Raniere told her to make a sorority website for *bar alpha mu*.

Meanwhile, more and more slaves were asking Salzman to return their collateral and come clean about Raniere's involvement. At

V-Week Raniere had claimed he had very little knowledge of DOS, that the group was "a little edgy" and "alternative," but that he supported a woman's right to express herself.

Salzman repeated this version of the story to anyone who asked and collected positive testimonials from the slaves who remained faithful.

THE VIDEO DEPICTING Sarah Edmondson's branding was also prepared for release. Salzman and actor Nicki Clyne had begun preparing for a number of possible outcomes in September 2017. They edited the recording of the branding, blurred out nudity, transcribed the audio, and edited audio files to see how best to present the ceremony to the public.

"We discussed among first-line DOS masters and Keith the idea of possibly releasing the branding video," Salzman recalled at Raniere's trial. "Keith said that he was considering whether we should show it to the media reporters or release it publicly." (The clip, which Raniere had described as another layer of collateral, was leaked to Mexican media after Salzman testified.)

"We edited out the dialogue portions of the branding ceremony from Sarah's branding video," Salzman said, "things like 'I'm committing my labor, my material possessions, my body for unconditional use to my master and that's my highest priority.'"

The edited version still retained the statement read by every slave before she was branded: "Master, please brand me. It would be an honor, an honor I want to wear for the rest of my life."

Salzman pulled together as much proof of consent as she could find, including some collateral, and met with a forensic psychologist and a former law enforcement agent. She repeated the same story Raniere wanted them to hear: that Raniere had no knowledge of the sorority, that seduction assignments were just dares, that all the women were thriving and achieving their goals.

Salzman and Mack told the NXIVM community the same thing. They said that ex-law-enforcement had vetted the situation and there was no need for concern. "I lied to the entire community about it," Salzman later testified. "I lied to the media about it. I lied to everybody about it." That included her own mother.

NXIVM then released a statement on its website: "Recently a media outlet unfoundedly, and incorrectly, linked NXIVM corporation, its founder and its related companies, with a social group. The allegations relayed in the story are built upon sources, some of which are under criminal investigation or already indicted, who act as a coordinated group. This story might be a *criminal product of criminal minds* who, in the end, are also hurting the victims of the story.

"Unfortunately, this media outlet fell prey to these coordinated, criminal efforts. NXIVM was not able to participate in this story because it painfully held true to the due process of our free world justice system."

Lauren Salzman's behind-the-scenes public relations outreach was working. The PR firm hired to get favorable media coverage secured a major profile with a writer who covers consent issues.

I MET SARAH Edmondson at an upscale vegetarian restaurant on May 30, 2018, seven months after my first interview with her and one year since she had mustered the courage to leave. It was the same day *The New York Times* dropped another bombshell story, this time giving NXIVM's top leaders more space to justify their therapies and minimize abuses. Salzman later testified that she and Allison Mack had lied to the reporter outright.

Edmondson asked me what I thought of the story. Instead of clear-cut villains, the latest piece painted Raniere, Salzman, and Clare Bronfman as athletic, smart, conventionally attractive, and in touch with their emotions. It placed NXIVM within a constellation of self-improvement regimens that didn't sound all that different. Allison Mack was quoted as saying that it had been her idea to brand women recruits; that, in her mind, a tattoo wasn't meaningful enough. "I was like, 'Y'all, a tattoo? People get drunk and tattooed on their ankle,'" Mack told the *Times*. "I have two tattoos and they mean nothing."

Both Salzman and Mack knew this wasn't true, that it was Raniere who came up with the idea of branding. "She took credit for coming up with the idea of the brand and then was like, 'I don't know why I did that,'" Salzman testified. "She characterized it as this wonderful opportunity for women to explore their sexuality."

I didn't yet know about the lies, so I told Edmondson that more nuance was usually a good thing. The news story contained all the accusations against Raniere—that he may have created this twisted pyramid scheme, that he may have abused underage girls in the past—but left enough room for the idea that DOS slaves might just be very capable women using very powerful tools. Raniere stressed that no collateral had been released. He claimed he only had sex with two DOS slaves.

Every time a big story appeared, there'd be a flurry of ex-NXIVM chatter, Edmondson told me. Reactions in group chats were all over the map: some were outraged that America's newspaper of record would allow a cult accused of sex trafficking to put so much of its own spin on the scandal; others said the reporter's intimate access helped illustrate the extent of the psychological manipulation.

Outside of Edmondson's group chat, some readers wondered whether the world was overreacting to a chosen alternative lifestyle. Spend enough time scrolling on social media and anyone can find multi-level marketers, leadership seminar recruiters, BDSM practitioners, and, yes, polyamorous men. If the NXIVM fallout was going to add fuel to the #MeToo movement, the jury of public opinion was still out.

CHAPTER TWENTY-SEVEN

In Character

I can't pinpoint the exact moment my own sense of reality started to bend, but it was around one year into covering the NXIVM story for *Vice*. Keith Raniere had been locked up for just over six months, and I'd just learned that an episode of *Law & Order: Special Victims Unit* had been inspired by the cult.

By this time I was fully through the looking glass, nursing a level of paranoia I wasn't comfortable sharing with anyone but my closest friends. "Maybe they're following you," one of them had unhelpfully texted after I described a NXIVM-related coincidence that left me feeling unsettled.

The coincidence I'd recounted went like this: I was standing with another friend half a block away from my apartment one Saturday night, updating her on the stories I was working on. I told her about the branding, the actors, the FBI investigation—all of it. Then a striking blond woman with an iPhone pinned to her ear dramatically announced to the person she was speaking to that we were talking about Sarah Edmondson, someone she considered a close acquaintance.

The woman quickly hung up. Then she proceeded to walk alongside us as we crossed a street and headed toward a bar, chatting us up along the way. She asked us questions about what we knew about

NXIVM, and when I revealed that I was a journalist who'd been reporting on the self-help organization for many months, she started feeding me several NXIVM-related story tips.

Because of the Vancouver neighborhood I live in, it made sense to me that we were likely surrounded by people who probably knew things about NXIVM. It was strangely serendipitous, but not mind-blowing. We were about a fifteen-minute walk from the yoga studio where people like Sarah Edmondson, Jenn Kobelt, and Kristin Kreuk did regular vinyasa and hot yoga classes. Surely others lived nearby. But something about the conversation still seemed off.

The stranger suggested that I look into the misdeeds of the people who'd blown the whistle on the branding and cooperated with the FBI. I made a mental note to look into her allegations, especially something about NXIVM men supposedly being encouraged to "stallion" on their wives and girlfriends.

I thanked the woman for her suggestions and attempted to exchange contact information. I ended up giving her my Twitter handle, and in return she gave me what I thought was hers. A few minutes later, while waiting for a round of drinks on a Kitsilano patio, I plugged in every combination and spelling of the compound word she'd given me. I guessed I was about to find the musings of a bubbly yoga teacher/actor, but nothing came up on any social platform. It seemed she'd given me a fake name.

More unnerving than that were her parting words to me. Before disappearing around a corner, she warned that I should be careful about who I talked to and what I told them. This was after she'd invited me to describe my research process. I had named some of the people I'd interviewed with an understanding that she could potentially help uncover new aspects of the secretive group. Yet instead of feeling energized about new leads, I couldn't help feeling something spooky had just happened.

I already knew from court records that Clare Bronfman had paid private investigators to spy on perceived enemies. I would later hear testimony about actors sent on spy missions, instructed to drum up conversations with Raniere's targets.

I told my friend, "I don't need that level of paranoia in my life," but the damage was more or less done. Suddenly many terrible things seemed possible. Could the potential sources I'd already contacted be reporting back to NXIVM leadership? Was Clare paying to access my bank account and inbox? What was real and what was a product of gut feeling, suspicion, and thin air? I worried that what I thought were the facts of the case, ones I'd been poring over for months, could turn out to be a figment of my overactive imagination.

ALL OF THIS was bouncing around in my head when I arrived at Edmondson's door on November 12, 2018. It had been months since our last conversation. I didn't bring wine this time because she'd just recently announced her second pregnancy. Edmondson's four-year-old was playing around on the carpet, showing us his Ninja Turtle sunglasses and Transformers as we cued up the NXIVM-based episode of *Law & Order*.

Edmondson told me about her latest acting role: a journalist investigating a secretive women's empowerment group that turned criminal. I remember thinking it was fitting and confusing and hilarious at the same time. We later joked that it was too bad I wasn't able to show her the ropes at my desk job. The episode began with a disclaimer insisting that the story did "not depict any actual person, entity or event," which put a half-smile on my face. Then the *Law & Order* sound, an auditory meme in its own right, finished the job. I'll admit that I was excited.

One of the first scenes looked like a NXIVM recruitment session, except the group was called Accredo. About a dozen slim, beautiful women in blazers and minidresses sat in an open-concept living room with high ceilings, long golden curtains, and a grand piano. There was a sameness among the women, all with long hair down their backs, modest sleeves and necklines, and postures that minimized their already tiny frames. They applauded as a woman with sweeping dark hair moved to the front of the room.

"Barf," Edmondson said at the familiar scene. We were only two minutes in and for her it was already too on-the-nose.

Then she recognized the actor playing the blond woman directing the pitch meeting. "That's Sarah Carter," she told me. She reached for her phone to double check. Of course this actor was also named Sarah. Who better to stand in Sarah Edmondson's fictionalized shoes, pitching empowerment and success to would-be recruits? By the end of the episode, her character would be charged for "carrying out a murder at the behest of a manipulative guru."

"We were slick like that, with the power suits," Edmondson said as one woman onscreen recounted how she'd been in an abusive relationship and stalling in her career before she discovered Accredo. "And testimonials were a big part of it," she added.

The members of this slick empowerment group talked about subsisting on cucumber water and where to find the best gluten-free pasta. There was talk of step counts, intensive programs, facing fears, and gaining permission to love themselves. When the SVU detectives interviewed a woman dressed in red robes on the set of a *Handmaid's Tale*–like TV show, the line "This is so surreal" resonated on too many levels.

"Who knew there was so much money in insecurity?" Detective Amanda Rollins asked as she approached a mansion standing in for the NXIVM mothership.

Of course there were plenty of details that strayed far from the truth. The fictionalized Keith Raniere was a different flavor of creepy—in real life he's a calculating listener who hides what he thinks behind big questions, but the show presented an amateur mind reader, spouting off invasive assessments of the SVU detectives' personal lives.

When Detective Rollins stumbled on a sea of mattresses in a pool house, Edmondson pointed out that in her twelve years in NXIVM she'd seen no bare mattresses. Then again, she was never invited to what the *New York Post* called Raniere's "sex den," known to his associates as the executive library. "That was never on the table," she said. Edmondson was married, and she'd never taken Raniere up on his business offers, which would have placed her much closer to Albany and his harem.

Those points and the murder angle aside, Edmondson was impressed by the way the show handled some things, the branding in particular. Arlo, the Raniere stand-in, was quick to mention that it was a woman's idea to burn her skin with *AHM*, standing, in this fictional universe, for At His Mercy. "It's to symbolize her progress," said Arlo. "Something she'd never forget." The women onscreen insisted that Arlo didn't make any decisions for them; they found strength within themselves. That resonated for Edmondson.

A climactic scene had a detective question one of the women in a Rikers Island interrogation room. The detective says, "You know most of the women are in here because they believed a man's lies. Ask them. They'll be happy to tell you."

Edmondson cut in, "I hope Moira said that to Allison." I hadn't yet met prosecutor Moira Kim Penza, but I knew she had a stranger-than-fiction trial ahead of her.

THERE WAS STILL so much that was up in the air, but Edmondson was finally starting to feel secure in her decision to leave, she told me. There had been many times over the previous year when she'd questioned her decision to walk through fire on the way to justice and accountability. But those moments were becoming fewer and further between.

She still occasionally got obscenity-laced emails from strangers accusing her of seeking fame by going to *The New York Times* with her branding story. But by now she was incredulous at the suggestion: "Like, why?" she fumed. "Of all the things I could do, I'm not doing this to be famous."

She was right, of course, and I fumed with her. But I also wondered if a sense of personal exceptionalism was what attracted many NXIVM students in the first place. Followers wanted to be the best in their chosen field, whether that was acting, running, dancing, writing, public speaking, or filmmaking. And they all dared to believe greatness, if not fame, was possible.

Edmondson said she wanted to start a foundation to help victims of similar manipulation. Enough time had elapsed that she'd become more certain of her ethical principles, and living those values meant telling the truth about what had happened and letting the public decide what was good, bad, or criminal.

The irony wasn't lost on Edmondson: it took leaving and challenging NXIVM to finally uphold the world-changing ideals she thought Keith Raniere had taught her.

Vanguard on Trial

Nancy Salzman was the first to plead, in mid-March 2019.

Suddenly, after months of silence from lawyers and whistleblowers, case developments started coming, one after another.

Salzman, once a feared disciplinarian to many inner-circle women, appeared deflated as she entered the Brooklyn courthouse. She pleaded guilty to one count of racketeering conspiracy. In a short statement she apologized to her daughter, Lauren, and the other defendants for her actions. "Some of the things I have done weren't only wrong, they were criminal," she told the court. "If I could go back and change things, I would. But I can't." Salzman also admitted to conspiring to commit identity theft and doctoring video evidence in a civil court case against cult educator Rick Ross.

Then, hours after Salzman's plea, the Department of Justice brought new child porn and child exploitation charges against Raniere. The explosive new indictment alleged that he'd had a sexual relationship with at least one fifteen-year-old victim and had taken photos that the feds called "child pornography."

After twenty years of working in lockstep atop a hierarchical web of companies, it seemed that Vanguard and his Prefect were facing the moment of collapse.

LAUREN SALZMAN PLEADED two weeks later, 364 days after Raniere's arrest.

I thought about the difference a year makes. On March 25, 2018, Salzman had been at that compound in Chacala, Mexico, with Nicki Clyne and Allison Mack. A year later she was officially convicted of one count of racketeering and one count of racketeering conspiracy. Her plea was sealed by the court on March 25, 2019, likely in an effort not to disrupt the ongoing plea negotiations with other defendants in the case.

As part of her plea, she admitted to confining Daniela in a room for nearly two years and threatening her with deportation. She said she'd committed forced labor as a DOS "master" and committed extortion when she collected "collateral" from her "slaves." She admitted to collecting credit card authorizations, sexually explicit photos and videos, and rights to cars and other property.

Lauren Salzman apologized for the harm she'd caused the witnesses who were about to testify as well as the hundreds of members of the NXIVM community. "Your Honor, in light of reviewing all the discovery and having many months to reflect, I came to the conclusion that the most moral and the most just course of action for me was to take full responsibility for my conduct, and that is why I am pleading guilty today."

MEANWHILE, CLARE BRONFMAN'S courtroom conduct nearly overshadowed the Salzmans' pleas. She'd shown her loyalty to NXIVM by staring daggers at prosecutor Moira Kim Penza during a March 19 hearing and setting up a $14.3 million trust to pay for some of the other defendants' legal fees.

Bronfman had as many as twelve lawyers working on her case. On March 27 she was asked whether she'd retained famed Stormy Daniels lawyer Michael Avenatti, who was already making headlines that week for his alleged role in a high-profile case in New York's Southern District that involved an attempt to extort $20 million from the Nike company. Judge Nicholas Garaufis questioned why Avenatti and Bronfman's main lawyer, Mark Geragos, had met with a federal prosecutor to negotiate on the NXIVM file. He also cast doubt on Bronfman's account that she found Geragos by internet search, as there happened to be a family connection between Raniere's and Bronfman's legal teams: Teny Geragos, Mark's daughter, was working on Raniere's defense.

Faced with such tough questions about her legal representation, Bronfman fainted, and an ambulance was called.

"As Your Honor is aware, Ms. Bronfman is not feeling well," one of her lawyers told the judge after the episode. "She is going to the hospital. . . . I believe she blacked out."

Judge Garaufis scolded Bronfman's lawyers for deflecting his questions. "I want answers. I want to know why I wasn't told last week that Mr. Avenatti had been retained," he said. "I should have been told who the lawyers are."

In a letter to the judge the next day, one of Bronfman's lawyers confirmed that Avenatti had worked for her "for a matter of days" and "for a limited purpose." Avenatti was charged and later convicted of extortion in the Nike case.

ALLISON MACK'S WAS the next plea to drop, on April 8, 2019. Mack began to cry as she started reading a list of her crimes.

She'd had a year, she said, to look back and re-examine her life and relationships. "Looking closely at the decisions I made, the people I trusted, and, more importantly, those who placed their trust in me . . . I am prepared to take responsibility for acts in which I was involved, some of which I now recognize were wrong.

"I became close with many individuals," she continued, "many of whom are wonderful people, and some of whom I now realize are not. . . . I joined NXIVM first to find purpose. I was lost and I wanted to find a place, a community in which I would feel comfortable. Over time, I truly believed that I had found a group of individuals who believed as I did and who were interested in trying to become better people and in doing so make those around them better."

Mack said it had been her motivation to help others, "misguided though it was," that brought her closer to Keith Raniere. "Through it all, I believed that Keith Raniere's intentions were to help people, and that my adherence to his system of beliefs would help empower others and help them."

As Lauren Salzman had done a few weeks earlier, Mack admitted that Raniere had founded, developed, and led DOS. "At Raniere's direction, I and other women sought to recruit other women to join DOS," she said.

Even though Salzman's plea had gone over many of the same facts of the case, it sounded different coming from Mack. She described the fear the scheme had intended to create, and the ruinous, embarrassing outcomes she'd threatened to set in motion if Nicole and others didn't comply.

Like Salzman, Mack admitted to forced labor, extortion, and obscuring the real purpose and leadership of DOS. "Specifically, I concealed Keith Raniere's role as the head of DOS and characterized DOS as a women's only organization, knowing that Keith Raniere was the head of the organization. . . .

"I am very sorry for the victims of this case. I am also very sorry for the harm that I caused to my family. They are good people who I have hurt through my misguided adherence to Keith Raniere's teachings."

Allison Mack thanked the judge, the lawyers, and her family. "I know that I am and will be a better person as a result of this," she said.

CLARE BRONFMAN PLEADED guilty on Good Friday, two weeks before the trial was scheduled to take place. She admitted to identity fraud and to harboring an undocumented migrant for financial gain. The charges stemmed from bogus job and work visa offers she'd extended to non-citizen students. One Mexican woman said she was offered a $3,600-per-month salary to work on a NXIVM venture, but was paid little more than $4,000 over two years, and was discouraged from taking other jobs. "Your Honor, I was afforded a great gift by my grandfather and father," she told Judge Garaufis. "With the gift comes immense privilege and more importantly, tremendous responsibility. It does not come with an ability to break the law." Sara Bronfman, whose husband, Basit Igtet, had helped secure Clare's $100 million bond, was not in attendance.

When Bronfman was finally sentenced in 2020, Judge Garaufis said she made promises she didn't keep, exacted labor she did not pay for, and "took advantage of these individuals' financial straights and immigration statuses." He stressed that her blindness to Raniere's crimes was willful, and her continued loyalty to him was concerning.

He sentenced her to six years and nine months in federal prison—three times the recommended guideline. Bookkeeper Kathy Russell pleaded to a separate fraud charge that same afternoon as Bronfman. Four out of five defendants had moved from the "not guilty" column to "guilty."

There was only one left.

WHEN KEITH RANIERE'S day in court finally arrived, on May 7, 2019, he was a lone defendant with the knowledge that his closest allies had all pleaded guilty.

Still, there was absolutely no certainty about what outcome Raniere might face. On the one hand, there was the moral outrage that comes with branding women with your initials, but on the other hand, there were extraordinary levels of compliance that raised questions about personal responsibility. There was surely a difference between consent and the coerced appearance of consent, but there was no guarantee a jury would agree on what that was.

Prosecutor Tanya Hajjar was straightforward in her assessment of Raniere. In her opening arguments she called him a con man and a crime boss. "He targeted people who were looking to improve their lives," she said. "He drew them in slowly with promises of success, of money, of better relationships, and once he gained their trust, he exploited it."

The speech did not dwell on any of NXIVM's redeeming qualities, instead alleging that it was all a facade. "The defendant pretended to be a guru but he was a criminal, and along with an inner circle of followers he committed crimes, crimes of extortion, forced labor, sex trafficking, fraud, and the production and possession of child pornography, and that's why we are here."

Hajjar told the story of Daniela coming to the United States only to be groomed, sexually exploited, and later confined to a room for nearly two years of her young life. She told the story of Daniela's younger sister, Camila, who was photographed naked at the age of fifteen and went on to become an accessory in DOS and other crimes.

She also made a distinction between the more mundane genre of naked photos sent by iPhone-owning men and women of the twenty-first century and the specific use of nudes in DOS. "In the defendant's hands, these photographs didn't just serve his sexual needs. These photographs became instruments of coercion and of control. He used them to blackmail and extort," Hajjar said. "He used them to increase his power."

IN THE HALLS of the courthouse, Barbara Bouchey later told me she thought the prosecutors had left a yawning gap in their opening arguments. She said they'd be better off if they had at least acknowledged that Raniere did improve lives.

"I submit that you haven't heard much about the truth so far," defense lawyer Marc Agnifilo countered in his opening argument. "What you've heard is a lot of conclusions. You've heard a lot of slogans. You've heard a lot about the names of certain crimes."

As might be expected, Agnifilo played to men's insecurities about after-the-fact sexual accusations. "People are going to come here and say, Look, Raniere is abusing me. That's what they're saying now. That's not what they said at the time," he told the jury.

He also talked about control—specifically, how it could be a good thing. "Every downhill skier who won a gold medal was controlled by some ski coach," he said. "Every eighteen-year-old kid who comes from Biloxi, Mississippi, or Hauppauge, Long Island, who becomes a marine is controlled by a drill instructor." Agnifilo talked about self-denial and vulnerability as noble concepts, not levers of extortion and blackmail.

I walked away that day thinking that Agnifilo had scored points. He got in front of some majorly distasteful aspects of NXIVM and took advantage of our current climate of fear around sexual assault and its impact on men. He reiterated that this was something these women had signed up for. They'd made choices, and at some point, there had to be a level of personal responsibility.

THE FIRST DOS witness testified without mention of the word trafficking. Afterwards I spoke with former prosecutor Krishna Patel, who specialized in sex trafficking cases in the state of Connecticut. When I described the day's testimony to her, she saw the basic elements of a sex trafficking conviction: proof of commercial sex, compelled by force, fraud, or coercion. The "collateral" handed over remained a threat throughout one's membership in the group, even if it was never released. "That's the gun to her head," Patel said. Money didn't need to be exchanged if nude photos served as a kind of currency.

As days turned into weeks, Agnifilo's assessment rang less true. Every day more testimony was given about Raniere's brazen bait-and-switch designs. The witnesses were remarkably consistent in their use of the phrase "not what I signed up for."

Agnifilo had a particularly tough time cross-examining Lauren Salzman, who would not budge on the fact that she'd lied and misrepresented Raniere's involvement in DOS, and that she'd known it was wrong. She wouldn't go along with Agnifilo's "good intentions" frame.

Salzman had just revealed yet another disturbing side of DOS: the group had been acquiring equipment for a BDSM dungeon and increasingly women were being paddled for their shortcomings. Salzman said she had no interest in BDSM but knew she had to go along with the humiliating punishment, which was usually filmed. "These things started to become scary for me," she testified. Among the dungeon orders was a $645 "steel puppy cage" that Raniere had said "was for the people who were the most committed to growth," according to Salzman. This possibility weighed on her heavily. She wanted to challenge herself, and she believed in choosing hard things, but Raniere seemed to be choosing assignments for maximum cruelty and degradation.

I was amazed at how perceptive Salzman was about all the layers of compliance and coercion. She could capably jump in and out of NXIVM's circular and extreme logic. "Once you have collateral over somebody's head, then the way they interact with the situation is entirely different," she testified.

Sitting on the witness stand, Salzman had unofficially joined the new mission that Mark Vicente and Sarah Edmondson had started two years earlier. When Agnifilo asked what her goal had been in NXIVM, Salzman said it was to raise the ethics of the world. "Ultimately that's why I'm sitting here, because I believed that in order to decide what's ethical and what's not, the truth has to come out," she said. "Lying and covering up everything we did is not ethical and it is not the mission that I was enrolled in."

Agnifilo asked Salzman if she'd changed her mind when she pleaded guilty. "As you sit here today, many of the things you thought were positive and good for the world, you no longer view them that way; correct? You view them as negative?"

Salzman was fiery in her response. "I still hold the same principles that I held before and I've had enough time away by myself, after I was indicted, to think about my own experiences and to be able to process them without other people talking me out of them or reframing them or leveraging my own fears or attachments," she said. "I decided to go forward the way I've always gone forward to uphold what I think is right and good in the best way that I can."

Agnifilo tried a half-dozen ways to get her to say that there'd been a time when she thought she was doing good things for the women she recruited. Instead of getting the answer he wanted—that she'd had no idea she was doing anything criminal—Salzman said, through sobs, that her sole intent had been to prove herself to Raniere, that she put his approval above everything else in her life. He was the one on trial, not her.

"Okay, that's it. We are done," Judge Garaufis told Agnifilo after the wrenching emotional outburst. After a few awkward exchanges with Agnifilo, he clarified his point: "So you can sit down."

Agnifilo questioned why the judge had cut off his cross-examination. "I am not going to have someone have a nervous breakdown on the witness stand," Garaufis said. "This is a broken person, as far as I can tell."

THE COURTROOM WAS stunned. Agnifilo later told me that in his twenty-nine years as a lawyer, he'd never seen anything like it.

Agnifilo had tried to frame Salzman as a scorned woman who was upset that she'd found out about Raniere's other relationships through the evidence prosecutors shared with her. He'd asked whether Salzman still loved Raniere, and implied that she'd taken a plea deal simply to avoid a drawn-out trial. This had angered Judge Garaufis.

"I have to sentence this defendant and what you did was, basically, ask her to make legal judgments about whether what she did in pleading guilty was farcical," Garaufis countered once the jury was out of the room. "I thought that really went pretty far beyond the pale, frankly."

Having spent the better part of two years studying Raniere's teachings, I knew how this must have looked from his seat at the defense table. A woman had an emotional outburst, and was promptly coddled by a man with authority. Raniere would see this as an injustice, and later his lawyers confirmed this. (Agnfilo filed for a mistrial the next day.)

Judge Garaufis was straightforward about why he'd cut off cross-examination. "I may not get everything right up here, but I will tell you, as a human being, it was the right decision. All right? And before I'm a judge, I'm a human being. And that goes for everybody in this room," he said. "I am not going to allow someone to be placed in this circumstance and then let it continue. I am the one who is disappointed. I'm done."

As I left the courtroom I noticed two missed calls from Sarah Edmondson. I'd been updating her on Salzman's testimony, and we were jointly piecing together all the secrets she'd missed living 3,000 miles from Albany. I told her what Salzman had said about telling the whole truth and letting a jury decide what's ethical. Edmondson said it sounded more like the friend she knew.

THE NEXT WITNESS was Daniela, who walked into the courtroom with such force that she seemed to cut the air with her elbows and hips. She'd lived claustrophobically close to Raniere—first as his hacker protégée and secret girlfriend, then as his caged emotional punching bag. She recounted how Raniere's pattern of psychological domination had torn her family apart. Her father and sister still shunned her after all the years of gaslighting, conditioning, and group influence.

Daniela testified that, after leaving Albany and despite her fears of going out on her own, she'd built a whole new life for herself. She'd worked at a computer store, she'd coached tennis, and she'd met a human rights lawyer who helped her get a new birth certificate so that she could travel and work more freely. She beamed when asked about her current job overseeing a company of 250 employees. Despite everything that had happened to her, she'd refused to suffer.

The testimony was a lot to take in. It spanned decades and international borders. There was striving and aspiration as well as starvation and deprivation. On the way out of the courtroom I heard more than one observer say they sensed an acute injustice, but didn't know what to name it. Raniere's actions sounded bad—like torture, even—but didn't easily fit between lines drawn by a legal system that disproportionately polices street crime and marginalized groups.

Raniere and his lawyers would later leverage this disconnect, writing that no one "was shot, stabbed, punched, kicked, slapped or even yelled at." NXIVM victims said guilt and shame were Raniere's weapons of choice, and he deployed them in systemic and calculated ways. His so-called "human behavior equation" amounted to a cruel premeditated subtraction—slashing women's opportunities to question, resist, or walk away without enormous risk. As the justice system faces serious questions about overpolicing, particularly in Black and Indigenous communities, it's also worth investigating what happens to powerful people who orchestrate harm on a mass scale. In the case of Raniere, I thought his whiteness and class privilege could have easily been part of the reason he was not adequately investigated for so long.

About halfway through the six-week trial I noticed that prosecutors hadn't asked any of the witnesses whether they thought NXIVM was a cult. It wasn't something the government was trying to prove or disprove, so the word rarely came up. I'd spoken to a handful of experts who had their own theories and definitions. I knew that Raniere had endless rebuttals and deflections, and I felt relieved that this can of worms didn't need to be opened.

By the fifth week, the mood in the courtroom had shifted. Nicole was on the stand, describing her impression of V-Week in 2015 and Nancy Salzman's overwrought introduction of Vanguard. "She would always refer to Keith as the smartest man in the world, which, like— it just strikes me as weird because how would you know who the smartest man in the world is?" she asked, her voice more than a touch incredulous. "Anyone who says that—it just sounds like bullshit to me." The entire room broke out laughing. Nicole apologized as the judge attempted to hold back his own laughter. "It just seems like a very arrogant thing to say," she added, to another round of low chuckles.

"Next question, please," Judge Garaufis said.

Of the twenty-three witnesses who testified, only four were in DOS, yet they left the impression that as many as 150 women had submitted nude photos of themselves as part of the scheme. Taken with Raniere's own collection of photos, emails, and messages presented as evidence, there was a strong suggestion that Raniere had been developing a porno-blackmail scheme as early as 2005. A folder that contained up-close photos of an underage girl's genitalia, as well as nudes of her two grown sisters, was entitled "Studies." If Raniere considered himself a scientist, this was his life's research.

The prosecution's last two pieces of evidence began with a video of Nancy Salzman that had been shown in the first days of the trial. In the clip she reads a disturbing sermon on child sexual abuse to a room of Jness members: "If you look at sexual abuse, there are different ways to determine if it's abuse. One of them is the age of consent." Salzman adds that in some parts of the world the age of consent was set at twelve. "But what is sexual abuse really? Is the person a child or is the person adult-like? . . . Often when you counsel people who are children of what you might call abuse, some little children are perfectly happy with it until they find out what happens later in life." Salzman concludes that society is the abuser for telling such children that something bad happened to them.

Prosecutors then showed their second and final piece of evidence: a separate clip of Raniere, filmed at another time, dictating this statement to Nancy Salzman and others, word for word.

IN HER CLOSING arguments, prosecutor Moira Kim Penza stood in front of an oversized chart with Raniere's face in the center, surrounded by a circle of thumbnail photographs of his closest allies. Penza was assembling elements of each crime like puzzle pieces, the acts spanning more than a decade.

The first racketeering act was the fake ID made for Daniela to cross the Canadian border into the United States. The two acts of sexual exploitation of a child happened on November 2 and 24, 2005, when Raniere took photos of fifteen-year-old Camila. The photos themselves counted as child pornography possession. The identity theft occurred after Daniela was told to hack into Edgar Bronfman's and others' emails.

Daniela herself was trafficked when she spent twenty-three months in a room, Penza said. That was different from the sex trafficking and attempted sex trafficking of Nicole and others. Then there was the DOS scheme itself, which Penza said constituted wire fraud conspiracy and forced labor conspiracy. Penza did not once say the word cult, and she didn't need to.

It wasn't guaranteed that all these pieces would fit neatly in jurors' heads, but when the jury emerged after less than five hours on the first day of deliberation, there was a sense that it was going that way.

"I hope he cries," I heard someone whisper. To my left and right were former slaves mentioned in testimony but spared from testifying themselves.

ID theft: guilty. Exploitation of a child: guilty. Trafficking: guilty. Extortion: guilty.

After hearing the word "guilty" four times in a row, your ears start to ring with anticipation waiting for the next one. I heard gasps behind me and saw people squeezing each other's arms in my peripheral vision.

Wire fraud conspiracy: guilty. Forced labor conspiracy: guilty. Sex trafficking: guilty. Sex trafficking conspiracy: guilty. Attempted sex trafficking: guilty.

MORE THAN A year went by before Keith Raniere faced Judge Nicholas Garaufis for sentencing in October 2020. Raniere's remaining followers, Nicki Clyne and four other DOS loyalists among them, lined up outside the courthouse at dawn as part of a coordinated effort to discredit the prosecutors and maintain their Vanguard's innocence. But after two years in federal custody, Raniere's influence had faded. The women who risked so much to expose his lies and manipulations no longer feared the "flat earthers" who held on.

Camila, who had been advised to "stay invisible" during the trial, was the first of fifteen victims to give a statement detailing the grooming, gaslighting, torment and isolation she endured for twelve years. "He hid his abuse behind ideas and concepts of nobility, but there is nothing noble about abusing a child," she said. "I never got to live like a normal teenager. I never went on a date until I was twenty-nine. I never went to college. I never—and this is where I go blank because I missed so much of my own life, I find it difficult to even conceptualize what I have missed."

Raniere told the judge that he did not feel remorse for crimes he did not believe he committed. "I believe I tried my best and I had good intent, but I see that I have led to this place where there is so much anger and so much pain," he said. Judge Garaufis was incensed when Raniere's lawyer circled around this point, implying that women's changing perceptions and feelings had manufactured a scenario of abuse in retrospect. "I am not going to tolerate spending time on what his intent was when he seduced a fifteen-year-old girl," Garaufis interjected. "It's an insult to the intelligence of anyone who listens."

Raniere's belief in his own innocence did not spare him. He was sentenced to 120 years in prison and ordered to pay a $1.75-million fine. Raniere's victims, no longer silenced by shame or blackmail, welcomed the lifetime judgment. "It has taken me three years and a substantial amount of space from your manipulation to realize that the shame that has been weighing so heavily on my shoulders is not mine to carry," Nicole said. "It's yours."

APPENDIX
LETTER TO RANIERE

Hi Keith,

I'm reaching out in the fourth month of COVID-19 lockdown at Brooklyn's Metropolitan Detention Center; I hope this letter makes it to you. I'm Sarah Berman, a reporter and editor based in Vancouver. I've been following NXIVM and the charges against you since 2017.

I'd like to offer a chance to respond to questions that I think only you can answer. I want to know more about what you actually think and believe. Forgive me for cutting to the chase:

Many people have put immense faith in your intellect and ability over the years. They have trusted you with their life savings, their psychological trauma, their medical decisions. Do you think they were right to place that faith in you? Why or why not?

When people say you are the smartest, most ethical man in the world, do you believe them? Why or why not?

You have said in various ways that adults having sex with children isn't necessarily wrong. A jury of your peers has found that you sexually exploited fifteen-year-old Camila in 2005. Do you look back at your relationship with her as wrong? Why or why not?

Do you believe you have done psychological harm to any of the women you were involved with?

Do you think, on balance, the good in NXIVM has outweighed the bad?

Do you think you were treated fairly by the criminal justice system?

Do you think your adversaries were treated fairly by the legal system?

Do you have anything to say to the people who testified at your trial?

ACKNOWLEDGMENTS

Writing about trauma and shame is hard, but opening up about trauma and shame to a journalist is a thousand times harder. So I am grateful first and foremost to everyone who trusted me with their stories as I struggled to figure this out. Thank you Sarah Edmondson, Anthony Ames, Barbara Bouchey, Maja Miljkovic, Toni Natalie, and others who I can't name here for going the extra mile to explain the unexplainable.

I'm indebted to the many reporters who went down this rabbit hole before me, especially Dennis Yusko, Michael Freedman, Suzanna Andrews, James Odato, and Chet Hardin. I know that each of you has faced the worst kind of journalistic headwinds and kept going. I've tried my best to carry that spirit forward.

Thank you Carolyn Forde for believing in me and this book. Your hunger to know what happened next propelled me on many occasions. Jennifer Croll, your advice and friendship have been indispensable. I hereby declare you godmother to this paperback. Harrison Mooney! You read fast and close and I will remember that forever. Can't wait to return the favor.

To my editors Diane Turbide, Helen Smith, Alex Schultz, and editorial assistant Alanna McMullen, thanks for coming on this wild journey with me. You knew where I was going when I didn't, asked brilliant questions, and made me laugh when I needed it. David Ball and Matt Chambers, thank you for looking at drafts that didn't yet have a beginning, middle, or end. Sorry about that.

I'm so lucky to have met extremely good and cool reporters while covering this trial. Sonia Moghe, Rob Gavin, Karim Amer, Claire Read, Jehane Noujaim, Yahia Lababidi, Grace McNally, Laura Sepulveda, Pilar Melendez, Molly Crabapple, EJ Dickson, Michael Blackmon, Mary Ann Georgantopoulos, Vanessa Grigoriadis, and Lucien Formichella right at the end. There was never enough time to unpack but I'm so glad we tried.

I owe a special thanks to Ryan McMahon for helping me recover my personal belongings after more than one late night of drinking at the Banff Centre in 2019. Thank you to everyone who read my work or listened to me think out loud while we were on Treaty 7 territory. Liz Howard, Cherie Dimaline, Syd Lazarus, Jean Hurtig, Christy-Ann Conlin, Shannon Webb-Campbell, Cody Caetano, Luciana Erregue, Silmy Abdullah, Kara Sievewright, Elizabeth Aiossa, Kerri Huffman, Razielle Aigen, Darlene Naponse, you're all legends.

Thanks to my *Vice* colleagues, who I won't call fam in public. Josh Visser and Chris Bilton, you gave this project a fighting chance in the beginning. Thank you Manisha Krishnan and Mack Lamoureux for hearing out my complaints in the home stretch. Tash Grzincic, Anya Zoleziowski, I miss your faces.

Blessed thanks to my actual family! My mom for being both a cheerleader and a critic as needed, my dad for teaching me about the power of belief at a young age, and my brother for not caring about Twitter at all. I love and thank you for putting up with me being perpetually, terminally busy since 2018.

To my friends who've heard about this nonstop for years now: it's over! Aurora, Jackie, Katie, Ashton, Mirit, Lex, Abeer, Robyn, Aziza, you were all so patient and kind as I descended into one-minded obsession.

Thank you to Janos, Carmen, Samuel, Lisa, and Davis for hosting me on my reporting trips in New York and Mexico. Because of you I had somewhere to watch the Raptors win the NBA championship and celebrate Our Lady of Guadalupe.

I'm alive and able to write earnest thank-yous in the back of a book because of a man who spends an admirable amount of time offline: Will Brown. You loved and supported me through the late nights, the sudden twists, the endless months of quarantine. With you I've always felt ready to face the end of the world. Love you!

NOTES

PROLOGUE: "THE MOST ETHICAL MAN"

slept only one or two hours: Irene Gardiner Keeney, "Troy Man Has a Lot on His Mind: IQ Test Proves What Many Suspected, He's One in 10 Million," Albany *Times Union*, July 1988.

$10,000-a-week vacation rental: Bail filings, *USA v. Raniere et al*, March 2018.

Raniere was napping: Lauren Salzman testimony, *USA v. Raniere et al*, May 21, 2019.

infinity pool: Interview with Chacala neighbors, December 2019.

wearing masks: Lauren Salzman testimony, *USA v. Raniere et al*, May 21, 2019.

accused in *The New York Times*: Barry Meier, "Inside the Secretive Group Where Women Are Branded," *The New York Times*, October 17, 2017.

feds had left business cards: Lauren Salzman testimony, *USA v. Raniere et al*, May 21, 2019.

disposable phones: Ibid.

might have included group sex: Ibid.

taking the red pill: Interview with Maja Miljkovic, July 2018.

dramatic scene unfolding: *NXIVM Founder Keith Raniere Arrested on Sex Trafficking Charges*, ABC News video, April 2018.

indicted for racketeering: Criminal complaint, *USA v. Raniere et al*, July 2018.

sexually explicit pictures: Superseding indictment, *USA v. Raniere et al*, March 2019.

CHAPTER 1: SECRET SISTERHOOD

one of the most successful satellite offices: NXIVM newsletter, April 2014.

wizard-like appearance: Maja Miljkovic interview, July 2018.

"master over the slave women": Latin scholars have called this translation misconceived pseudo-Latin. See Matthew Sullivan, "A Public Service Announcement About Sex Cults and Bad Latin," *Oldenhammer in Toronto* blog, May 10, 2018.

elite talent agency: Nicole testimony, *USA v. Raniere et al*, June 7, 2019.

lifers were mostly white: Sarah Edmondson interview, December 2019.

It was like a bad horror movie: First appeared in "Why I Joined a Secret Society That Branded Me," Sarah Edmondson as told to Sarah Berman, *Vice*, November 2, 2017.

summer camp for adults: Interview with former NXIVM student, February 2019.

heart rates are likely to match: Richard Bandler and John Grinder, *Patterns of the Hypnotic Techniques of Milton H. Erickson, M.D., Vol. I* (Soquel, CA: Meta Publications, 1975), 11.

"finding the ruin": Lawrence Wright, *Going Clear: Scientology, Hollywood, and the Prison of Belief* (New York: Alfred A. Knopf, 2013), 4.

preposterously proportioned home: Vanessa Grigoriadis, "Inside NXIVM, the 'Sex Cult' That Preached Empowerment," *The New York Times Magazine*, May 30, 2018.

CHAPTER 2: ONE IN TEN MILLION

1988 article in the *Times Union*: Irene Gardiner Keeney, "Troy Man Has a Lot on His Mind," Albany *Times Union*, 1988.

stacked with brainteasers: Scot Morris, "World's Most Difficult IQ Test," *Omni* magazine, April 1985, 128–132.

IQ cutoff for Mensa: Ibid.

multiple kinds of intelligence: Marie Winn, "New Views of Human Intelligence," *The New York Times*, April 29, 1990.

Racists and eugenicists are obsessed: Adam Shapiro, "The Dangerous Resurgence in Race Science," *American Scientist*, January 2020.

The *Guinness Book of Records*: *The Guiness Book of Records* 1989 edition, Guinness World Records Limited, 16.

retired the "highest IQ" contest: Sam Knight, "Is a High IQ a Burden As Much As a Blessing?" *Financial Times*, April 2009.

solutions were leaked: Darryl Miyaguchi, "Explanations," *Uncommonly Difficult IQ Tests* website.

shameful secret: Incident was first recounted to Bowen Xiao in *The Epoch Times*, May 28, 2018.

Raniere read the Isaac Asimov novel: Keith Raniere affidavit, *NXIVM v. Ross et al*, August 29, 2003, 7.

ready for a lifetime together: Barbara Bouchey, quoted in "Sex, Money and Nazis," *Uncover: Escaping NXIVM*, podcast, CBC, 2018.

CHAPTER 3: MOTHERSHIP, NEW YORK

both were allegedly molested: Interview with Heidi Hutchinson, February 2019. Gina's classmate did not respond to fact-finding requests.

encourage enlightenment simply by his presence: Karen Shafer and Gulshan Khakee, "Baba Muktananda: Meditation Revolution Continues Ten Years After His Passing," *Hinduism Today*, October 1992.

well-meaning therapists using trance states: Susan A. Clancy, *Abducted: How People Come to Believe They Were Kidnapped by Aliens* (Cambridge: Harvard University Press, 2005), 54–57.

found a programming job: Raniere deposition, *NXIVM v. Ross et al*, March 2009.

dubbed "the mothership": Interview with Sarah Edmondson, April 2018; *Uncover: Escaping NXIVM*, podcast, CBC.

the Flintlock house: Daniela testimony, *USA v. Raniere et al*, May 23, 2019.

met on a chairlift: Sarah Edmondson, *Scarred: The True Story of How I Escaped NXIVM, the Cult That Bound My Life* (San Francisco: Chronicle Prism, 2019), 22.

"defuser of bombs": Daniela testimony, *USA v. Raniere et al*, May 2019.

Ghislaine Maxwell: Maxwell was charged with enticing and transporting a minor with intent to engage in criminal sexual activity on July 2, 2020. She has not faced trial as of this writing.

actuary certification: Interviews with Heidi Hutchinson and Susan Dones; Nancy Salzman deposition, *NXIVM v. Ross et al*, June 9, 2009, 176.

make a lot of money: "Epiphany," *Uncover: Escaping NXIVM*, podcast, CBC, May 2018.

studied the sales techniques of Amway: Interview with Sarah Edmondson, as told by the late Barbara Jeske, March 2020.

Matol International: Raniere deposition, *NXIVM v. Ross et al*, March 12, 2009, 231.

Pre-Paid Legal: Ibid, 230.

other multi-level marketing companies were unethical: Ibid.

"new concept in marketing": Raniere affidavit, *NXIVM v. Ross et al*, August 2003, 10.

new company called Consumers' Buyline: Ibid.

"I had a small child": Toni Natalie interview with *Vice News* documentary producer Kathleen Caulderwood, quoted with permission, November 2017.

As she confessed in 2006: Chet Hardin, "Stress in the Family," *Metroland*, August 2006.

made $10,000 in their first few months: Interview with Toni Natalie, May 2020. First appeared in *The Program: Inside the Mind of Keith Raniere and the Rise and Fall of NXIVM*, Toni Natalie with Chet Hardin (New York: Grand Central Publishing, 2019), 17.

made to feel like family: Ibid.

playing arcade games: James Odato and Jennifer Gish, "Secrets of NXIVM," Albany *Times Union*, February 2012.

having sex in the Consumers' Buyline warehouse: Ibid.

CHAPTER 4: "MONEY SPILLING INTO YOUR WALLET"

look up his IQ record at the library: Interview with Toni Natalie, May 2020.

had grown an average of 40 percent: Raniere affidavit, *NXIVM v. Ross et al*, August 2003, 10.

"quite the creature": Keith Raniere address to followers, 2014.

he had a "type": Interview with Sarah Edmondson, October 2017.

$39 annual fee: *Rhodes v. Consumers' Buyline*, August 21, 1992.

long list of products and services: *Virginia v. Consumers' Buyline*, May 11, 1993.

1-800 number: Toni Natalie interview, May 2020.

a promotional video: Compilation video "NXIVM: Multi-Level Marketing," Albany *Times Union* YouTube channel, April 2019.

tell NXIVM recruiters the same thing: Sarah Edmondson interview, March 2020.

"one-time effort": "How to Raise Your Standard of Living Without Getting a Raise," Consumers' Buyline brochure. Exhibit in *Rhodes v. Consumers' Buyline*, August 1992.

"spilling into your wallet": Ibid.

rallied around wins and growth: Toni Natalie interview, May 2020.

pitching in with advertising: Ibid.

"her entire flock followed": Toni Natalie, *The Program: Inside the Mind of Keith Raniere and the Rise and Fall of NXIVM* (New York: Grand Central Publishing, 2019), 53.

Arkansas was one of the first: Attorney General complaint, *Arkansas v. Consumers' Buyline*, 1992.

sold $1 billion in products: Raniere affidavit, *NXIVM v. Ross et al*, August 2003.

nearly 300,000 members: Ibid.

signed settlements: Final judgment and order, *Arkansas v. Consumers' Buyline*, November 3, 1992.

lawsuits in twenty-three states: David Orenstein, "Consumers Buyline of Clifton Park Was Forced to Close After 25 Separate Investigations," Albany *Times Union*, August 24, 1997. (Note: The "25" in headline includes investigations by two federal agencies.)

Amway first came under fire: Jane Marie and Dann Gallucci, "The Mind Is a Fertile Field," *The Dream* podcast, October 2018.

successfully prosecuted by the FTC: Interview with Dann Gallucci, February 2019. First appeared in "Lazy, Stupid, Greedy or Dead," *The Dream* podcast, October 2018.

jars of avocado face cream: Steven Pressman, *Outrageous Betrayal: The Dark Journey of Werner Erhard from EST to Exile* (New York: St. Martin's Press, 1993), 35.

244,140,625 new recruits: Calculated by 5^12. Also illustrated in "Lazy, Stupid, Greedy or Dead," *The Dream* podcast, 2018.

forced to close in 1974: Order in *FTC v. Holiday Magic Inc et al*, October 15, 1974.

beaten, mock-crucified, or put in coffins: Steven Pressman, *Outrageous Betrayal*, 41.

inspired the creators of other leadership seminars: Ibid, 42.

Amway changed the game: Dann Gallucci interview; "The American Way," *The Dream* podcast, 2018.

"Bill Clinton's people": Mark Vicente testimony, *USA v. Raniere et al*, May 9, 2019.

millions of dollars on legal fees: Raniere affidavit, August 2003, 12.

CHAPTER 5: WHEN KEITH MET NANCY (AND LAUREN)

a new multi-level marketing company: Toni Natalie interview, October 2017. Also in Toni Natalie, *The Program: Inside the Mind of Keith Raniere and the Rise and Fall of NXIVM* (New York: Grand Central Publishing, 2019), 83.

wasn't living up to relationship agreements: Toni Natalie interview, April 24, 2018.

husband of six years came out: Interview with Barbara Bouchey, March 13, 2019.

as a nurse and a hypnotherapist: Nancy Salzman deposition, June 2009, 9.

studied under NLP's two founders: Nancy Salzman deposition, June 2009, 186.

second husband was a doctor: Barbara Bouchey interview, March 2019.

depressive episode: Ibid.

teaching communications courses: Toni Natalie, *The Program*, 2019, 137.

testing out various self-help methodologies: Heidi Hutchinson interview, March 2019.

he didn't want to teach it to me: Nancy Salzman deposition, June 2009, 201.

talked about Werner Erhard: Heidi Hutchinson interview, March 2019.

The likes of John Denver: Steven Pressman, *Outrageous Betrayal: The Dark Journey of Werner Erhard from EST to Exile* (New York: St. Martin's Press, 1993), 93.

no such thing as a "victim": Ibid, 71–73.

used Scientology terminology: i.e., "overt" in Keith Raniere letter to Toni Natalie, May 12, 1999.

denied being influenced by Dianetics: Raniere deposition, March 2009, 362.

raised almost $50,000: "The Concept School," Raniere affidavit, August 2003, 8.

the ideal person: Raniere affidavit, August 2003, 13.

incorporated in July 1998: Nancy Salzman deposition, June 2009, 197.

it would become NXIVM: Complaint, *O'Hara v. Raniere et al*, 2012, 8.

Salzman was a senior: Lauren Salzman testimony, *USA v. Raniere et al*, May 2019.

a patent application: Keith Raniere, The Rational Inquiry Method, Application number 09/654,423, filed September 4, 2000, rejected August 19, 2004.

early trial run of classes: Lauren Salzman testimony, *USA v. Raniere et al*, May 2019; Toni Natalie interview, May 2020.

set of curious rules and rituals: Rational Inquiry patent application; exhibits in *USA v. Raniere et al*, May 2019.

the "Self-esteem" module: Coach notes, Rational Inquiry patent application.

never explicitly reveal his own position: Interview with Anthony Ames, March 2020.

twice a week, or daily: Coach notes, Rational Inquiry patent application.

no psychologists or psychiatrists: Interview with Susan Dones, July 2019; Nancy Salzman deposition, June 2009, 320.

"all they want to do is argue": Susan Dones interview, July 2019.

a great human invention: Lauren Salzman testimony, May 2019.

early test subject: Toni Natalie interview, April 2018.

hundreds of sessions: Ibid.

unifying theory of her "issues": Ibid; Raniere letter, May 1999.

dispute over laundry: Toni Natalie interview, October 2017.

showed up at her workplace: Ibid.

I was raped repeatedly: Filing by Toni Natalie, *NXIVM v. Dones*, August 26, 2011, 4.

very small playbook: Toni Natalie interview, April 2018.

CHAPTER 6: ALBANY SHRUGGED

out of the Yellow Pages: Barbara Bouchey interview, May 2020.

claimed they had visions: Bouchey deposition, October 2009, 23.

she was his Dagny: Bouchey interviews, 2018–2020.

watching her closely: Ibid.

Proctors earned 10 percent: Exhibit in *NXIVM v. Ross et al*, October 2009.

both lived past lives: Bouchey deposition, October 2009, 216–217.

she had been Reinhard Heydrich: "Sex, Money and Nazis," *Uncover: Escaping NXIVM*, podcast, CBC, May 2019.

Hitler reincarnated: Susan Dones interview, July 2019.

repetitive suggestion: Ibid.

around a hundred pounds: Lauren Salzman testimony, *USA v. Raniere et al*, May 2019.

more than a dozen other relationships: Barbara Bouchey interviews, 2018–2020.

go along with the wrong answer: Solomon Asch, "Effects of Group Pressure on the Modification and Distortion of Judgments," in *Groups, Leadership and Men: Research in Human Relations*, ed. Harold Guetzkow (Pittsburgh: Carnegie Press, 1951), 177–190.

personal assistant role: Sarah Edmondson and Barbara Bouchey interviews, 2018–2020.

she actually has the highest IQ: Susan Dones interview, July 2019.

paralegal internship: Complaint, *O'Hara v. Raniere et al*, 2012, 7.

CHAPTER 7: THE GIRLS

massive family legacy: Edgar Bronfman, *Good Spirits: The Making of a Businessman* (New York: GP Putnam and Sons, 1998).

unspoken social boundaries: Suzanna Andrews, "The Heiresses and the Cult," *Vanity Fair*, November 2010.

living out of a suitcase: Nicholas Kohler, "How to Lose $100 Million," *Maclean's* magazine, September 2010.

money made people bad: Vanessa Grigoriadis, "Inside the 'Sex Cult' That Preached Empowerment," *The New York Times Magazine*, May 2018.

"the girls": Interviews with Barbara Bouchey and Frank Parlato; Stephen Herbits testimony, 2019; Bouchey deposition, 2009.

unverified April 2003 testimonial: Quoted by Will Yakowicz, "From Heiress to Felon: How Clare Bronfman Wound Up in 'Cult-Like' Group NXIVM," *Forbes*, May 2019.

"parasite strategies": Rational Inquiry patent application, 2000.

the first thing I had earned: Michael Freedman, "Cult of Personality," *Forbes*, October 2003.

anti-NXIVM conspiracies: Barbara Bouchey deposition, *Precision v. Plyam et al*, June 2, 2009, 58–59.

kiss him and sit at his feet: Nicholas Kohler, *Maclean's*, 2010.

novelty check: Bouchey deposition, *NXIVM v. Ross et al*, October 2009, 79.

$11 million private jet: Suzanna Andrews, *Vanity Fair*, 2010.

CHAPTER 8: US VS. THEM

Michael had refused: Michael Sutton deposition, *NXIVM v. Ross et al*, October 21, 2008.

long hours, secrecy: John Hochman, "A Forensic Psychiatrist Evaluates ESP," Cult Education Institute (formerly Ross Institute) website.

highly critical report: Paul Martin, "Robert Jay Lifton's Eight Criteria of Thought Reform as Applied to the Executive Success Programs," Ross website.

$10 million lawsuit: Complaint, *NXIVM v. Ross et al*, August 22, 2003.

more than twenty factual falsehoods: Raniere affidavit, *NXIVM v. Ross et al*, August 2003.

joyous interdependent civilization: Keith Raniere quoted in Dennis Yusko, "Group Gathers Both Acolytes, Doubters," Albany *Times Union*, August 28, 2003.

complete radical shift: Kristin Keeffe, quoted in Ibid.

campaign contributions: Government exhibit GX 1482, in *USA v. Raniere et al*, June 2019.

$30,000 in private jet travel: James Odato, "Political Connections Take to the Air," Albany *Times Union*, September 14, 2007.

Snyder had gone missing: Dennis Yusko, "An Espian's Brief Life," Albany *Times Union*, February 1, 2004.

low self-esteem could have contributed to their illness: Maja Miljkovic interview, July 2018; Complaint, *Edmondson v. Raniere et al*, January 28, 2020, 179.

subject to an ethical review: Raniere deposition, September 2009, 259.

attack might not have happened: Susan Dones interview, July 2019.

hallucinating and suffered a nervous breakdown: Michael Freedman, "Cult of Personality," *Forbes*, October 2003.

"resort hopping": Michael Weniger testimony, *USA v. Raniere et al*, June 14, 2019.

CHAPTER 9: SUNK COSTS

theory for everything: Psychology, mathematics, biology, world markets, spirituality, parenting, childhood development, athletics, art, journalism, philosophy, history, gender, sexuality, criminal justice, and weight loss, to name a few areas of claimed specialty and innovation.

buy land and start a new society: Barbara Bouchey deposition, *NXIVM v. Ross et al*, October 2009, 83.

asking to open a $50,000 trading account: Bouchey interviews and records, 2009–2020.

more wealthy followers: Ibid.

develop a winery: Complaint, *O'Hara v. Raniere et al*, February 2012, 19.

$2,000 per hour: Frank Parlato. "Bronfman Sisters Join NXIVM and Lose Millions," *Niagara Falls Reporter*, December 2015.

"passive investors": Clare Bronfman testimony, *Precision v. Plyam et al*, March 2011.

getting a driver's license: Mark Vicente testimony, May 9, 2019.

blamed the sisters' father: Bronfman deposition, *Precision v. Plyam et al*, 2009, 58.

CHAPTER 10: MISSION IN MEXICO

she got it right: Daniela testimony, May 2019.

wrote a story for *Vice*: Sarah Berman, "Keith Raniere's 'Sex Cult' Was Powered by Gaslighting, Experts and Witnesses Testify," *Vice*, June 11, 2019.

CHAPTER 11: THE HEIST

multibillion-dollar self-help industry: The U.S. self-improvement market was worth an estimated $11 billion in 2018. "The U.S. Market for Self-Improvement Products and Services," Marketdata Enterprises, October 2019.

excitement made people better communicators: Rational Inquiry patent application, 2001.

didn't understand these concepts: Mark Vicente testimony, May 2019.

It doesn't have a hold on you: Interviews with Sarah Edmondson, 2018–2020.

"Abuse, Rights and Injury": Michael Weniger testimony, quoting module from "The Human Experiment," June 14, 2019.

"confusion techniques": Richard Bandler and John Grinder, *Patterns of the Hypnotic Techniques of Milton H. Erickson, M.D., Vol. I* (Soquel, CA: Meta Publications, 1975), 50–63.

CHAPTER 12: WHAT THE BLEEP

a process called "auditing": Lawrence Wright, *Going Clear: Scientology, Hollywood, and the Prison of Belief* (New York: Alfred A. Knopf, 2013), 15–17.

a running joke in the community: Susan Dones interview, July 2019.

CHAPTER 13: "CRACKED OPEN"

most active and star-studded centers: Sarah Berman, "How NXIVM Ripped Through This Group of Canadian Actors," *Vice*, September 2018.

"seal bark" coughs: "Epiphany," *Uncover: Escaping NXIVM*, podcast, CBC May 2018.

I want to bring this to Canada: Sarah Edmondson interview, October 2017.

rolled out the VIP treatment: Scott Johnson and Rebecca Sun, "Her Darkest Role: Actress Allison Mack's Descent from 'Smallville' to Sex Cult," *The Hollywood Reporter*, May 2018.

CHAPTER 14: AN ETHICAL BREACH

collection of miniskirts: Lauren Salzman testimony, May 21, 2019.

a 2015 phone call: Exhibit for Bouchey motion to dismiss, *New York State v. Bouchey*, May 28, 2015.

TV mounted on the ceiling: Daniela testimony, May 23, 2019.

CHAPTER 15: GOLDEN BOY

wish for a family only grew stronger: Lauren Salzman testimony, May 2019.

what he called the "golden child": Rodger Kirsopp interview with *Vice* News documentary producer Kathleen Caulderwood (quoted with permission), October 27, 2017.

"bespoke, in-home service": Fred Quick, "The New Frontiers of Education," Quintessentially Education, July 7, 2017, Quintessentially Education website.

"epitome of a Rainbow child": Maja Miljkovic interview, July 2018.

operations had been halted: Jerry Iannelli, "State Closes Midtown Miami School Tied to NXIVM 'Sex Cult' Leader," *Miami New Times*, April 27, 2018.

CHAPTER 16: HIS HOLINESS

earning the nickname "Forlorn": Lauren Salzman testimony, May 2019.

had become a "suppressive": See also: a "suppressive person" in Lawrence Wright, *Going Clear: Scientology, Hollywood, and the Prison of Belief* (New York: Alfred A. Knopf, 2013), 99–100.

making out in a hot tub: Catherine Oxenberg with Natasha Stoynoff, *Captive: A Mother's Crusade to Save Her Daughter from a Terrifying Cult* (New York: Gallery Books, 2018).

Dhonden would be forced to step down: Katherine Ellison and Rory Carroll, "Revealed: Dalai Lama's Personal Emissary Suspended Over Corruption Claims," *The Guardian*, October 2017.

leaked eight-minute video clip: Jeane MacIntosh, "Creepy Cultist's 'Killing' Confession," *New York Post*, October 2010.

CHAPTER 17: SPY GAMES

compromising poses: Transcript read in Raniere deposition, *NXIVM v. Ross et al*, March 12, 2009.

sixty attorneys at thirty firms: Edmondson et al. v. Raniere et al, January 2020; Will Yakowicz, "From Heiress to Felon: How Clare Bronfman Wound Up in 'Cult-Like' Group NXIVM," *Forbes*, May 2019.

what extent I was being surveilled: Sarah Berman, "What It's Like to Be Surveilled and Sued by NXIVM," *Vice*, June 2019.

victim's advocate: James Odato, "NXIVM Pressed District Attorney," Albany *Times Union*, March 6, 2012.

investigated for professional misconduct: James Odato, "Private Eye Lands in Public Trouble," Albany *Times Union*, September 17, 2012.

CHAPTER 18: ROOM

one of his other young victims: Camila texts, exhibit GX 1702, *USA v. Raniere et al*, June 6, 2019.

he didn't pick up: Ben Myers did not respond to interview requests.

CHAPTER 19: THE ACT

"all students would make a vow": Mark Vicente testimony, May 9, 2019.

"control panel": Richard Bandler, Design Human Engineering lectures, 1997.

Tourette's syndrome research: Sarah Berman, "I Tried to Make Sense of an Alleged Sex Cult's Bizarre Health Claims," *Vice*, May 1, 2018.

"philosophical founder": Mark Vicente testimony, May 9, 2019.

You could say I don't know what I'm talking about: *Keith Raniere Conversations* on YouTube.

CHAPTER 20: SLAVE NUMBER ONE

more emotionally mature: Daniela testimony, May 2019.

secret boyfriend for nearly nine years: Camila texts, *USA v. Raniere et al*, June 2019.

palms once turned orange: Maja Miljkovic interview, July 2018; Sarah Berman, "I Followed the NXIVM 'Sex Cult' Diet for a Week," *Vice*, August 2018.

if someone is threatening to hurt you: Sarah Berman, "A BDSM Educator Tells Us Why NXIVM Sex Cult Allegations Aren't Consensual Kink," *Vice*, May 2018.

CHAPTER 21: THE CALL

Barbara Bouchey was speechless: Interview with Barbara Bouchey, August 2018; Sarah Berman, "The Alleged Plot to Put NXIVM's Critics in Mexican Prison," *Vice*, September 2018.

chase her with lawsuits: *Bronfman v. Bouchey et al* (Los Angeles), February 2010; *NXIVM v. Bouchey* (New York), May 2011; *Bronfman v. Bouchey Asset Management* (New York), May 2011; *New York State v. Bouchey*, March 2014.

unloaded her knowledge: Exhibit for motion to dismiss, *New York State v. Bouchey*, May 28, 2015.

102 women were initiated: Lauren Salzman testimony, May 2019.

CHAPTER 22: THE VOW

Hildreth told her: Mark Hildreth did not respond to interview requests for this book.

CHAPTER 23: "THIS IS NOT THE ARMY"

through a trapdoor: Nicole testimony, June 2019.

envisioned thousands or maybe even a million members: Lauren Salzman testimony, May 2019.

CHAPTER 24: "MASTER, PLEASE BRAND ME"

get over your body issues: Sarah Edmondson interview, October 2017.

obedience experiments of the 1960s: Stanley Milgram, "Behavioural Study of Obedience," *Journal of Abnormal and Social Psychology*, 1963.

CHAPTER 25: RECKONING

episode of *Black Mirror*: Charlie Brooker, "Shut Up and Dance," *Black Mirror*, season 3, 2016.

ten-hour train ride: First recounted on "The Suppressives," *Uncover: Escaping NXIVM*, podcast, CBC 2018.

texted Raniere "911": Lauren Salzman testimony, May 2019.

allegations appeared on *Frank Report*: Frank Parlato, "Sources: Human Branding Part of Raniere-Inspired Women's Group," *Frank Report*, June 5, 2017.

the BDSM dungeon: Lauren Salzman testimony, May 2019.

CHAPTER 26: "ME TOO"

abuses of film producer Harvey Weinstein: Jodi Kantor and Megan Twohey, "Harvey Weinstein Paid Off Sexual Harassment Accusers for Decades," *The New York Times*, October 5, 2017.

an investigation into Keith Raniere: Barry Meier, "Inside the Secretive Group Where Women Are Branded," *The New York Times*, October 2017.

the U.S. Declaration of Independence: Lauren Salzman testimony, May 2019.

actor Nicki Clyne prepared: Nicki Clyne did not respond to requests for comment on her involvement in NXIVM.

CHAPTER 27: IN CHARACTER

episode of *Law & Order*: Dick Wolf, "Accredo," *Law & Order: Special Victims Unit*, season 20, 2018.

EPILOGUE: VANGUARD ON TRIAL

conspiring to commit identity theft: Sarah Berman, "NXIVM President Nancy Salzman Pleads Guilty to Racketeering Conspiracy," *Vice*, March 13, 2019.

Bronfman fainted: Sarah Berman, "'Slave' to NXIVM 'Sex Cult' Leader Pleads Guilty to Racketeering," *Vice*, March 29, 2019.

Mack said it had been her motivation to help others: Allison Mack did not respond to interview requests for this book.

INDEX

Note: KR = Keith Raniere

© Jackie Dives

SARAH BERMAN is an investigative journalist based in Vancouver covering crime, drugs, cults, politics, and culture. She is a former senior editor at *Vice* and past contributor to *Adbusters*, *Reuters*, *Maclean's*, *The Globe and Mail*, the *Vancouver Sun*, and other publications.